Lofts

Living, Working and Shopping in a Loft
Vivir, trabajar y comprar en un loft
Vivere, lavorare e comprare in un loft

To My Honeybears
Diane for her
Birthday!
Love, Alex
Sep 4th 2005

Lofts

Living, Working and Shopping in a Loft
Vivir, trabajar y comprar en un loft
Vivere, lavorare e comprare in un loft

© 2003 Feierabend Verlag oHG
Mommsenstr. 43, D-10629 Berlin

Translation into English: Mary Cecelia Black
Traduzione all'italiano: Paola Consolaro, Maurizio Siliato
Editing of the Spanisch text, typesetting and project coordination:
LocTeam S.L., Barcelona

Editorial project by
LOFT Publications
Domènech, 7-9, 2°-2ª
E- 08012 Barcelona
e-mail: loft@loftpublications.com
www.loftpublications.com

Author
Arco Editorial S.A., Barcelona

Editing
Lola Gómez & Susana González Torras

Graphic design
Mireia Casanovas Soley, Jaume Martinez Coscojuela, Emma Termes Parera

Printing and binding
Centro Poligrafico Milano S.p.A.

Printed in Italy

ISBN 3-936761-07-8
37-06024-1

Living in a loft
Vivir en un loft
Vivire in un loft

Light-filled Atmosphere	Peter Tow Studios	18
Ambiente luminoso		
Ambiente luminoso		
Dualities	Dean/Wolf Architects	24
Dualidades		
Dualità		
Visual Freedom	Alexander Gorlin	30
Liberación visual		
Liberazione visiva		
Chelsea District	Kar-hwa Ho Architecture & Design, S. Sirefman	36
Distrito Chelsea		
Distretto di Chelsea		
Spatial Privacy	Kar-hwa Ho Architecture & Design	44
Intimismo del espacio		
Intimismo dello spazio		
K-Loft in New York	George Ranalli	50
K-Loft en Nueva York		
K-Loft a New York		
Potter's Loft	Resolution: 4. Architecture	56
Potter's Loft		
Potter's Loft		
Monolithic Structure	Resolution: 4. Architecture	60
Estructura monolítica		
Struttura monolitica		
Renaud Residence	Cha & Innerhofer	66
Residencia Renaud		
Residenza Renaud		
Spatial Flexibility	Kar-hwa Ho Architecture & Design	72
Flexibilidad espacial		
Flessibilità spaziale		
New Trends	Hardy Holzman Pfeiffer Associates	78
Nuevas tendencias		
Nuove tendenze		
Apartment in Manhattan	Shelton, Mindel & Associates	86
Apartamento en Manhattan		
Appartamento a Manhattan		
Artists' Residence	Abelow Connors Sherman Architects	92
Residencia para artistas		
Residenza per artisti		
Urban Interface	Dean/Wolf Architects	98
Urban Interface		
Urban Interface		
Industrial Feel	Alexander Jiménez	106
Aire industrial		
Aria industriale		
A Blank Canvas	Vicente Wolf	112
Un lienzo en blanco		
Una tela in bianco		
A Play of Lights	Moneo Brock Studio	116
Juego de luces		
Gioco di luci		
Rosenberg Residence and Studio	Belmont Freeman Architects	122
Residencia y estudio Rosenberg		
Residenza e studio Rosenberg		
Minimalist Continuity	Form Werkstatt	128
Continuidad minimalista		
Continuità minimalista		
Multi-purpose Space	Abelow Connors Sherman Architects	134
Espacio polivalente		
Spazio polivalente		

16

O'Malley Residence	Carpenter/Grodzins Architects	140
Residencia O'Malley		
Residenza O'Malley		
Accessibility	Paul Guzzardo, Ray Simon	146
Accesibilidad		
Accessibilità		
1709 Studio	Paul Guzzardo, David Davis	152
1709 Studio		
1709 Studio		
Sophisticated Innovation	Cecconi Simone Inc.	158
Innovación sofisticada		
Innovazione sofisticata		
Private Residence	Cecconi Simone Inc.	164
Residencia privada		
Residenza privata		
Workshop and Living Space	Fernando Campana	172
Taller y vivienda		
Laboratorio e abitazione		
Formal Unities	Knott Architects	178
Unidades formales		
Unità formali		
Transparent Floors	Fraser Brown McKenna Architects	184
Suelos transparentes		
Pavimenti trasparenti		
Blank and Empty	Hugh Broughton Architects	188
Blanco y vacío		
Bianco e vuoto		
New Concordia Wharf	Mark Guard Architects	192
New Concordia Wharf		
New Concordia Wharf		
Oliver's Wharf	McDowell + Benedetti Architects	198
Oliver's Wharf		
Oliver's Wharf		
Post Office in London	Orefelt Associates	204
Oficina postal en Londres		
Ufficio postale a Londra		
Home for a Painter	Simon Conder Associates	210
Vivienda para una pintora		
Abitazione per una pittrice		
FOA London	FOA. Foreign Office Architects	214
FOA London		
FOA London		
Conversion of a Warehouse	Adam Caruso, Peter St. John	220
Conversión de un almacén		
Conversione di un magazzino		
Lofts on Wall Street	Chroma AD. Alexis Briski + Raquel Sendra	224
Lofts en Wall Street		
Loft a Wall Street		
Top Floors on Wardour Street	CZWG Architects	230
Áticos en Wardour Street		
Attici a Wardour Street		
Lee House	Derek Wylie	234
Casa Lee		
Casa Lee		
Loft in Clerkenwell	Circus Architects	242
Loft en Clerkenwell		
Loft a Clerkenwell		
Unit 203	Buschow Henley & Partners	248
Unit 203		
Unit 203		
Chromatic Treatment	AEM	254
Tratamiento cromático		
Trattamento cromatico		

Interior Landscape Paisaje interior Paesaggio interno	Florian Beigel Architects	260
Neutral Space Espacio neutral Spazio neutrale	Felicity Bell	266
No Restrictions Sin restricciones Senza restrizioni	Blockarchitecture: Graeme Williamson + Zoe Smith	272
Kopf Loft Kopf Loft Kopf Loft	Buschow Henley	278
Multidirectional Light Luz multidireccional Luce multidirezionale	Buschow Henley	282
Piper Building Piper Building Piper Building	Wells Mackereth Architects	288
Spatial Contrast Contraste espacial Contrasto spaziale	María Rodríguez-Carreño Villangómez	294
Leisure and Business Ocio y negocio Tempo libero e affari	Ramón Úbeda/Pepa Reverter	302
La Nau La Nau La Nau	Carol Iborra, Mila Aberasturi	308
Urban Panorama Panorámica urbana Panoramica urbana	Antoni Arola	316
Vapor Llull Vapor Llull Vapor Llull	Cirici & Bassó, Inés Rodríguez, Alfonso de Luna, Norman Cinamond, Carla Cirici	324
Apartment for an Actress Apartamento para una actriz Appartamento per un'attrice	Franc Fernández	330
Verticality Verticalidad Verticalità	Pere Cortacans	336
Austerity or Design Austeridad o diseño Austerità o design	Joan Bach	342
Working at Home Trabajar en casa Lavorare a casa	Helena Mateu Pomar	348
Effective Layout Distribución eficaz Distribuzione efficace	Joan Bach	354
Camden Lofts Camden Lofts Camden Lofts	Cecconi Simone Inc.	360
House in Igualada Casa en Igualada Casa a Igualada	Pep Zazurca i Codolà	366
Renovation of a Top Floor Reforma de un ático Restauro di un attico	A-cero estudio de arquitectura y urbanismo SL	372
Interior Garden Jardín interior Giardino interno	Alain Salomon	378
Visual Connection Conexión visual Connessione visuale	Christophe Pillet	386

Living Space and Studio **Vivienda y estudio** **Abitazione e studio**	Christophe Pillet	392
A Cluster of Lofts **Agrupación de lofts** **Gruppo di loft**	Alain Salomon	398
Spaciousness **Espacialidad** **Spazialità**	Patrizia Sbalchiero	404
House for a Painter **Casa para una pintora** **Casa per una pittrice**	Antonio Zanuso	412
House in San Giorgio **Casa en San Giorgo** **Casa a San Giorgio**	Studio Archea	418
Transparencies **Transparencias** **Trasparenze**	Rüdiger Lainer	424
Ecological Apartment **Apartamento ecológico** **Appartamento ecologico**	Lichtblau & Wagner	430
Loft in Bruges **Loft en Brujas** **Loft a Bruges**	Non Kitch Group	436
Old Spinning Mill **Antigua nave de hilatura** **Un vecchio capannone per la filatura**	Ernst & NiklausArchitekten ETH/SIA	442
Sopanen/Sarlin Loft **Sopanen/Sarlin Loft** **Sopanen/Sarlin Loft**	Marja Sopanen + Olli Sarlin	450

Working in a loft
Trabajar en un loft
Laborare in un loft
456

@radical.media **@radical.media** **@radical.media**	Rockwell Group	458
Connors Communications **Connors Communications** **Connors Communications**	Lee H. Skolnick Architecture + Design	464
Design Studio in Tribeca **Estudio de diseño en Tribeca** **Studio di design a Tribeca**	Parsons + Fernández-Casteleiro	470
Sunshine Interactive Network **Sunshine Interactive Network** **Sunshine Interactive Network**	Gates Merkulova Architects	474
Miller-Jones Studio **Estudio Miller-Jones** **Studio Miller-Jones**	LOT/EK	478
Stingel Studio **Stingel Studio** **Stingel Studio**	Cha & Innerhofer	482
Triple Space **Triple espacio** **Triplo spazio**	Tow Studios Architecture	488
WMA Engineers **WMA Engineers** **WMA Engineers**	Valerio Dewalt Train Architects	494
BBDO West **BBDO West** **BBDO West**	Beckson Design Associates	498

Rhino Entertainment	Beckson Design Associates	504
Rhino Entertainment		
Rhino Entertainment		
MTV Networks	Felderman + Keatinge Associates	510
MTV Networks		
MTV Networks		
Praxair Distribution Inc.	Herbert Lewis Kruse Blunck Architecture	516
Praxair Distribution Inc.		
Praxair Distribution Inc.		
German Design Center	Norman Foster & Partners	520
Centro Alemán del Diseño		
Centro Tedesco del Design		
Nuremberg	Wirth	524
Núremberg		
Norimberga		
Michaelides & Bednash	Buschow Henley	528
Michaelides & Bednash		
Michaelides & Bednash		
Shepherd's Bush Studios	John McAslan & Partners	534
Shepherd's Bush Studios		
Shepherd's Bush Studios		
London Merchant Securities	John McAslan & Partners	538
London Merchant Securities		
London Merchant Securities		
Advertising Agency	John McAslan & Partners	544
Agencia de publicidad		
Agenzia di pubblicità		
Derwent Valley Holding	John McAslan & Partners	550
Derwent Valley Holding		
Derwent Valley Holding		
Offices Thames & Hudson	John McAslan & Partners	554
Oficinas Thames & Hudson		
Uffici di Thames & Hudson		
Williams Murray Banks	Pierre d'Avoine Architects	560
Williams Murray Banks		
Williams Murray Banks		
Metropolis Studios Ltd.	Powell-Tuck, Connor & Orefelt	564
Metropolis Studios Ltd.		
Metropolis Studios Ltd.		
Studio in Glasgow	Anderson Christie Architects	570
Estudio en Glasgow		
Studio a Glasgow		
Labotron. Offices and workshops	Pep Zazurca i Codolà	574
Labotron. Oficinas y talleres		
Labotron. Uffici e atelier		
Double You	Marc Viader i Oliva	580
Double You		
Double You		
Hispano 20	José Ángel Rodrigo García	586
Hispano 20		
Hispano 20		
Montardit SA	Josep Juvé & Núria Jolis	592
Montardit SA		
Montardit SA		
GCA	GCA Arquitectes Associats	598
GCA		
GCA		
Casadesús Studio	Antoni Casadesús	604
Estudio Casadesús		
Studio Casadesús		
B&B Studio Home	Sergi Bastidas	610
B&B Estudio vivienda		
Studio e abitazione B&B		

Studio in Madrid	Enrique Bardají	618
Estudio en Madrid		
Studio a Madrid		
Empty SA	Víctor López Cotelo	624
Empty SA		
Empty SA		
Salamanca Neighborhood	Manuel Serrano, Marta Rodríguez Ariño	630
Barrio de Salamanca		
Quartiere di Salamanca		
Ciclorama	Manuel Serrano, Marta Rodríguez Ariño	636
Ciclorama		
Ciclorama		
Architectural Studio	José Miguel Usabiaga Bárcena	642
Estudio de arquitectura		
Studio di architettura		
Central Headquarters of IU-EB	José Miguel Usabiaga Bárcena	650
Sede central IU-EB		
Sede centrale dell'IU-EB		
Studio Naço Offices	Studio Naço	658
Oficinas Studio Naço		
Uffici Studio Naço		
Silos in Amsterdam	Die architectengroep	664
Silos en Amsterdam		
Silo ad Amsterdam		
Architecture Office	Jacob Zeilon & Partners	672
Oficina de arquitectura		
Studio di architettura		
Shopping in a loft		676
Comprar en un loft		
Comprare in un loft		
R 20th Century	Mike Solis + Nick Dine/Dinersan Inc.	678
R 20th Century		
R 20th Century		
Spazionavigli	RBA. Roberto Brambilla & Associates	686
Spazionavigli		
Spazionavigli		
Shin Choi in New York	Wormser + Associates	694
Shin Choi en Nueva York		
Shin Choi a New York		
Géneros de punto	Bailo + Rull. ADP. Arquitectes Associats	700
Géneros de punto		
Géneros de punto		
Round Store	Pep Zazurca i Codolà	706
Round Store		
Round Store		
Joan Lao Mobiliario	Joan Lao	710
Joan Lao Mobiliario		
Joan Lao Mobiliario		
Esprit	Citterio & Dwan	716
Esprit		
Esprit		
Preu bo	Joan Lao	722
Preu bo		
Preu bo		
La Farinera del Clot	Josie Abascal	730
La Farinera del Clot		
La Farinera del Clot		
ArtQuitect	Francesca Ricós Martí	736
ArtQuitect		
ArtQuitect		

In Mat. ArtQuitec	José Luis López Ibáñez	742
In Mat. ArtQuitec		
In Mat. ArtQuitec		
Magna Pars	Luciano Maria Colombo	750
Magna Pars		
Magna Pars		
Progetto Lodovico	Luciano Maria Colombo	756
Progetto Lodovico		
Progetto Lodovico		
Nani Marquina Showroom	Nani Marquina	762
Nani Marquina Showroom		
Nani Marquina Showroom		
Montaje 97	Estudi Metro	768
Montaje 97		
Allestimento 97		
Montaje 96	Francesc Rifé & Associats	774
Montaje 96		
Allestimento 96		
Two showrooms en Italia	King-Miranda Associati	780
Dos *showrooms* en Italia		
Due *showroom* en Italia		
P.S.1 Museum	Frederick Fisher, David Ross, Joseph Coriaty	788
Museo P.S.1		
Museo P.S.1		
Dromokart	Florencia Costa Architecture	794
Dromokart		
Dromokart		
Talls Tallats	Eugeni Boldú, Orlando González	800
Talls Tallats		
Talls Tallats		
Bar Zoom	Pau Disseny Associats	808
Bar Zoom		
Bar Zoom		
Club Cabool	Lorens Holm, Ray Simon	814
Club Cabool		
Club Cabool		
Taxim Nightpark	Branson Coates	820
Taxim Nightpark		
Taxim Nightpark		
Paci Restaurant	Roger Ferris + Partners Llc.	826
Paci Restaurant		
Ristoranti Paci		
Porto Colom Restaurant	B&B Estudio de arquitectura	832
Restaurante Porto Colom		
Ristorante Porto Colom		
Thèatron Restaurant	Philippe Starck	836
Restaurante Thèatron		
Ristorante Thèatron		
Belgo Centraal	Ron Arad, Alison Brooks	842
Belgo Centraal		
Belgo Centraal		
Belgo Restaurant	FOA. Foreign Office Architects	848
Belgo Restaurant		
Ristorante Belgo		

Stripped Loft
Loft depurado / Loft depurato

Based on the exercise suggested in the manual, various lofts that correspond to a number of representative persons have appeared, and we have decided to illustrate the stripped loft.

To strip means to eliminate excesses.

The stripped loft is also the result of a process of spatial recycling, but in this we are referring more to a qualitative degree in the operation: stripping, which affects the type of transformation made. One who strips a loft basically clears away excesses and always chooses on the basis of a certain criteria, which is retained during the transformation.

The stripped loft can be located anywhere. In this case we have chosen a top floor; it will be large, but not too large, and it will have an aesthetically controlled shape; it will have an excess of cubic meters, a disproportion, since the person who defined it is very coherent and knows what is essential.

In the stripped loft there will be little of everything—intervention, furniture, objects—but everything will be painstakingly chosen, allowing for a quick description. There will probably be a lot of light, and it is certain that in the recycling process many of the initial elements will probably have been chosen and appropriately adapted.

A partir del ejercicio propuesto por el manual, han aparecido varios lofts correspondientes a un número de personas representativas y hemos escogido ilustrar el loft depurado.

Depurar significa despojar de impurezas.

El loft depurado es también el resultado de un proceso de reciclaje espacial, pero en éste definimos un grado cualitativo más en la operación: depurar, que afecta al tipo de transformación realizada. El depurador fundamentalmente limpia y selecciona siempre sobre la base de un criterio determinado, el mismo que se sigue manteniendo a la hora de intervenir.

El loft depurado puede tener cualquier emplazamiento. En este caso hemos elegido un ático; será grande, pero no demasiado, y tendrá una forma estéticamente controlada; tendrá un exceso de metros cúbicos, una desproporción, ya que la persona que lo ha definido es muy coherente y conoce aquello que le es esencial.

En el loft depurado habrá poco de todo −intervención, mobiliario, objetos− pero seleccionado cuidadosamente, lo cual permitirá un recorrido veloz. Probablemente habrá mucha luz y es seguro que en el proceso de reciclaje se habrán escogido y adecuado convenientemente muchos de los elementos iniciales.

Partendo dall'esercizio proposto dal manuale, sono comparsi vari loft corrispondenti a un numero di persone rappresentative ed abbiamo scelto di illustrare il loft depurato.

Depurare significa liberare da impurità.

Il loft depurato è pure il risultato di un processo di riciclaggio spaziale; tale processo è caratterizzato comunque da un ulteriore grado qualitativo che riguarda il tipo di depurazione e di trasformazione realizzata. Fondamentalmente, il depuratore pulisce e seleziona sempre sulla base di un criterio determinato, lo stesso criterio che si mantiene quando si realizza l'intervento.

Il loft depurato può avere qualsiasi ubicazione. In questo caso abbiamo scelto un attico; sarà grande, ma non troppo, e avrà una forma esteticamente controllata; avrà un eccesso di metri cubici, una sproporzione, in quanto la persona che l' ha definito è molto coerente e conosce ciò che per lei è essenziale.

Nel loft depurato ci sarà un po' di tutto − intervento, mobili, oggetti − ma verrà rigorosamente selezionato, consentendo così di percorrerlo velocemente. Probabilmente ci sarà molta luce ed è sicuro che nel processo di riciclaggio si saranno scelti e adeguati convenientemente molti degli elementi iniziali.

Top view
Planta
Pianta

living vivir vivere

in a loft   en un loft   in un loft

"A house, even more than a landscape, is a psychological state"

Gaston Bachelard, "The Poetry of Space"

«La casa, incluso más que el paisaje, es un estado psíquico»

Gaston Bachelard, *La poética del espacio*

«La casa, persino più del paesaggio, è uno stato psichico»

Gaston Bachelard, *La poetica dello spazio*

Light-filled Atmosphere
Ambiente luminoso / Ambiente luminoso

Peter Tow Studios

On the west shore of Manhattan, above the Hudson River, this loft lies at the entrance to the Holland Tunnel which connects the island of Manhattan with New Jersey. The exterior industrial aesthetic serves as a counterpoint to the loft's interior, which has deliberately been designed to have a spare, light-filled feeling

In this apartment, this building's original concrete surface by a maple wood surface. In the entrance, limestone has been installed on the floor, extending as far as he kitchen. A grained glass wall runs from north to south, separating the bedrooms from the rest of the space. All the closets and shelves have been manufactured in varnished wood and light maple.

With an almost square floor plan, the loft is surrounded by windows on three sides. The dining room is located in middle of the living room and is symbolically the heart of the space.

The bathrooms are simple and white, with views to the industrial sector where the loft is located. The kitchen is located in the north-eastern corner of the loft such that it intersects with the translucent glass panel.

En la orilla oeste de Manhattan, sobre el río Hudson, se encuentra este loft a la entrada del túnel Holland, que conecta la isla de Manhattan con Nuerva Jersey. La estética industrial del exterior sirve de contrapunto al interior del loft, que ha sido deliberadamente diseñado para dar sensación de limpio y luminoso.

La original solera de hormigón del edificio está cubierta dentro del apartamento por una superficie de madera de arce. En la entrada se ha dispuesto piedra caliza en el suelo y se ha extendido hasta conectar con la cocina. Una pared de cristal arenado corre de norte a sur separando los dormitorios del resto del espacio. Todos los armarios y estanterías han sido fabricados en madera lacada y arce claro.

Con una planta más o menos cuadrada, el loft está rodeado de ventanas en tres de sus lados. El comedor se ubica en el centro de la sala y constituye simbólicamente el corazón del espacio.

Los baños son sencillos y blancos, con vistas al sector industrial del emplazamiento. La cocina se sitúa en la esquina nordeste del lugar de forma que hace intersección con el panel de vidrio translúcido.

Nella riva occidentale della penisola di Manhattan, sul fiume Hudson, si trova questo loft, all'entrata del tunnel Holland, che collega Manhattan con il New Jersey. L'estetica industriale dell'esterno serve da contrappunto alla parte interna del loft, che è stata deliberatamente disegnata per dare una sensazione di pulizia e luminosità.

L'originario dormiente di cemento dell'edificio è rivestito, all'interno dell'appartamento, da una superficie di legno acero. All'ingresso il pavimento è stato rivestito di pietra calcare, estendendolo fino a raggiungere la cucina. Una parete in vetro sabbiato scorre da nord a sud separando le stanze da letto dal resto dello spazio. Tutti gli armadi e gli scaffali sono stati fabbricati in legno laccato e acero chiaro.

Con una pianta più o meno quadrata, il loft è circondato da finestre in tre dei suoi lati. La sala da pranzo si trova al centro del salone e costituisce simbolicamente il cuore dello spazio.

I bagni sono semplici e bianchi, con vedute sulla zona industriale dell'ubicazione. La cucina si trova nell'angolo a nord-est dell'appartamento, in modo tale che interseca il pannello in vetro traslucido.

Architects: Peter Tow Studios
Location: New York, United States
Photographs: Björg Amarsdoottir

Floor plan layout   Planta de distribución   Pianta di distribuzione

A sliding panel in this wall acts as a shoji-like screen controlling the degree to which the loft is open.

Un panel deslizante en esta pared funciona como pantalla tipo shoji que controla su grado de abertura al loft.

Un pannello scorrevole in questa parete funziona come uno schermo di tipo «shoji» che controlla il suo grado di apertura al loft.

Dualities
Dualidades / Dualità

Dean / Wolf Architects

The main characteristic of this loft, located in the New York neighborhood of Tribeca, is the light coming in from the windows on the south façade.

The open space was adapted to accommodate the duality involved in living and working in the same space. The first problem faced by the architects was the presence of two small rooms in the back part, which interrupted the apartment's open space. Demolishing these spaces and creating a single volume allowed the activities in the new scheme to be included. In the interior, minimalist furniture was chosen.

The strategy that governs the entire design views a loft as a collage of functions, a system of movable components, and a series of connections that expand in both real space and the feeling of greater spaciousness.

The wall/office duality constitutes the border and the visual connection between the work area and the living room. Other dualities include the room/table and the bathroom/stairway.

La característica principal de este loft, ubicado en el barrio neoyorquino de Tribeca, era la luz procedente de las ventanas de la fachada sur.

El espacio abierto se adaptó para acomodar la dualidad que supone trabajar y vivir en un mismo espacio. El primer problema con que se encontraron los arquitectos fue la presencia de las dos pequeñas habitaciones de la parte posterior, que interrumpían la planta diáfana del apartamento. La demolición de estas estancias y la creación de un solo volumen permitió insertar las actividades previstas por el nuevo programa. En el interior se eligió un mobiliario de tendencia minimalista.

La estrategia que rige todo el diseño entiende el loft como un collage de operaciones, un sistema de componentes móviles y una serie de conexiones que expanden tanto el espacio real como la sensación de mayor espacialidad.

La dualidad muro/despacho constituye el límite y la conexión visual entre el área de trabajo y el comedor. Otras dualidades son la habitación/mesa y el baño/escalera.

La caratteristica principale di questo loft, ubicato nel quartiere newyorkese di Tribeca, era la luce proveniente dalle finestre della facciata sud.

Lo spazio aperto è stato adattato per confarsi alla dualità che presuppone lavorare e vivere in uno stesso spazio. Il primo problema al quale si sono trovati di fronte gli architetti è stata la presenza delle due piccole stanze della parte posteriore, che interrompevano la pianta diafana dell'appartamento. La demolizione di questi due vani e la creazione di un unico ambiente ha permesso di inserire le attività previste dal nuovo programma. Per l'interno sono stati scelti dei mobili di tendenza minimalista.

La strategia che regge tutto il progetto concepisce il loft come un collage di operazioni, un sistema di componenti mobili e una serie di connessioni che estendono sia lo spazio reale che la sensazione di una maggiore spazialità.

La dualità muro/ufficio costituisce il limite e la connessione visiva tra l'area di lavoro e la sala da pranzo. Altre dualità sono la stanza/il tavolo e il bagno / la scala.

Architects: Dean/Wolf Architects

Location: New York, United States

Photographs: Dean/Wolf Architects

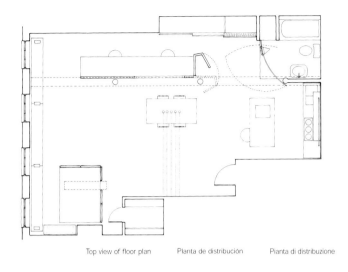

Top view of floor plan   Planta de distribución   Pianta di distribuzione

The three dualities created are office/wall, room/table and bathroom/stairway

Las tres dualidades creadas son despacho/muro, habitación/mesa y baño/escalera.

Le tre dualità create sono ufficio/muro, stanza/tavolo e bagno/scala

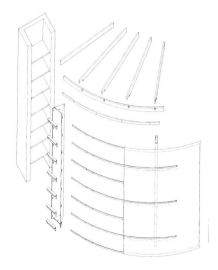

Visual Freedom
Liberación visual / Liberazione visiva

Alexander Gorlin

This loft on Hudson Street in the New York neighborhood of Tribeca, is a project for 1994 in which the architect, Alexander Gorlin, very aptly drew a floor plan that allowed for the freedom and visual continuity of the entire façade. The building's triangular layout is yet another element in the diversity of shapes that coexist in the interior of this apartment.

The western-facing façade receives a lot of light, which is in turn reflected by the stainless steel material of the kitchen furniture, located in one of the angles in this triangular floor plan. Also covered with stainless steel panels, a work island in the kitchen zone is reminiscent of the triangular shape of the apartment's floor plan, which in turn coincides with that of the building.

On the other side of the apartment, the curved wall containing the spiral staircase serves to separate the common spaces and the more private areas. This succession of spaces contains the library, the master bedroom, a dressing room and a full bathroom, where we find a bathtub whose shape is generated by the sinuosity of the wall bordering on the common spaces.

Este loft de Hudson Street, en el barrio neoyorquino de Tribeca, es una obra de 1994 en la que el arquitecto Alexander Gorlin traza con gran habilidad una distribución en planta que permite la liberación y continuidad visual de toda la fachada. La planta triangular del edificio es una anécdota más de la diversidad de formas que conviven en el interior de este apartamento.

La fachada orientada a poniente recibe una gran iluminación que es reflejada por el material de acero inoxidable que conforma los muebles de cocina, situados en uno de los ángulos de la planta triangular. Igualmente revestida de chapas de acero inoxidable, una isla de trabajo en la zona de la cocina recrea la forma triangular que tiene la planta del apartamento y que coincide con la del edificio.

En el otro extremo de la planta, el muro curvo que contiene la escalera en espiral sirve de separación entre el espacio común y las estancias más privadas. Esta sucesión de espacios contiene la biblioteca, el dormitorio principal, un vestidor y el baño completo, donde encontramos una bañera generada por la sinuosidad de la pared fronteriza con los espacios comunes.

Questo loft di Hudson Street, nel quartiere newyorkese di Tribeca, risale al 1994. È un'opera dove l'architetto Alexander Gorlin traccia con grande abilità una distribuzione in pianta che consente la liberazione e la continuità visiva di tutta la facciata. La pianta triangolare dell'edificio è un ulteriore esempio della diversità di forme che convivono all'interno di questo appartamento.

La facciata rivolta a ponente riceve una grande quantità di luce che viene riflessa dal materiale in acciaio inossidabile dei mobili di cucina, situati in uno degli angoli della pianta triangolare. Anch'essa rivestita da lamiere di acciaio inossidabile, un'isola di lavoro nella zona della cucina, ricrea la forma triangolare della pianta dell'appartamento e che coincide con quella dell'edificio.

All'altra estremità della pianta, il muro curvo che contiene la scala a chiocciola funge da separazione tra lo spazio comune e gli ambienti più intimi. Questa successione di spazi contiene la biblioteca, la stanza da letto principale, uno stanzino e il bagno completo, dove troviamo una vasca da bagno generata dalla sinuosità della parete limitrofa agli spazi comuni.

Architects: Alexander Gorlin

Location: New York, United States

Photographs: Peter Aaron/Esto

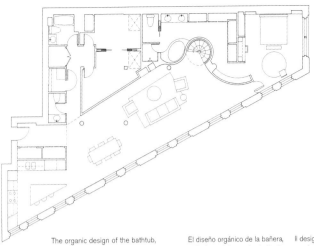

The organic design of the bathtub, which is covered in imported cobalt blue tiles, contrasts with the angular triangle-shaped geometry of the loft's floor plan, which is reflected in the kitchen's stainless steel cabinets.

El diseño orgánico de la bañera, revestida de azulejos azul cobalto de importación, contrasta con la geometría triangular angulosa de la planta del loft, que se refleja en el mueble de cocina de acero inoxidable.

Il design organico della vasca da bagno, rivestita da piastrelle di importazione di colore blu cobalto, contrasta con la spigolosa geometria triangolare della pianta del loft, che si riflette nel mobile da cucina in acciaio inossidabile.

Chelsea District
Distrito Chelsea / Distretto di Chelsea

Kar-Hwa Ho
Architecture & Design,
S. Sirefman

This loft in New York's Chelsea district has a surface area of almost 214 m², and the main aim was to let in as much daylight as possible. Architect Kar-Hwa Ho's team, working along with Susanna Sirefman, was in charge of the layout and design. They attempted to define and connect the different spaces with their functions so that despite the spatial continuity, the spaces did not affect each other. The distinction between the more private spaces was critical. Likewise, they considered the possibility of each area being distinguished from the others through specific design characteristics.

The design proposals were translated into the use of translucent windows which convey the depth of the spaces through their uniform distribution of light. The lack of natural light led to the creation of a quite effective and responsive system of artificial lighting. The proper placement of the furniture helps to further define the spaces.

Este loft, en el distrito Chelsea de Nueva York, cuenta con una superficie de casi 214 m² y el objetivo principal es captar la máxima entrada de luz posible del exterior. El equipo del arquitecto Kar-Hwa Ho se encargó, junto con Susanna Sirefman, de la distribución y el diseño. Intentaron definir y conectar los diferentes espacios con sus funciones para que, aunque tuvieran una continuidad espacial, no se vieran afectadas unas por otras. La distinción entre las que constituían zonas privadas fue primordial. Igualmente se planteó la posibilidad de que cada una de las áreas se distinguiera de las otras por unas características determinadas de diseño.

Las propuestas en el diseño se tradujeron en el empleo de cristales translúcidos que, con su reparto homogéneo de luz, transmiten la profundidad de los espacios. La falta de luz natural indujo a la creación de un sistema de iluminación artificial bastante eficaz y resolutorio. La disposición adecuada del mobiliario previsto ayuda a una mejor definición de los espacios.

Questo loft, nel distretto newyorkese di Chelsea, ha una superficie di quasi 214 m² e l'obiettivo principale è di far entrare quanta più luce possibile dall'esterno. Lo staff dell'architetto Kar-Hwa Ho è stato responsabile, assieme a Susanna Sirefman, della distribuzione e del design. Insieme hanno cercato di definire e di collegare i diversi spazi con le loro relative funzioni affinché ognuna di queste, sebbene avessero una continuità spaziale, non incidesse sull'altra. La distinzione tra quelle che costituivano le zone private è stata primordiale. Allo stesso modo si era presa in considerazione la possibilità che ciascuna delle aree si distinguesse dalle altre in base a delle determinate caratteristiche di design.

Le proposte di design si sono tradotte nell'impiego di vetri traslucidi che, con la loro distribuzione omogenea della luce, trasmettono la profondità degli spazi. La mancanza di luce naturale ha portato alla creazione di un sistema di illuminazione artificiale abbastanza efficace e risolutore. L'adeguata disposizione dei mobili previsti aiuta ad ottenere una migliore definizione degli spazi.

Architects: Kar-Hwa Ho Architecture & Design, S. Sirefman

Location: New York, United States

Photographs: Björg/Photography

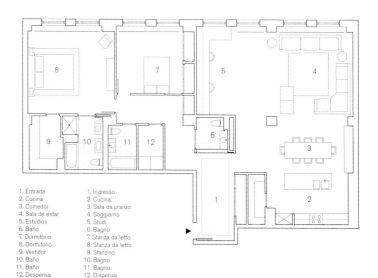

1. Entrance	1. Entrada	1. Ingresso
2. Kitchen	2. Cocina	2. Cucina
3. Dining room	3. Comedor	3. Sala da pranzo
4. Living room	4. Sala de estar	4. Soggiorno
5. Studies	5. Estudios	5. Studi
6. Bathroom	6. Baño	6. Bagno
7. Bedroom	7. Dormitorio	7. Stanza da letto
8. Bedroom	8. Dormitorio	8. Stanza da letto
9. Dressing room	9. Vestidor	9. Stanzino
10. Bathroom	10. Baño	10. Bagno
11. Bathroom	11. Baño	11. Bagno
12. Pantry	12. Despensa	12. Dispensa

The project's architect designed the lower kitchen cabinets on wheels in maple wood with translucent glass doors.

El arquitecto del proyecto diseñó en madera de arce y frontales de cristal translúcido los armarios bajos sobre ruedas del comedor.

L'architetto del progetto ha disegnato gli armadi della sala da pranzo bassi, con ruote, in legno acero e con frontale di vetro trasparente.

The desktop is made of translucent glass and is supported by the table's maple wood structure, the legs of which lie on stainless steel feet.

El sobre del escritorio es de cristal translúcido y se apoya en la estructura de madera de arce de la mesa, cuyas patas descansan sobre pies de acero inoxidable.

Il piano della scrivania è di vetro traslucido e si appoggia sulla struttura in legno acero del tavolo, i cui piedi riposano su basi in acciaio inossidabile.

Spatial Privacy
Intimismo del espacio / Intimismo dello spazio

Kar-Hwa Ho
Architecture & Design

This loft in the Chelsea district of New York is located in an old sewing workshop approximately 112 m² in area and is the work of architect Kar-Hwa Ho.

This project was focused on privacy and the internal contemplation of the space, given the fact that the views to the outside were not particularly interesting.

Spatial depth is achieved through transparencies based on layers of translucent materials and matte grained glass, all of which are united through a light color palette. The apartment's layout was conceived for just one inhabitant, such that the space between the different activities to be performed in each area of the house are allowed to flow into one another. The full and half bathrooms have no windows, which is counterbalanced through the use of luminous, translucent materials such as mirrors, treated glass, limestone and indirect lighting, the placement of which provides glamour and comfort to these areas.

In general, all the elements were designed in the same spirit in order to convey luminosity and fluidity throughout the entire space.

En un antiguo almacén de costura de alrededor de 112 m² se ubica este loft, obra del arquitecto Kar-Hwa Ho, en el barrio Chelsea de Nueva York.

Este proyecto se centró en el intimismo y la contemplación interior del espacio, dado que las vistas al exterior no resultaban de gran interés.

La profundidad espacial se consigue mediante transparencias a base de capas de materiales translúcidos y cristales mates arenados, todo ello unido a una paleta muy clara de colores. La distribución del apartamento está pensada para un solo inquilino, de modo que se dejó fluir el espacio entre las diferentes actividades atribuidas a cada área. El baño y el aseo no tienen ventanas, lo cual se compensa mediante el empleo de materiales muy luminosos y translúcidos como espejos, vidrios tratados, piedra caliza y luz indirecta, cuya disposición aporta *glamour* y comodidad a las zonas de servicio.

En general, el diseño de todos los elementos mantiene el mismo espíritu con la intención de transmitir luminosidad y fluidez a todo el espacio.

In un antico magazzino tessile di circa 112 m² si trova questo loft, opera dell'architetto Kar-Hwa Ho, nel quartiere Chelsea di New York.

Questo progetto si è concentrato sull'intimismo e sulla contemplazione interna dello spazio, dato che all'esterno, le viste non erano di grande interesse.

La profondità spaziale si ottiene mediante trasparenze a base di strati di materiali traslucidi e vetri sabbiati opachi, il tutto associato a una palette di colori molto chiara. La distribuzione dell'appartamento è stata pensata per un unico inquilino, quindi si è lasciato fluire lo spazio tra le diverse attività attribuite ad ogni ambiente. Il bagno e la toilette non hanno finestre, per cui si ovvia a questo inconveniente mediante l'impiego di materiali molto luminosi e trasparenti come per esempio specchi, vetri trattati, pietra calcare e luce indiretta, la cui disposizione aggiunge glamour e comodità alle zone di servizio.

In generale, il design di tutti gli elementi mantiene lo stesso spirito con l'intenzione di trasmettere luminosità e fluidità a tutto lo spazio.

Architects: Kar-Hwa Ho Architecture & Design

Location: New York, United States

Photographs: Björg/Photography

<table>
<tr><td>1. Entrance</td><td>1. Recibidor</td><td>1. Ingresso</td></tr>
<tr><td>2. Closet</td><td>2. Ropero</td><td>2. Guardaroba</td></tr>
<tr><td>3. Living/dining room</td><td>3. Salón comedor</td><td>3. Salone e sala
da pranzo</td></tr>
<tr><td>4. Kitchen</td><td>4. Cocina</td><td>4. Cucina</td></tr>
<tr><td>5. Half bathroom</td><td>5. Aseo</td><td>5. Toilette</td></tr>
<tr><td>6. Dressing room</td><td>6. Vestidor</td><td>6. Stanzino</td></tr>
<tr><td>7. Bedroom/study</td><td>7. Estudio dormitorio</td><td>7. Studio e stanza
da letto</td></tr>
<tr><td>8. Library</td><td>8. Biblioteca</td><td>8. Biblioteca</td></tr>
<tr><td>9. Full bathroom</td><td>9. Baño</td><td>9. Bagno</td></tr>
</table>

K-Loft in New York
K-Loft en Nueva York / K-Loft a New York

The project consists of remodeling an approximately 200 m² space in the New York district of Chelsea for an artist couple and their son. The building, an old sewing factory, is 90 years old and perfectly exemplifies the type of construction used in lower Manhattan at the turn of the century: deep, narrow corridors, structural brick walls, hand-wrought vaulting.

The original structure has been highlighted in the design of this loft. All extraneous coverings have been stripped from the original construction elements, which in this case consist of brick and metal beams that form the vaulted ceiling. With the new materials, volumes of contoured shapes containing the loft's functions have been created. White plasterboard walls join at the ceiling and walls, echoing some of the already-existing shapes at their seams.

The wooden panels are the material that starts from the floors, which are covered in wood as well, and which climb the walls using the same panels as on the floor.

The loft only has windows on two sides. Ranalli proposed a succession of large spaces (exhibition galleries, living room, bedrooms) separated by small utility areas conceived with furniture (half bathroom, elevator shaft/ stairwell, kitchen, full bathroom, dressing room).

El proyecto consiste en la remodelación de un espacio de aproximadamente 200 m² en el barrio neoyorkino de Chelsea para una pareja de artistas y su hijo. El edificio, una antigua fábrica de costura, tiene 90 años y responde perfectamente al tipo de construcción que se practicó en la parte baja de Manhattan durante el cambio de siglo: crujías profundas y estrechas, muros estructurales de ladrillo, forjados de bovedillas manuales.

La estructura original se ha enfatizado al desarrollar este proyecto. Los elementos constructivos originales, que aquí son el ladrillo y la vigueta metálica que conforma el techo de bovedillas, se han despojado de cualquier otro revestimiento. Con los nuevos materiales se han creado volúmenes de formas contorneadas que contienen las funciones. Blancas paredes de cartón yeso se unen a techo y paredes reproduciendo en los encuentros algunas formas ya existentes.

Los paneles de madera son el material que llega desde el suelo, igualmente entarimado, y que trepa, con un mismo lenguaje de cortes, por las paredes blancas.

El loft sólo dispone de ventanas en sus dos extremos. Ranalli ha planteado una sucesión de grandes espacios (galerías de exposición, sala de estar, dormitorios) separados por pequeñas áreas de servicio concebidas con mobiliario (aseo, caja de comunicaciones verticales, cocina, baño, vestidor).

Il progetto consiste nella ristrutturazione di uno spazio di circa 200 m² nel quartiere newyorkese di Chelsea, per una coppia di artisti e il proprio figlio. L'edificio, una vecchia fabbrica tessile, ha 90 anni e risponde perfettamente al tipo di costruzione eretto nella parte bassa di Manhattan durante il cambio di secolo: intercapedini profonde e strette, muri strutturali in mattoni, solette dalle piccole volte manuali.

Grazie allo sviluppo di questo progetto, ci è dato più rilievo alla struttura originale. Gli elementi costruttivi originali, che qui sono il mattone e la longarina metallica cha forma il tetto di gusci, sono stati privati di qualsiasi altro rivestimento. Con i nuovi materiali si sono creati volumi dalle forme delineate che contengono le varie funzioni. Pareti bianche di cartongesso si uniscono al soffitto e alle pareti, riproducendo nei punti di incontro delle forme già esistenti.

I pannelli di legno sono il materiale che arriva dal pavimento, anch'esso parchettato, e che si arrampica, con uno stesso linguaggio fatto di tagli, lungo le pareti bianche.

Il loft dispone di finestre soltanto nelle due parti estreme. Ranalli ha previsto una successione di grandi spazi (gallerie di esposizione, soggiorno, stanze da letto) separati da piccole aree di servizio pensate con dei mobili (toilette, vano delle comunicazioni verticali, cucina, bagno, stanzino).

Architects: George Ranalli

Location: New York, United States

Photographs: Paul Warchol

50

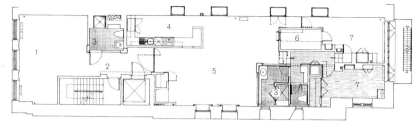

1. Gallery	1. Galería	1. Veranda
2. Vestibule	2. Vestíbulo	2. Atrio
3. Bathroom	3. Baño	3. Bagno
4. Kitchen	4. Cocina	4. Cucina
5. Living room	5. Sala de estar	5. Soggiorno
6. Storage	6. Almacén	6. Deposito
7. Bedroom	7. Dormitorio	7. Stanza da letto

The doors and closets are made of laminated beech wood. Corners have also been covered in this beech. Rough-edged wooden panels introduce a more detailed-oriented scale of design, vaguely reminiscent of Scarpa and Steven Holl, into the house.

Las puertas y los armarios son de madera laminada de haya. Los cantos también se han revestido con este material. Paneles de madera con límites quebrados introducen en la casa una escala de proyecto más próxima al detalle, que recuerda ligeramente a Scarpa y Steven Holl.

Le porte e gli armadi sono in legno faggio laminato. Anche gli spigoli sono stati rivestiti con questo materiale. Dei pannelli in legno dai tratti irregolari introducono nella casa una scala progettuale più vicina ai particolari, che ricorda leggermente Scarpa e Steven Holl.

Potter's Loft

Located in the Chelsea district of New York, the renovation of this loft reflects the client's practical lifestyle. The floor plan is divided according to the open volume that crosses the centrally-located kitchen and the nucleus that runs from the bathrooms to the back bedrooms. Concrete panels identify the living room. A light-covered ceiling with a wedge of lighting is located in the dining room, while a flat stone surface uncovers the space on one of its sides.

Both the kitchen and the dining room are lit by approximately twenty strips or segments of light connected to individual dimmer switches, which can be adjusted at the occupant's will.

Situado en el distrito de Chelsea, en Nueva York, la renovación de este loft responde al práctico estilo de vida de su cliente. La planta se distribuye en función de un volumen abierto que atraviesa la cocina central y el núcleo formado por los baños hasta alcanzar los dormitorios en la parte posterior. Unos paneles de hormigón identifican la zona de estar. Un techo de luces con una cuña de iluminación ubica el comedor, mientras que un plano de piedra descubre el hogar por una de sus caras.

Tanto la cocina como el comedor están iluminados con unas veinte barras o segmentos de luz conectados a unos controles de sordinas ajustables de forma individual, según la voluntad del ocupante.

Situato nel distretto di Chelsea, a New York, questo loft è stato ammodernato seguendo lo stile di vita pratico del suo cliente. La pianta si distribuisce in funzione di un volume aperto che attraversa la cucina centrale e il nucleo formato dai due bagni fino ad arrivare alle stanze da letto nella parte posteriore. Dei pannelli di calcestruzzo contraddistinguono la zona soggiorno. Un soffitto di luci con una struttura di illuminazione cuneiforme individua la sala da pranzo, mentre un plano di pietra scopre l'angolo cucina da uno dei suoi lati.

Sia la cucina che la sala da pranzo sono illuminate con circa venti sbarre o segmenti di luce collegati in modo individuale a dei controlli con sordine regolabili, a seconda dei gusti dell'occupante.

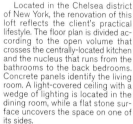

Architects: Resolution: 4. Architecture

Location: New York, United States

Photographs: Eduard Hueber

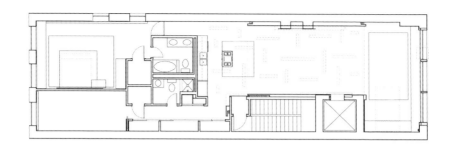

Monolithic Structure
Estructura monolítica / Struttura monolitica

Resolution: 4.
Architecture

Located in New York's financial district, this 158 m² apartment occupies the third floor of what was once an industrial building. The Resolution: 4 team, led by architects Joseph Tanney and Robert Luntz, were hired to remodel the kitchen space.

The building, which is long and narrow, a typical model of a New York loft, divided the apartment's floor plan through the placement of the elevator and the stairwell. The remodeling project extended to both sides of these shafts, differentiating the more public and private spaces of the layout through their depth. Thus, new, larger areas were designed near the elevator and stairway, including two bathrooms and a series of storage cabinets. The area devoted to sleep, a new projecting foldaway bed specially designed by the architect which remains hidden behind a wooden panel can also be found in this part of the loft.

The progression of spaces runs from the bedroom, through the kitchen and dining room, past the living room until finally reaching the workshop or study in the front of the apartment, where the guest bedroom is located.

Situado en el distrito financiero de Nueva York, este apartamento de 158 m² ocupa el tercer piso de un edificio de origen industrial. El equipo de Resolution: 4, dirigido por los arquitectos Joseph Tanney y Robert Luntz, fue contratado para reformar el espacio destinado a cocina.

El edificio, largo y estrecho, típico modelo del loft neoyorquino, dividía la planta del apartamento a través de la disposición del ascensor y la caja de la escalera. El proyecto de reforma se extendió a ambos lados de estos núcleos de comunicaciones verticales, diferenciando en la profundidad de la planta unas zonas más públicas de otras más privadas. De esta forma, se configuraron en las zonas adyacentes al ascensor y la escalera unas nuevas áreas ampliadas que contienen dos cuartos de baño y una serie de muebles para almacenar. En esta parte del loft se encuentra el espacio destinado al sueño, una nueva cama plegable en voladizo, especialmente diseñada por el arquitecto, que queda oculta tras una placa de madera.

La progresión de los espacios se extiende desde el dormitorio, pasando por la cocina y el comedor, hasta la zona de estar para finalmente llegar hasta el taller o estudio, donde se ubica la habitación de invitados, en la parte frontal del apartamento.

Situato nel distretto finanziario di New York, questo appartamento di 158 m² occupa il terzo piano di un edificio di natura industriale. Lo staff di Resolution: 4, diretto dagli architetti Joseph Tanney e Robert Luntz, è stato assunto per restaurare lo spazio destinato alla zona cucina.

L'edificio, lungo e stretto, il tipico modello di loft newyorkese, divideva la pianta dell'appartamento mediante l'ubicazione dell'ascensore e la tromba delle scale. Il progetto di restauro si estese ad entrambi i lati di questi nuclei di comunicazioni verticali, distinguendo lungo la profondità della pianta, delle zone di uso comune da altre più intime. In questo modo, nelle zone adiacenti all'ascensore e alle scale, si sono configurate delle nuove aree, ampie, che contengono due bagni e una serie di mobili che fanno da ripostiglio. In questa parte del loft si trova lo spazio destinato al riposo, con un nuovo letto ribaltabile a sbalzo, appositamente disegnato dall'architetto, che rimane nascosto dietro una lastra di legno.

La progressione degli spazi si estende dalla stanza da letto, passando dalla cucina e dalla sala da pranzo, fino alla zona soggiorno, per poi arrivare al laboratorio o studio, dove si trova la stanza degli ospiti, nella parte frontale dell'appartamento.

Architects: Resolution: 4. Architecture

Location: New York, United States

Photographs: Eduard Hueber

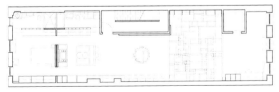

The walls have been painted white, and the dividers in the bathroom are made of Durock insulating panels, as are the ceiling coverings, all following the structural composition of layers that give the walls depth and texture.

Las paredes se han pintado de blanco y las separaciones de los cuartos de baño se han hecho de paneles aislantes de Durock, con los que también se ha cubierto el techo siguiendo una composición escultural de capas que dan relieve y textura al paramento.

Le pareti sono state dipinte di bianco e le divisioni dei bagni sono state realizzate con pannelli isolanti di Durock, con i quali è stato coperto anche il soffitto, seguendo una composizione scultorea a strati che danno rilievo e texture al paramento.

Sliding polycarbonate panels uniformly diffuse the light through to the back of the apartment.

Unos paneles correderos de policarbonato difunden de forma homogénea la luz hasta el fondo del apartamento.

Dei pannelli scorrevoli in policarbonato diffondono in modo omogeneo la luce, fino in fondo all'appartamento.

Renaud Residence
Residencia Renaud / Residenza Renaud

Cha & Innerhofer

This refuge in the middle of New York's Soho neighborhood is an almost 372 m² house chosen by a young banker. It is both a refuge and an elegant meeting point for his guests. The architecture of this peaceful loft allows for both atmospheres to coexist in the same space.

This five-story building, on the top floor of which lies the Renaud residence, was previously used for commerce but has now been totally renovated for living. This loft is evidence of the environment's diversity and complexity. The design makes references to traditional issues that defined modernity as viewed in a previous era.

The first division was planned to differentiate public from private functions. Cherry wood envelops the private areas, which are also covered by a hanging ceiling punctuated by skylights and which let light enter even the most private areas.

Un refugio en pleno Soho neoyorquino es la vivienda de casi 372 m² elegida por un joven banquero. Un lugar de reposo y un elegante punto de encuentro para sus invitados. La arquitectura de este loft apacible permite la combinación de ambas atmósferas en un mismo espacio.

El edificio, de cinco plantas, en lo alto del cual se ubica la residencia Renaud, tuvo anteriormente un destino comercial ahora convertido totalmente en residencial. El loft es testimonio de la diversidad y complejidad de su entorno. El diseño hace referencia a los temas tradicionales que definieron la modernidad planteada en una época anterior.

La primera división planteada diferencia las funciones públicas de las privadas. La madera de cerezo envuelve los ambientes privados, que quedan también cubiertos por un falso techo interrumpido por tragaluces que cuelan la luz hasta las zonas más privadas.

Un rifugio nel cuore di Soho, a New York, è l'abitazione di quasi 372 m² scelta da un giovane banchiere. Un luogo di riposo e un elegante punto di incontro per i suoi ospiti. L'architettura di questo loft tranquillo permette la coesistenza di entrambe le atmosfere in un unico spazio.

L'edificio è di cinque piani, e nell'ultimo di questi si trova la residenza Renaud. Anticamente era adibito ad un uso commerciale, che adesso si è tramutato completamente in residenziale. Il loft è testimone della diversità e della complessità dell'ambiente circostante. Il suo design fa riferimento agli elementi tradizionali che hanno definito la modernità concepita in un'epoca anteriore.

La prima divisione ideata differenzia le funzioni pubbliche da quelle private. Il legno di ciliegio avvolge gli ambienti privati, che inoltre rimangono coperti da un controsoffitto interrotto da lucernari che fanno passare la luce fino alle zone più intime.

Architects: Cha & Innerhofer

Location: New York, United States

Photographs: Dao-Lou Zha

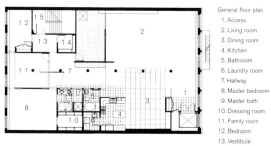

General floor plan	Planta general	Pianta generale
1. Access	1. Acceso	1. Accesso
2. Living room	2. Sala de estar	2. Soggiorno
3. Dining room	3. Comedor	3. Sala da pranzo
4. Kitchen	4. Cocina	4. Cucina
5. Bathroom	5. Baño	5. Bagno
6. Laundry room	6. Lavandería	6. Lavanderia
7. Hallway	7. Distribuidor	7. Disimpegno
8. Master bedroom	8. Dormitorio principal	8. Stanza da letto principale
9. Master bath	9. Baño principal	9. Bagno principale
10. Dressing room	10. Vestidor	10. Stanzino
11. Family room	11. Habitación familiar	11. Stanza familiare
12. Bedroom	12. Dormitorio	12. Stanza da letto
13. Vestibule	13. Vestíbulo	13. Anticamera
14. Storage room	14. Almacén	14. Dispensa
15. Service stairway	15. Escalera de servicio	15. Scala di servizio

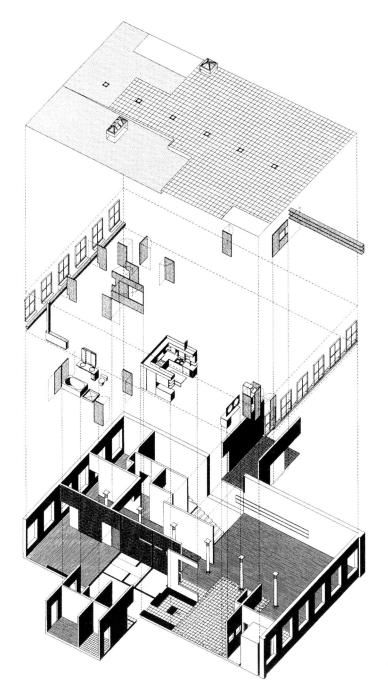

Spatial Flexibility
Flexibilidad espacial / Flessibilità spaziale

Kar-Hwa Ho
Architecture & Design

An old warehouse in the Flatiron district of New York houses this 195 m² loft located near the Empire State Building.

The original layout was considered appropriate, and the aim was to bring comfort and serenity to the space. The objectives of the improvement were mainly centered on including large spaces to be used exclusively for storage and integrated into the wall architecture. Likewise, the artificial lighting system adds to the uniform natural daylight that comes in through the north-facing windows that open the loft onto the street.

The walls were covered with panels with skirting boards incorporated into the same surface. Using a simple range of colors, the walls were painted in a light, luminous cream-like color, as were the doors. The design of the glass bar is an original, colorful element that defines the connection between the kitchen and the dining room. The care taken when designing each detail can especially be appreciated when noting the decision to avoid handles on the closet doors in an effort to integrate them into the walls.

Un antiguo almacén del distrito Flatiron de Nueva York alberga este loft de 195 m² junto al Empire State Building.

Se consideró adecuada la distribución original y se buscó aportar comodidad y serenidad al lugar. Los objetivos de mejora se centraron en ubicar espacios generosos para almacenaje de uso exclusivo integrados en la arquitectura de las paredes. Igualmente, el sistema de iluminación artificial incrementa la luz natural homogénea que llega de las ventanas de orientación norte que abren el loft a la calle.

Las paredes fueron revestidas con paneles que incorporan en su disposición la presencia del zócalo en un mismo plano. En una gama de colores muy sencilla, los paramentos se han pintado en tono claro color crema, muy luminoso, que también se ha aplicado a las puertas. El diseño del mueble bar de cristal es el elemento original y colorista que articula la conexión entre la cocina y el comedor. El cuidado del diseño en cada detalle se aprecia en gran medida al observar la decisión de evitar los tiradores en las puertas de los armarios con tal de integrarlos en las paredes.

Un antico magazzino del distretto di Flatiron di New York, ospita questo loft di 195 m², vicino all'Empire State Building.

La distribuzione originale si ritenne adeguata e si cercò di apportare al luogo comodità e serenità. Gli obiettivi delle migliorie si sono concentrati nell'ubicazione di spazi ampi, per l'alloggio esclusivo di determinati oggetti, integrati nell'architettura delle pareti. Allo stesso modo, il sistema di illuminazione artificiale incrementa la luce naturale omogenea che arriva dalle finestre orientate a nord, che proiettano il loft sulla strada.

Le pareti sono state rivestite con pannelli la cui struttura presenta già incorporato, su uno stesso piano, lo zoccolo. In una gamma di colori molto semplice, i paramenti sono stati dipinti in un tono chiaro color crema, molto luminoso, che si è applicato pure alle porte. Il design del mobile bar in vetro, è l'elemento originale e coloristico che articola il collegamento tra la cucina e la sala da pranzo. L'attenzione riposta nel design, curato nei minimi particolari, si fa evidente in gran parte nella decisione di non utilizzare nessun pomello nelle ante degli armadi, al fine di integrarli nelle pareti.

Architects: Kar-Hwa Ho Architecture & Design

Location: New York, United States

Photographs: Björg/Photography

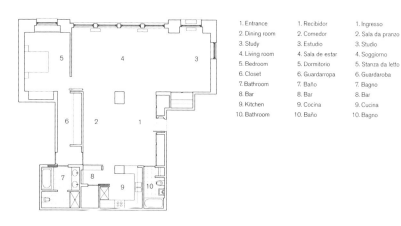

1. Entrance	1. Recibidor	1. Ingresso
2. Dining room	2. Comedor	2. Sala da pranzo
3. Study	3. Estudio	3. Studio
4. Living room	4. Sala de estar	4. Soggiorno
5. Bedroom	5. Dormitorio	5. Stanza da letto
6. Closet	6. Guardarropa	6. Guardaroba
7. Bathroom	7. Baño	7. Bagno
8. Bar	8. Bar	8. Bar
9. Kitchen	9. Cocina	9. Cucina
10. Bathroom	10. Baño	10. Bagno

The hanging lights in the dining room, cylinders of milky hand-blown glass suspended on a stainless steel rings, were designed by the architect Kar-Hwa Ho.

Las luminarias suspendidas del comedor son diseño del arquitecto Kar-Hwa Ho, un cilindro de cristal lechoso soplado manualmente y soportado por un collar de acero inoxidable.

Le lampade da sospensione della sala da pranzo sono opera dell'architetto Kar-Hwa Ho, e sono costituite da un cilindro di vetro latteo soffiato a mano e sorretto da un collare di acciaio inossidabile.

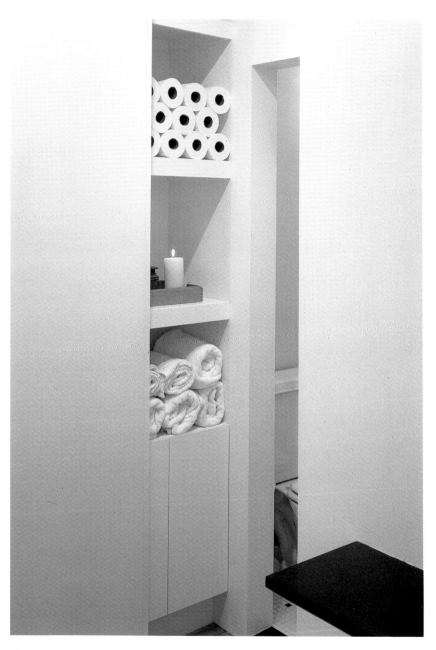

New Trends
Nuevas tendencias / Nuove tendenze

Hardy Holzman
Pfeiffer Associates

This building at 117 East 24th Street is located in the heart of New York's historic district and predates its more famous neighboring buildings: the Flatiron Building by the architect Burnham, Le Brun and Corbett's Metropolitan Life building, and Hardenburg's Western Union building.

Many elements were left just as they had been found: these include the beams and ceilings that were found in a state of ruin in order to show off the installation of a freight elevator. The skylight was re-covered with translucent glass similar to Fersnel, which was originally used in the building's construction. The flooring, which had been found in pieces and very damaged, was repaired, polished, and dyed in a dark reddish tone. Ondulating, fine-structured fiberglass panels were installed, allowing for the transparency and brightness created by the fluorescent light installed inside them to shine through and dramatically transform the space. A neon light heralds the kitchen space.

The loft is the backdrop and gallery for some prestigious paintings and works of art such as that by Philip Pearlstein and Jack Beal, as well as of rugs from different places and eras. Landsman and Holzman's loft, for they are both renters and architects, is a stimulating, attractive place where a new perspective on the concept of housing is set forth.

El edificio de la 117 East 24th Street se encuentra en el corazón histórico de Nueva York y precede a sus más conocidos edificios vecinos: el Flatiron Building, del arquitecto Burnham, el Metropolitan Life, de Le Brun y Corbett, o el Western Union, de Hardenberg.

Muchos de los elementos se dejaron tal y como se encontraron; entre ellos, vigas y techos que se hallaban en un estado ruinoso, para mostrar la instalación del montacargas. El lucernario se ha cubierto nuevamente con cristal translúcido tipo Fersnel, original de la construcción del edificio. El pavimento, que se encontró a pedazos y bastante castigado, se ha reparado, pulido y teñido de un tono rojizo oscuro. Se han montado paneles ondulados de fibra de vidrio con una fina estructura que permite la transparencia y el brillo creados por la luz fluorescente instalada en su interior y que transforma dramáticamente el espacio. Una luz de neón anuncia el espacio de la cocina.

El loft es escenario y galería de algunas pinturas y obras de prestigio como la de Philip Pearlstein y Jack Beal, o alfombras de diferentes orígenes y épocas. El loft de Landsman y Holzman, inquilinos y arquitectos, es un lugar estimulante y atractivo donde se sugiere una nueva perspectiva en el concepto de vivienda.

L'edificio al numero 117 Est della 24ª Strada, si trova nel centro storico di New York e precede i suoi, più noti, edifici limitrofi: il Flatiron Building, dell'architetto Burnham, il Metropolitan Life, opera di Le Brun e Corbett, o il Western Union, di Hardenberg.

Molti elementi sono stati lasciati così come li hanno trovati; tra questi, travi e soffitti che si trovavano in uno stato rovinoso, per mostrare l'installazione del montacarichi. Il lucernario è stato nuovamente coperto con vetro traslucido di tipo Fersnel, che risaliva alla costruzione originaria dell'edificio. Il pavimento, trovato a pezzi e alquanto danneggiato, è stato riparato, lisciato, e tinto in un tono rossiccio scuro. Si sono montati dei pannelli ondulati, in fibra di vetro, con una fine struttura che consente la trasparenza e la luminosità create dalla luce fluorescente installata all'interno e che trasforma drammaticamente lo spazio. Una luce al neon annuncia lo spazio riservato alla cucina.

Il loft è sfondo e galleria di alcuni dipinti ed opere di prestigio come quelle di Philip Pearlstein e Jack Beal, o tappeti di provenienze ed epoche diverse. Il loft di Landsman e Holzman, al contempo inquilini e architetti, è un luogo stimolante ed attraente che suggerisce una prospettiva nuova nel concetto di abitazione.

Architects: Hardy Holzman Pfeiffer Associates

Location: Manhattan, New York, United States

Photographs: Hardy Holzman Pfeiffer Associates

Panels of galvanized sheet metal with a brick-like texture cover the perimeter walls.

Paneles de chapa galvanizados con un relieve semejante al ladrillo de obra cubren las paredes envolventes.

Pannelli in lamiera galvanizzati con un rilievo simile al mattone a vista coprono le avvolgenti pareti.

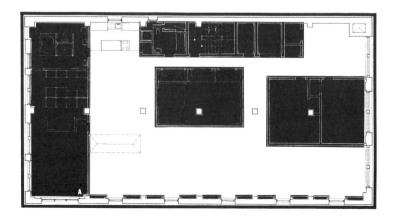

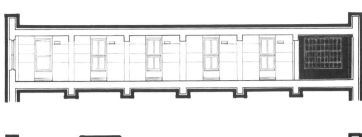

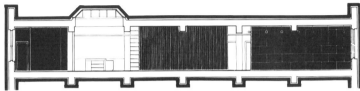

Apartment in Manhattan
Apartamento en Manhattan / Appartamento a Manhattan

Shelton, Mindel
& Associates

The first step in the process of designing this almost 200 m² apartment was to identify the problems that required specific solutions. Thus, the priorities of integrating the design into the city, making the best use of the ceiling, and housing a collection of furniture and decorative arts pieces by 20th century artists and architects were set.

The lower level of this apartment very clearly differentiates between public and private spaces. The area for social relations is organized on the southern façade around a central element shaped like a water tank. A large living room with a chimney and a dining room with an adjacent seating zone are located on either side of the central artifact, made up of a circular space and a glass box with a stainless steel spiral staircase.

The movable panels are an important element in the home since the possibility of opening and closing them modifies the perception of the space. Aluminum, stainless steel, white structural glass, oak and cherry wood on the floors constitute some of the materials used in this apartment, while Prouve, Richard Serra, Hoffman, Jacobsen, Aalto, Charles Eames, Caldés, Wagner and Robert Ryman are some of the artists, sculptors, potters and architects whose works can be found in its interior.

El proceso de proyección seguido en este apartamento de casi 200 m² tenía como primer paso detectar los problemas que requerían soluciones concretas. Así, se establecieron como prioridades integrar el proyecto en la ciudad, sacar el máximo provecho de las cuatro fachadas y de la cubierta y albergar una colección de mobiliario y piezas de artes decorativas de artistas y arquitectos del siglo xx.

El nivel inferior del apartamento tiene diferenciados muy claramente los ámbitos público y privado. La zona propicia para las relaciones sociales se organiza ocupando la fachada sur y en torno a un elemento central con forma de depósito de agua. Una gran sala de estar con chimenea y un comedor con zona anexa para sentarse se sitúan a ambos lados del artefacto central, formado por un espacio circular y una caja de vidrio con una escalera de acero inoxidable de doble hélice.

En la vivienda los paneles móviles adquieren cierta relevancia, pues la posibilidad de abrirlos o cerrarlos modifica la percepción del espacio. Aluminio, acero inoxidable, vidrio blanco estructural, madera de roble y de cerezo en los suelos constituyen algunos de los materiales utilizados en este apartamento, mientras que Prouve, Richard Serra, Hoffman, Jacobsen, Aalto, Charles Eames, Caldés, Wagner y Robert Ryman son algunos de los artistas, escultores, ceramistas o arquitectos cuyas obras podemos encontrar en su interior.

Il processo progettuale seguito per questo appartamento di quasi 200 m² prevedeva come fase iniziale individuare i problemi che richiedevano delle soluzioni concrete. Così, si stabilirono come priorità: integrare il progetto nella città, trarre il massimo vantaggio dalle quattro facciate e dalla copertura, e accogliere una collezione di mobili e di pezzi di arti decorative, di artisti e architetti del XX secolo.

La parte inferiore dell'appartamento distingue molto chiaramente le zone comuni da quelle più intime e private. La zona che si presta alle relazioni sociali si organizza occupando la facciata sud e attorno a un elemento centrale a forma di cisterna. Un ampio soggiorno provvisto di un caminetto, e una sala da pranzo con una zona attigua per sedersi occupano ambedue i lati di questa zona centrale, formata da uno spazio circolare e una cassa di vetro, con una scala in acciaio inossidabile a doppia elica.

Nell'abitazione i pannelli mobili acquisiscono una certa rilevanza, visto che la possibilità di aprirli o chiuderli modifica la percezione dello spazio. Alluminio, acciaio inossidabile, vetro strutturale bianco, legno di rovere e ciliegio nei pavimenti, costituiscono alcuni dei materiali utilizzati in questo appartamento. All'interno del quale possiamo trovare opere di artisti, scultori, ceramisti ed architetti come per esempio Prouve, Richard Serra, Hoffman, Jacobsen, Aalto, Charles Eames, Caldés, Wagner e Robert Ryman.

Architects: Shelton, Mindel & Associates

Location: Manhattan, New York, United States

Photographs: Michael Moran

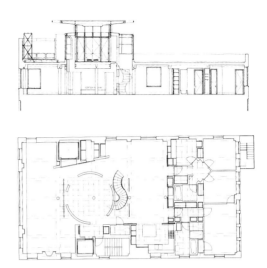

On the west façade, an irregular volume contains the elevator and a storage closet. In addition, a L-shaped swath of utility areas separates this more public space from the private space. Part of the L, which contains the stairwell and elevator shaft, the entrance to the apartment, the half-bathroom and the kitchen —which opens out onto the dining room—occupies the east façade. The other part, with a bathroom and dressing room for the two single bedrooms and another for the larger bedroom, creates an intermediate area between the bedrooms—with excellent panoramic views on the north façade—and the rest of the home.

En la fachada oeste, un volumen irregular contiene un ascensor y el almacén. Además, una franja de servicios en forma de L separa este entorno más público del privado. Una parte de la L, la que contiene el núcleo vertical de comunicaciones, la entrada al apartamento, un aseo y la cocina —que se abre al comedor—, ocupa la fachada este; la otra, con un baño y un vestidor para las dos habitaciones simples y otro tanto para la doble, crea una zona intermedia entre los dormitorios —con excelentes panorámicas en la fachada norte— y el resto de la vivienda.

Nella facciata ad ovest, una zona dai volumi irregolari contiene l'ascensore e la dispensa. Inoltre, un blocco di servizi a forma di L separa questo ambiente comune da quello più intimo e privato. Una parte della L, quella che contiene il nucleo verticale di comunicazioni, l'ingresso all'appartamento, una toilette e la cucina, – che dà sulla sala da pranzo – occupa la facciata ad est; l'altra, con un bagno e uno stanzino per le due stanze da letto singole, e un altro bagno per la camera doppia, crea una zona intermedia tra le stanze da letto – con eccellenti panoramiche nella facciata a nord- e il resto dell'abitazione.

Artists' Residence
Residencia para artistas / Residenza per artisti

Abelow Connors
Sherman Architects

The writer Joel Siegel and his wife, the painter Ena Swansea, acquired this loft in New York City with the intention of creating a unified space that they could use for both living and working.

The design respected the vaulted ceilings and industrial details. Similar materials and products were used to restore the different surfaces, and the electrical installations and tubing were left exposed.

The painting studio is located in the northern part of the house. Thus, the painter can enjoy the panoramic views through the large windows and take advantage of the balanced, cool, and constant light provided by a northward orientation. The office is located in the middle of the loft.

The more private areas (bedrooms, bathrooms and dressing room) are located in the perimeter area and are separated from the common areas by walls. The kitchen, dining room and living room merge with the painting studio, the entrance and the hallways.

El escritor Joel Siegel y su esposa, la pintora Ena Swansea, adquirieron este loft en la ciudad de Nueva York con la intención de crear un espacio unificado que les sirviera como vivienda y lugar de trabajo.

El proyecto fue respetuoso con los techos abovedados y los detalles industriales. Para restaurar las distintas superficies se utilizaron materiales y productos similares y se dejaron al descubierto las instalaciones eléctricas y el sistema de tuberías.

El estudio para pintar está ubicado en la parte norte de la casa. Así, la pintora puede disfrutar de las vistas panorámicas que ofrecen los grandes ventanales y aprovechar la luz equilibrada, fría y constante que proporciona esta orientación. El despacho ocupa el centro del loft.

Las zonas más privadas (las habitaciones, los baños y el vestidor) están ubicadas en el área perimetral y separadas de las zonas comunes mediante tabiques. La cocina, el comedor y la sala de estar se funden con el estudio para pintar, la entrada y los espacios de circulación.

Lo scrittore Joel Siegel e la sua sposa, la pittrice Ena Swansea, acquistarono questo loft nella città di New York con l'intenzione di creare uno spazio unificato che servisse loro da abitazione e luogo di lavoro.

Il nuovo progetto rispettò i tetti a volta e i particolari industriali originari. Per restaurare le diverse superfici sono stati utilizzati materiali e prodotti simili, lasciando allo scoperto le istallazioni elettriche e il sistema di condutture.

Lo studio di pittura si trova nella parte a nord della casa. Così, la pittrice può godersi le viste panoramiche offerte dai finestroni e sfruttare la luce equilibrata, fredda e costante che dona questa orientazione. L'ufficio occupa la parte centrale del loft.

Le zone più intime (le stanze da letto, i bagni e lo stanzino) si trovano nell'area perimetrale e sono separate dalle zone di uso comune mediante dei tramezzi. La cucina, la sala da pranzo e il soggiorno si fondono con lo studio di pittura, l'ingresso e gli spazi di circolazione.

Architects: Abelow Connors Sherman Architects

Location: New York, United States

Photographs: Michael Moran

1. Bedroom	1. Habitación	1. Stanza da letto
2. Living room	2. Sala de estar	2. Soggiorno
3. Dining room	3. Comedor	3. Sala da pranzo
4. Multimedia space	4. Espacio multimedia	4. Spazio multimediale
5. Kitchen	5. Cocina	5. Cucina
6. Painting studio	6. Taller de pintura	6. Studio di pittura
7. Bathroom	7. Baño	7. Bagno
8. Dressing room	8. Vestidor	8. Stanzino

Urban Interface

Dean/Wolf Architects

The Urban Interface loft works within the idea of a home contained within an imaginary plane which represents the new skyline within the same city. This new skyline is made by the outline of the roofs of the six-story buildings that make up the urban environment of Duane Park. The roof surface is carved and open to the sky, uncovering and juxtaposing different landscapes between the city and the sky. At the same time, this lower city skyline is allowed to enter the loft and generates a visual and physical link that through this connection only serves to increase the contrast existing between lower and higher levels in the urban context.

The universe created at a lower level is capable of creating a new center of tensions. The depth inherent in the interior generates a special external domain stolen from the cityscape. Cutting the original wall that defined the building allows for the insertion of a domestic scale in the private sphere of the loft. This new copper-covered roof wall belongs to both the outside and the inside space at the same time, thus linking both parts of the public sphere that form part of this loft.

El loft Urban Interface desarrolla la idea de vivienda contenida en un plano imaginario base que representa el nuevo plano horizonte dentro de una misma ciudad. Este nuevo horizonte está formado por el perfil que dibujan las cubiertas de los edificios de seis pisos de altura que conforman el entorno urbano de Duane Park. El plano de cubierta está recortado y abierto al cielo, descubriendo y enfrentando diferentes paisajes entre el cielo y la ciudad. A un mismo tiempo, esta nueva planta de la ciudad recortada en las alturas se deja caer en el interior del loft y genera un enlace visual y físico que va aumentando, a través de esta conexión, el contraste que existe entre un nivel inferior y otro superior en un mismo contexto urbano.

El universo creado a un nivel más bajo es capaz de originar un nuevo centro de tensiones. La profundidad inherente a lo interior genera un particular reino exterior robado al paisaje de la ciudad. El recorte de la original envolvente que define el edificio permite la inserción de la escala doméstica en la esfera privada del loft. Esta nueva envolvente de la cubierta revestida de cobre pertenece al espacio exterior e interior a un mismo tiempo enlazando ambas partes de la esfera pública que forman parte del loft.

Il loft Urban Interface sviluppa l'idea dell'abitazione contenuta in un piano di base immaginario che rappresenta il nuovo piano orizzonte all'interno di una stessa città. Questo nuovo orizzonte è formato dal profilo che disegnano i tetti degli edifici, alti sei piani, che formano l'ambiente urbano di Duane Park. Il piano del tetto, ridotto e aperto al cielo, scopre e mette di fronte paesaggi diversi tra il cielo e la città. Allo stesso tempo, questa nuova pianta della città, ridotta in termini di altezza, si insinua all'interno del loft e crea un legame visivo e fisico che fa aumentare, mediante questo collegamento, il contrasto che esiste tra un livello inferiore e un altro superiore in uno stesso contesto urbano.

L'universo creato a un livello più basso è in grado di originare un nuovo centro di tensioni. La profondità insita nella parte interna genera un particolare regno esterno rubato al paesaggio della città. La riduzione dell'involucro originario consente di inserire la scala domestica nella sfera privata del loft. Questo nuovo involucro ricoperto di rame appartiene contemporaneamente allo spazio esterno ed interno, collegando entrambe le zone di uso comune che fanno parte del loft.

Architects: Dean/Wolf Architects

Location: New York, United States

Photographs: Peter Aaron/Esto

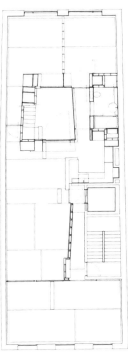

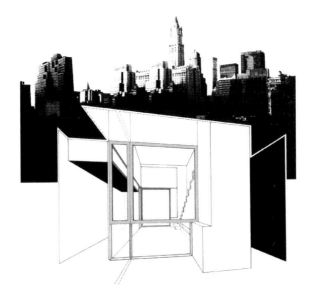

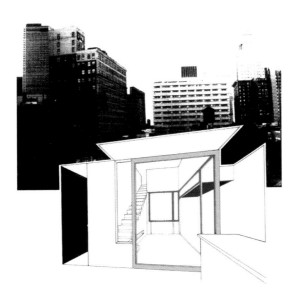

Industrial Feel
Aire industrial / Aria industriale

Alexander Jiménez

Far from being as spectacular as some of the designs in this book, this New York home does not stand out for its size or luxurious finishes, but for its simplicity and the effectiveness of the constructional and functional solutions used.

The living room and dining room are located in the same space and are differentiated through the use of large rugs placed beneath the furniture. This gesture allows for both spaces to be clearly delimited without the need to install flooring. The space gets plenty of natural daylight through its windows to the outside.

The kitchen, bedroom and bathroom are located in the inside of a structure placed into the surroundings as if it were a piece of furniture. In addition, this part of the home houses all the electrical, water and heating utilities. The walls only close off the bathroom and bedroom, and the kitchen is open to the rest of the house.

It was possible to restore the exposed brick finish on the walls and between the wooden ceiling beams, but the light wood floor was anew design since the original surface was severely damaged and refinishing it was unfeasible.

Lejos de la espectacularidad de algunos de los proyectos de este libro, esta vivienda neoyorquina no destaca por sus dimensiones o acabados lujosos, sino que despunta por la sencillez y la eficacia de las soluciones funcionales y constructivas utilizadas.

La sala de estar y el comedor están ubicados en el mismo habitáculo y se diferencian gracias a las alfombras que se colocan debajo del mobiliario. Este gesto permite, sin la necesidad de levantar paramentos, una delimitación notable de ambos espacios. La estancia recibe abundante luz natural de los ventanales que dan al exterior.

La cocina, el dormitorio y el cuarto de baño se encuentran ubicados en el interior de una estructura colocada a modo de mueble en la envolvente. Además, esta parte de la vivienda alberga todas las instalaciones eléctricas, de agua y de calefacción. Los tabiques levantados sólo cierran el baño y la habitación, y la cocina se abre al resto de la casa.

Fue posible restaurar el acabado de ladrillo visto en las paredes y el entramado de vigas de madera del techo pero el suelo de madera clara se ha proyectado de nuevo, ya que el original estaba seriamente dañado y su recuperación era inviable.

Lontani dalla spettacolarità di alcuni progetti di questo libro, questa abitazione newyorkese non spicca per le sue dimensioni o rifiniture di lusso, quanto per la semplicità e l'efficacia delle soluzioni funzionali e costruttive utilizzate.

Il soggiorno e la sala da pranzo si trovano nello stesso ambiente e si differenziano grazie ai tappeti disposti sotto i mobili. Questa soluzione permette, senza bisogno di costruire paramenti, una marcata delimitazione di entrambi gli ambienti. Tutta la stanza riceve luce naturale in abbondanza dai finestroni che danno all'esterno.

La cucina, la stanza da letto e il bagno, si trovano all'interno di una struttura collocata a guisa di mobile nell'involucro. Inoltre, in questa parte dell'abitazione si trovano tutti gli impianti elettrici, di acqua e riscaldamento. I tramezzi eretti chiudono solo il bagno e la stanza da letto, mentre la cucina rimane aperta proiettandosi verso il resto della casa.

È stato possibile restaurare la finitura in mattoni a vista delle pareti e l'intelaiatura delle travi di legno del soffitto, mentre si è dovuto progettare nuovamente il pavimento in legno chiaro, visto che quello originale era seriamente danneggiato e il suo recupero non era fattibile.

Architect: Alexander Jiménez
Location: New York, United States
Photographs: Jordi Miralles

The bathroom is the only enclosed space in the design.

El baño es la única estancia cerrada del proyecto.

Il bagno è l'unica stanza chiusa del progetto.

A Blank Canvas
Un lienzo en blanco / Una tela in bianco

Vicente Wolf

Vicente Wolf's Manhattan loft is, in his own words: "A constant surrounding where I experiment with things that I love that form part of my work." He travels two months out of the year and always comes back laden with highly diverse objects that fit admirably well into his house. At almost 150 m², this loft has impressive southern, northern and eastern views of Manhattan.

Wolf's skill lies in combining all types of unique sculptural objects in a seemingly haphazard way.

A Gilda-style Louis XVI bench is placed across from a refined 1940s French armchair. Likewise, across from a wooden 19th century table we find a simple stool bought in a Tebas flea market.

Despite the ever-changing furniture in this loft's life, what is constant is the presence of the designer's collection of 20th century photos. These include black and white images by great figures such as Man Ray, Robert Mapplethorpe, Alexander Rodchenko and Diane Arbus.

El loft de Vicente Wolf en Manhattan es, según sus propias palabras: «Una envolvente constante donde experimento con las cosas que quiero que formen parte de mi trabajo». Se dedica a viajar unos dos meses al año, y siempre regresa cargado de objetos muy diversos que admirablemente encajan en su casa. De casi 150 m², este loft dispone de unas vistas impresionantes del sur, norte y este de la isla de Manhattan.

La destreza de Wolf está en combinar todo tipo de piezas esculturales de una fuerte presencia en una forma aparentemente fortuita.

Un banco estilo Gilda modelo Luis XVI se dispone en ángulo frente a un refinado sillón francés de 1940. Igualmente, frente a una mesa de madera del siglo XIX encontramos un sencillo taburete comprado en un mercadillo de Tebas.

A pesar del mobiliario siempre cambiante en la vida de este loft, es constante la presencia de la colección de fotos del siglo XX que tiene el diseñador. Imágenes en blanco y negro de grandes figuras como Man Ray, Robert Mapplethorpe, Alexander Rodchenko o Diane Arbus.

Il loft di Vicente Wolf a Manhattan è, come afferma lui stesso: «Un involucro costante dove faccio esperimenti con le cose che desidero facciano parte del mio lavoro». Per circa due mesi l'anno viaggia, e rientra sempre carico di oggetti molto diversi tra loro ma che, ammirevolmente, si addicono alla sua abitazione. Con quasi 150 m², questo loft dispone di impressionanti vedute della zona sud, nord ed est dell'isola di Manhattan.

La destrezza di Wolf consiste nell'abbinare qualsiasi tipo di pezzo scultoreo dalla forte presenza in un modo apparentemente fortuito.

Una panca in stile Gilda, modello Luigi XVI, si dispone ad angolo, di fronte a una raffinata poltrona francese del 1940. Di seguito troviamo, di fronte a un tavolo in legno del XIX secolo, un semplice sgabello comprato in un mercatino di Tebe.

Nonostante la mobilia sia un elemento variabile nella vita di questo loft, è costante la presenza della collezione di fotografie del XX secolo, appartenente al disegnatore. Immagini in bianco e nero di grandi artisti come Man Ray, Robert Mapplethorpe, Alexander Rodchenko o Diane Arbus.

Designer: Vicente Wolf

Location: Manhattan, New York, United States

Photographs: Vicente Wolf

A Play of Lights
Juego de luces / Gioco di luci

Moneo Brock Studio

The original structure showed the characteristics of having been an industrial warehouse: a central row of columns, enormous windows in the different walls and a ceiling more than three meters high. The design of the project had to bear in mind the modest budget and the possibility of adding higher quality finishes in the future.

The architects' strategy was to place the utility spaces along the windowless northern and southern façades. In order for these spaces to not appear totally separated from the others, they were treated as volumes that had been inserted inside the container. Their walls do not reach the ceiling and the materials used are iridescent, creating magnificent plays of reflections and highlighting the airiness of the modules.

In order to divide the open spaces according to the changing needs of the moment, translucent movable panels were chosen. The rail system for sliding the panels is comprehensive and multiple, such that they can change directions or be superimposed in order to achieve opacity.

La estructura original reunía las características de haber sido un almacén industrial: una hilera central de columnas, enormes ventanales en los distintos cerramientos y un techo de más de tres metros de altura. El desarrollo del proyecto debía tener en cuenta el ajustado presupuesto y la posibilidad de que en un futuro se pudieran añadir acabados de mejor calidad.

La estrategia de los arquitectos fue colocar las estancias de servicio en las fachadas norte y sur, que no tenían aberturas. Para que dichas estancias no aparecieran totalmente desligadas del resto se trataron como volúmenes insertados en el contenedor. Sus paredes no llegan al techo y los materiales utilizados son iridiscentes, crean magníficos juegos de reflejos y enfatizan la sensación de ligereza de los módulos.

Para distribuir el espacio abierto según las necesidades del momento, se eligieron unos paneles translúcidos y móviles. El sistema de raíles para deslizar los paneles es completo y múltiple, con lo que se pueden cambiar de dirección o sobreponer para conseguir opacidad.

La struttura originaria riuniva le caratteristiche tipiche di un magazzino industriale: una fila centrale di colonne, enormi finestroni nei diversi tramezzi e un soffitto alto più di tre metri. Lo sviluppo del progetto doveva tenere in considerazione il budget alquanto limitato e la possibilità di aggiungere, in futuro, finiture di una migliore qualità.

La strategia degli architetti consistette nel collocare le stanze di servizio nelle facciate nord e sud, prive di aperture. Affinché le suddette stanze non apparissero completamente separate dal resto, sono state trattate come volumi inseriti nello stesso contenitore. Le loro pareti non arrivano fino al soffitto e i materiali usati sono iridescenti, creano magnifici giochi fatti di riflessi e enfatizzano la sensazione di leggerezza dei moduli.

Per distribuire lo spazio aperto secondo le esigenze del momento, si è scelto di usare dei pannelli traslucidi e mobili. Il sistema a rotaie per far spostare i pannelli è comodo e multiplo, e consente di cambiare la loro direzione o di sovrapporli l'uno all'altro per ottenere opacità.

Architects: Moneo Brock Studio

Location: Manhattan, New York, United States

Photographs: Michael Moran

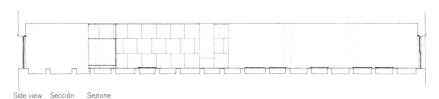

Side view   Sección   Sezione

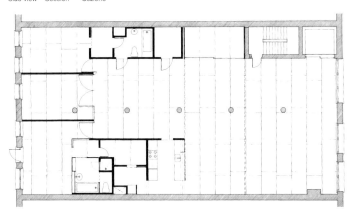

Top view   Planta   Pianta

Some of the design's vertical partitions are movable and make it easy to create different layouts within the home. The panels' translucence allows for a certain interaction between spaces, such that compartmentalization is never complete.

Algunas de las particiones verticales del proyecto son móviles y facilitan crear distintas distribuciones en la vivienda. El carácter translúcido de los paneles permite una cierta relación entre espacios, así que la compartimentación no es nunca definitiva.

Alcune divisioni verticali del progetto sono mobili e agevolano la creazione di varie distribuzioni all'interno dell'abitazione. Il carattere trasparente dei pannelli consente una certa relazione tra gli spazi, cosicché la compartimentazione non è mai definitiva.

Rosenberg Residence and Studio
Residencia y estudio Rosenberg / Residenza e studio Rosenberg

Belmont
Freeman Architects

Living and working in a lower Manhattan neighborhood can be a challenge in the city of skyscrapers. This loft was designed in a commercial building dating from 1900 that was converted into a home in the 1980s.

Two 140 m² apartments, each with a single bedroom, are vertically combined in order to place an office, a study and a living space for an art-loving renter.

The upper floor is a living space made up of a living room, a kitchen and two bedrooms. No partition interrupts the outside wall, which maintains the generous light coming from its northern orientation. The lower floor, with a recovered original floor surface of sand-blasted concrete and covered with cast zinc, is devoted to an office and a studio area. Two movable walls, one made of plasterboard and the other of milky glass, allow for different configurations within the loft. Finally, a ship's staircase connects both levels while at the same time distinguishing the working area from the private spaces in the living quarters above.

Vivir y trabajar en el barrio bajo de Manhattan de Nueva York puede convertirse en un reto en la ciudad de los rascacielos. El proyecto de este loft se encuentra en un edificio comercial del año 1900 que fue convertido en vivienda en los años ochenta.

Dos apartamentos de una sola habitación, de 140 m² cada uno, se combinan verticalmente para ubicar una oficina, un estudio y el lugar donde vivir para un inquilino enamorado del arte.

El piso superior es una vivienda formada por una sala de estar, una cocina y dos habitaciones. Ninguna partición interrumpe el muro exterior, que mantiene la generosa claridad que da la luz de orientación norte. El piso inferior, con una original superficie de suelo recuperado de hormigón chorreado a la arena y cubierto de fundición de zinc, está destinado a oficina y zona de estudio. Dos paramentos móviles, uno de cartón yeso y otro de cristal lechoso, permiten las diferentes configuraciones del loft. Finalmente, una escalerilla de barco conecta ambos niveles, al tiempo que distingue la zona de trabajo de las estancias privadas de la vivienda de arriba.

Vivere e lavorare nel quartiere di Manhattan a New York, la città dei grattacieli, può diventare una sfida. Il progetto di questo loft riguarda un edificio commerciale del 1900, riconvertito in abitazione negli anni '80.

Due appartamenti con un unico ambiente, ciascuno di 140 m², si uniscono verticalmente per configurare un ufficio, uno studio, e il luogo dove vivere per un inquilino innamorato dell'arte.

Il piano superiore è un'abitazione formata da un soggiorno, una cucina e due stanze da letto. Nessuna divisione interrompe il muro esterno, che mantiene la generosa luminosità che dà la luce dell'orientazione a nord. Il piano inferiore, dove si è potuta recuperare la superficie del pavimento, in calcestruzzo spruzzato di sabbia e ricoperto di zinco fuso, è adibito a ufficio e zona di studio. Due paramenti mobili, uno di cartongesso e l'altro in vetro latteo, rendono possibili le diverse configurazioni del loft. In ultimo, un'apposita scaletta a scomparsa collega tutti e due i livelli, distinguendo contemporaneamente la zona di lavoro dalle stanze private dell'abitazione del piano di sopra.

Architects: Belmont Freeman Architects

Location: Manhattan, New York, United States

Photographs: Christopher Wesnofske

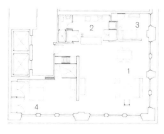

1. Living room	1. Sala de estar	1. Soggiorno
2. Kitchen	2. Cocina	2. Cucina
3. Bedroom	3. Dormitorio	3. Stanza da letto
4. Master bedroom	4. Dormitorio principal	4. Stanza da letto principale
5. Studio	5. Estudio	5. Studio
6. Wheeled wall	6. Pared rodante	6. Parete mobile
7. Office	7. Oficina	7. Ufficio
8. Pantry	8. Despensa	8. Dispensa
9. Security storage	9. Almacén de seguridad	9. Magazzino di sicurezza
10. Utility room	10. Sala de instalaciones	10. Sala impianti

Minimalist Continuity
Continuidad minimalista / Continuità minimalista

Form Werkstatt

The German architect, Siggi Pfundt, is the renter and designer of the renovation of this loft, which located in an old sewing machine factory in the center of Munich. After the remodeling, which was finished in 1997, this 70 m² space had been converted into a working and living space. "In order to conserve the original character of the old factory, the loft's renovation was carried out with the use of simple materials and construction methods," claims the architect.

In accordance with the design, the loft contains a main space extending along the entire façade devoted to a living room and studio; the bathroom and the bedroom are located in the back part of the apartment. Light and privacy in the more private zones are controlled through five birch wood covered plywood panels which hang from a steel track which virtually and physically marks a separation along the space's longitudinal axis. This ingenious and flexible solution maximally preserves the continuity and unification of the space while resolving all the practical considerations on a low budget.

La arquitecta alemana Siggi Pfundt es la inquilina y autora de la rehabilitación de este loft, ubicado en una antigua fábrica de máquinas de coser del centro de Munich. Tras la remodelación, terminada en el año 1997, este espacio de 70 m² quedó convertido en lugar de trabajo y vivienda. «Para conservar el carácter original de la antigua fábrica, la renovación del loft se llevó a cabo con el uso de materiales y métodos constructivos sencillos», comenta la arquitecta.

De acuerdo con el proyecto, el loft tiene un espacio principal destinado a zona de estar y estudio que se extiende a lo largo de la fachada; el baño y el dormitorio están situados en la parte posterior del apartamento. El control de la luz y la privacidad de las estancias más íntimas queda garantizado por cinco paneles de madera contrachapada de abedul, suspendidos de un riel de acero, que marcan virtual y físicamente una separación según el eje longitudinal del espacio. Esta ingeniosa y flexible solución preserva al máximo la continuidad y globalidad del espacio, al tiempo que resuelve todas las consideraciones prácticas con un modesto presupuesto.

L'architetto tedesco Siggi Pfundt è l'inquilina e l'autrice del restauro di questo loft, ubicato in un'antica fabbrica di macchine da cucire del centro di Monaco. In seguito alla ristrutturazione, ultimata nel 1997, questo spazio di 70 m² si trasformò in luogo di lavoro ed abitazione. «Per conservare il carattere originario dell'antica fabbrica, la ristrutturazione del loft si è portata a termine usando materiali e metodi costruttivi semplici», dichiara l'architetto.

Secondo quanto prevedeva il progetto, il loft dispone di uno spazio principale, destinato a soggiorno e studio, che si estende lungo l'intera facciata; il bagno e la stanza da letto si trovano nella parte posteriore dell'appartamento. Il controllo della luce e la privacy degli ambienti più intimi sono garantiti grazie all'uso di cinque pannelli in compensato di betulla, appesi a una riloga di acciaio, che segna sia virtualmente che fisicamente una separazione secondo l'asse longitudinale dello spazio. Questa ingegnosa e flessibile soluzione mantiene al massimo la continuità e la globalità dello spazio, risolvendo allo stesso tempo tutte le problematiche pratiche mediante un budget modesto.

Architects: Form Werkstatt

Location: Munich, Germany

Photographs: Karin Hessmann/Artur

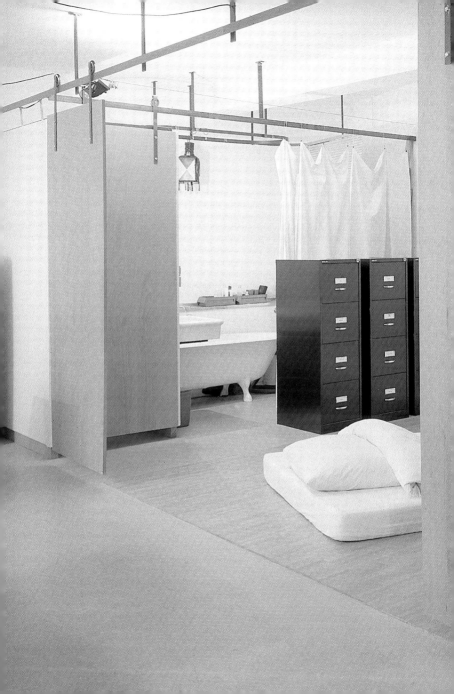

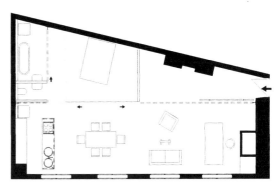

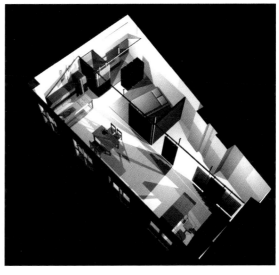

The majority of the furniture is second hand and comes from flea markets or has been recovered from the factory itself, such as the dining room, which used to be a tailor's table.

During the day, the movable birch-covered plywood separators allow the light and the privacy of the more private zones to be controlled.

La mayoría de los muebles son de segunda mano y proceden de mercadillos o han sido recuperados de la misma fábrica, como la mesa del comedor, antaño una mesa de sastrería.

De día, las separaciones móviles de madera contrachapada de abedul permiten el control de la iluminación y la privacidad de las zonas más íntimas.

La maggior parte dei mobili sono di seconda mano e provengono da mercatini o sono stati recuperati dalla stessa fabbrica, come il tavolo della sala da pranzo, prima un tavolo da sartoria.

Di giorno, le separazioni mobili in compensato di betulla consentono di controllare l'illuminazione e di gestire la privacy delle zone più intime.

Multi-purpose Space
Espacio polivalente / Spazio polivalente

Abelow Connors
Sherman Architects

The space retains the basic structure of the original building, which had been used as a warehouse and a horse stable. The slanted ceiling, the framework of wooden beams and pillars and the weight-bearing walls have been conserved. The interior had been left virtually intact since its construction in 1880. The architects decided to conserve the spirit of the building. The floor plan was designed through the abstraction of radial diagrams and formalizations based on the musical scale.

The agenda set forth by the client, a musician and producer, required all the conventional household elements, as well as an office and a complete recording studio including all the specific apparatuses needed.

A large multi-purpose studio, located on the lower floor and connected to an interior patio, is used as a living room and recording studio. It is three-stories high, thus benefitting from the acoustic advantages of open spaces. Aside from the studio, the lower floor also houses the kitchen, the dining room, a library and a space for computers. The two upper levels contain the bedrooms and other working zones, such as the control and editing rooms. The uses, both private and public, co-exist on all floors.

El local mantiene la estructura básica del edificio original, que se había utilizado como almacén y como establo para caballos. Se conservaron el techo inclinado, el entramado de vigas y pilares de madera y los muros portantes de ladrillo. El interior se mantuvo virtualmente intacto desde su construcción en 1880. Los arquitectos optaron por conservar el espíritu del edificio. La distribución se llevó a cabo mediante la abstracción de diagramas radiales y formalizaciones basadas en la escala musical.

El programa del cliente, un músico y productor, precisaba todos los elementos domésticos convencionales, un despacho y un completo estudio de grabación que incluyera todos los aparatos específicos necesarios.

Un gran estudio polivalente, ubicado en la planta baja y relacionado con un patio interior, se utiliza como sala de estar y estudio de grabación. Ocupa la altura de los tres pisos, aprovechando las ventajas acústicas de los espacios abiertos. Aparte del estudio, la planta baja también acoge la cocina, el comedor, una biblioteca y una estancia para los ordenadores. Los dos niveles superiores contienen las habitaciones y otras zonas de trabajo como la sala de control o de edición. Los usos, privados o públicos, conviven en todos los pisos.

Il locale mantiene la struttura di base dell'edificio originario, anticamente utilizzato come magazzino e come stalla per cavalli. Sono stati mantenuti il soffitto inclinato, l'intelaiatura fatta di travi e pilastri di legno, e i muri portanti in mattone. L'interno è stato mantenuto virtualmente intatto sin dalla sua costruzione nel 1880. Gli architetti hanno optato per mantenere lo spirito dell'edificio. La distribuzione si è realizzata mediante l'astrazione di diagrammi radiali e formalizzazioni basate sulla scala musicale.

Il programma del cliente, un musicista e produttore, aveva bisogno di tutti gli elementi domestici convenzionali, un ufficio e un completo studio di registrazione che includesse tutte le corrispondenti apparecchiature necessarie.

Un grande studio polivalente, ubicato a pian terreno e connesso a un cortile interno, viene utilizzato come soggiorno e studio di registrazione. Questo ambiente occupa un'altezza pari a tre piani, sfruttando i vantaggi acustici degli spazi aperti. A parte lo studio, a pian terreno si trova pure la cucina, la sala da pranzo, una biblioteca e una stanza per i computer. I due livelli superiori contengono le stanze da letto e altre zone di lavoro come la sala di controllo o di edizione. Gli usi, privati o comuni, convivono in tutti i piani.

Architects. Abelow Connors Sherman Architects
Location: Jersey City, New Jersey, United States
Photographs: Michael Moran

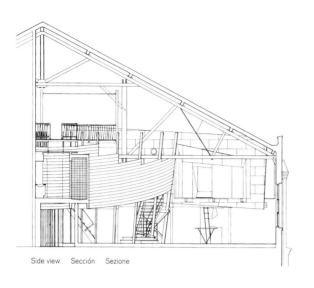

Side view   Sección   Sezione

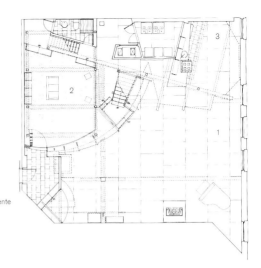

First floor

1. Multi-purpose
   room
2. Living room
3. Kitchen

Planta primera

1. Sala polivalente
2. Sala de estar
3. Cocina

Primo piano

1. Sala polivalente
2. Soggiorno
3. Cucina

O'Malley Residence
Residencia O'Malley / Residenza O'Malley

Carpenter/
Grodzins Architects

The O'Malley residence is located in Avoca, a small city located on the outskirts of Scranton, Pennsylvania. The building was originally a warehouse, and although its perimeter was demolished, the internal structure made up of columns, beams and walls which comprised an open, airy virtual volume remained.

The loft, around 140 m², is devoted to accommodating a single renter, whose main requirement consisted of retaining the maximum possible open space by including large storage zones. Thus, the floor plan was organized along the north wall, which houses the closets, and the south wall, which contains the kitchen and the bathroom.

In order to get as much natural daylight as possible from the southern orientation, both the bathroom and the kitchen were planned as interchangeable elements that connect spaces with light. This was achieved through the incorporation of translucent glass panels and a large horizontal cutout which becomes an eating counter.

La residencia O'Malley se encuentra en Avoca, una pequeña ciudad situada a las afueras de Scranton, en Pensilvania. En sus orígenes el edificio constituyó un almacén, y aunque su perímetro fue demolido, permaneció la estructura de columnas, vigas y muros que conformaba un diáfano volumen virtual.

El loft, de alrededor de 140 m², está destinado a acomodar a un solo inquilino, cuyo principal requerimiento consistió en mantener el mayor espacio abierto posible con la incorporación de importantes zonas de almacenaje. De este modo, la distribución se organizó según el muro norte, que alberga los armarios, y la fachada sur, que concentra la cocina y el baño.

Para sacar el mayor rendimiento posible de la luz natural de la orientación sur, tanto el baño como la cocina se plantean como elementos intercambiadores que comunican los espacios con el paso de la claridad. El primero lo consigue mediante la incorporación de paneles de cristal translúcido, y el segundo, con un gran corte horizontal que se convierte en mostrador para comer.

La Residenza O'Malley si trova ad Avoca, una cittadina situata nella periferia di Scranton, in Pensilvania. Anticamente l'edificio era un magazzino, e sebbene il suo perimetro sia stato abbattuto, è rimasta la struttura di colonne, travi e muri che formava un diafano volume virtuale.

Il loft, di circa 140 m², accoglierà un solo inquilino, la cui principale richiesta è stata quella di mantenere quanto più spazio aperto possibile, introducendo comunque notevoli zone di stoccaggio. In questo modo, la distribuzione è stata organizzata secondo il muro a nord, che comprende gli armadi, e la facciata a sud, che concentra la cucina e il bagno.

Per trarre il maggior rendimento possibile dalla luce naturale dell'orientazione a sud, sia il bagno che la cucina vengono concepiti come elementi «di scambio», che mettono in comunicazione gli spazi con il passaggio della luminosità. Il bagno ci riesce mediante l'incorporazione di pannelli di vetro traslucido, mentre la cucina, con un grande taglio orizzontale che si trasforma in un banco da cucina dove si può mangiare.

Architects: Carpenter/Grodzins Architects

Location: Avoca, Pennsylvania, United States

Photographs: Chun Y. Lai/Photography

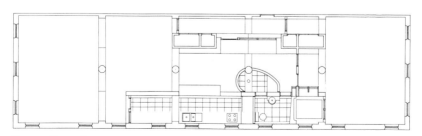

Top view   Planta   Pianta

Accessibility
Accesibilidad / Accessibilità

Paul Guzzardo,
Ray Simon

The objective was to convert the second floor of an old industrial building into a loft. The building had originally been a four-story shoe factory in Saint Louis.

The second floor, which is approximately 420 m², is a deep space which is compressed between large brick walls and divided down the middle by five thick concrete columns. The designer's response consisted of retaining the entire width of the floor, minimizing the partitions, and avoiding the visual obstructions produced by the columns.

Isolation and accessibility were crucial issues to be resolved, given that the agenda called for a separation of the first and second floors, as well as a direct entryway from the street through the building's back stairway. This outdoor stairway led directly from the first floor to the second, but there was no connection with the outside since a chimney blocked access from the street.

Thus, a curved wall was built to connect the second floor with the first, where a night club was located, and the chimney was sealed with a skylight.

The apartment conserves and has reused many of the tools from the shoe factory, such as the assembly benches, which are now used as wooden tables, and the metallic staircase. Even the window shutters and the fire doors are original elements from the building.

El objetivo era convertir el segundo piso de un antiguo edificio industrial en una fábrica de zapatos de cuatro plantas en Saint Louis.

La segunda planta, de alrededor de 420 m², es un espacio profundo, comprimido entre largas paredes de ladrillo y dividido en su eje central por cinco gruesas columnas de hormigón. La respuesta del diseñador consistió en mantener toda la amplitud de la planta, minimizando las particiones y evitando las obstrucciones visuales que producen las columnas.

Aislamiento y accesibilidad eran temas cruciales que resolver, dado que el programa requería la separación del segundo y el primer piso, así como una entrada directa desde la calle a través de la escalera trasera del inmueble. Una escalera al aire libre conducía directamente de la primera planta a la segunda, pero no había comunicación con el exterior, ya que una chimenea bloqueaba el acceso desde la calle.

A tal efecto se construyó un muro curvo que comunica la segunda con la primera planta, donde hay un *night club*, y se selló la chimenea con un tragaluz.

El apartamento conserva y ha reutilizado muchos de los utensilios de la fábrica de zapatos como las banquetas usadas en los montajes, que se han convertido en mesas de madera, o la escalera metálica. Incluso los postigos de las ventanas o las puertas contra incendios son elementos originales del edificio.

L'obiettivo era trasformare il secondo piano di un antico edificio industriale in un loft. Originariamente, era una fabbrica di scarpe di quattro piani, a Saint Louis.

Il secondo piano, di circa 420 m², è uno spazio profondo, compresso tra lunghe pareti di mattone e diviso nel suo asse centrale da cinque grosse colonne di cemento. La risposta del designer consistette nel mantenere tutta l'ampiezza del piano, minimizzando le divisioni ed evitando le ostruzioni visive che producono le colonne.

Isolamento e accessibilità erano questioni cruciali da risolvere, visto che il programma richiedeva la separazione del secondo e del primo piano, così come un'entrata diretta dalla strada attraverso la scala posteriore dell'immobile. Una scala all'aria aperta conduceva direttamente dal primo al secondo piano, ma non c'era nessuna comunicazione con l'esterno, visto che un caminetto bloccava l'accesso dalla strada.

A questo scopo venne costruito un muro curvo che comunica il secondo piano con il primo, dove si trova un *night club*, e si sigillò il caminetto con un lucernaio.

L'appartamento conserva ed ha riutilizzato molti degli attrezzi della fabbrica di scarpe come le panche usate nei montaggi, che sono diventate tavole di legno, o la scala metallica. Persino le imposte delle finestre o le porte antincendio sono elementi che risalgono all'edificio originario.

Architects: Paul Guzzardo, Ray Simon

Location: Saint Louis, Missouri, United States

Photographs: Jeffery Johnston/Photography

Top view:
1. Vestibule, living room and music room
2. Unit divided into bathroom and laundry room
3. Bath/shower stall
4. Kitchen cupboards and storage
5. Kitchen working counter
6. Building's interior staircase
7. Drainage conduit
8. Metallic shutters
9. Freight elevator
10. Curved wall
11. Cabool office
13. Stairway to Club Cabool

Planta
1. Vestíbulo, sala de estar y sala de música
2. Unidad dividida en baño y lavandería
3. Pabellón de baño con ducha
4. Armarios de cocina y almacén
5. Mostrador de trabajo de cocina
6. Escalera interior del inmueble
7. Conducto de saneamiento
8. Contraventanas metálicas
9. Montacargas
10. Zona dormitorio
11. Pantalla curva
12. Bufete Cabool
13. Escalera al Club Cabool

Pianta
1. Atrio, soggiorno e sala da musica
2. Unità divisa in bagno e lavanderia
3. Padiglione da bagno con doccia
4. Armadi da cucina e dispensa
5. Piano di lavoro della cucina
6. Scala interna dell'immobile
7. Condotto di scarico
8. Controfinestre metalliche
9. Montacarichi
10. Zona stanza da letto
11. Pannello curvo
12. Ufficio Cabool
13. Scala di accesso al Club Cabool

The ceilings and circular support pillars are made of concrete. The floor was covered in maple wood panels treated with oil and a special urethane preparation.

Los techos y la estructura de pilares circulares son de hormigón. El suelo se cubrió con un entarimado de madera de arce tratada con un aceite y un preparado especial de uretano.

I soffitti e la struttura a pilastri circolari sono in cemento. Il pavimento è stato ricoperto con una parchettatura in legno di acero trattato con dell'apposito olio e un preparato speciale di uretano.

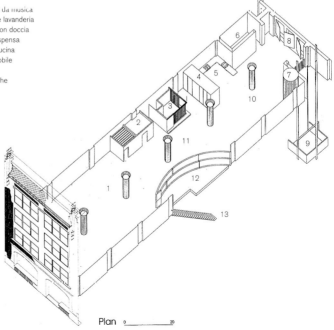

Plan 0_____20

1709 Studio

Paul Guzzardo,
David Davis

At 1709 Washington Street we find this early 20th century building which had been used for trade in leather goods.

The story that was renovated for this loft occupies the fourth floor and is a 8 x 12 meter rectangle. Flanked by large windows that make up the corner façade, the space is a continuum where the concrete structural pillars mark the rhythm in which the different spaces are located.

The designer's main consideration consisted of providing the inhabitant with all the comforts of home while respecting the space's maximum width, the views of the city, and the building's industrial heritage.

A semi-circle built of corrugated sheet metal contains the bathroom and the dressing room and creates a gallery of plexi-glass panels in the upper part that allow light to enter from outside.

The kitchen area is located between two transparent walls running perpendicular to the façade which are propped up on metal and glass bases. In the area chosen as the bedroom, we find a new mechanism for providing privacy when sleeping: it consists of bedspreads hung from tubes, handkerchief-style, which when spread out enclose the bed as if they were curtains. This invention for an enclosure is at once decorative, while it also provides acoustic insulation.

En el número 1709 de la calle Washington se encuentra ubicado este edificio de principios de siglo (1903) cuya actividad fue el comercio de pieles.

La planta objeto de la reforma ocupa el cuarto piso del edificio y tiene una forma rectangular de 8 x 12 metros. Flanqueado por grandes ventanales que conforman la fachada en esquina, el espacio es un continuo donde la estructura de columnas de hormigón marca un ritmo en el que se van ubicando las diferentes estancias.

La consideración principal del diseño consistió en proveer al inquilino con todas las comodidades, respetando siempre la máxima amplitud del espacio, las vistas de la ciudad y la herencia industrial del edificio.

Un semicírculo construido con chapa corrugada de metal contiene el baño y el vestidor y crea en lo alto una galería de paneles de plexiglás que permite la entrada de luz desde el exterior.

La zona destinada a cocina se ubica entre dos paredes transparentes y perpendiculares a la fachada, levantadas sobre montantes de metal y vidrio. En el área elegida como dormitorio encontramos un mecanismo nuevo para dar privacidad al sueño: consiste en unas colchas colgadas de unos tubos, como si fueran pañuelos de mano, que al abrirse cercan la cama como lo harían unas cortinas. Este invento envolvente, a la vez que decorativo, también aísla acústicamente.

Al numero 1709 di via Washington si trova questo edificio che risale agli inizi del secolo (1903), la cui attività era stata il commercio delle pelli.

La pianta oggetto del restauro occupa il quarto piano dell'edificio e ha una forma rettangolare di 8 x 12 metri. Fiancheggiato da grandi finestre che formano una facciata ad angolo, lo spazio è un insieme dove la struttura di colonne di cemento segna un ritmo che scandisce l'ubicazione progressiva delle diverse stanze.

La considerazione principale del disegno consistette nel fornire all'inquilino tutte le comodità, rispettando sempre la massima spaziosità, le viste della città e il passato industriale dell'edificio.

Un semicircolo costruito in lamiera corrugata di metallo contiene il bagno e lo stanzino, creando nella parte alta, una galleria di pannelli di plexiglas che consente l'entrata della luce dall'esterno.

La zona destinata alla cucina si trova tra due pareti trasparenti e perpendicolari alla facciata, erette su montanti di metallo e di vetro. Nell'area scelta come stanza da letto troviamo un meccanismo nuovo, ideale per la privacy delle ore di riposo. Questo è formato da leggeri drappi appesi, come se fossero foulard, a dei tubi; quando lo si apre, i drappi, al pari di una tenda, avvolgono il letto. Questa soluzione decorativa, funge al tempo stesso da isolante acustico.

Architects: Paul Guzzardo, David Davis

Location: Saint Louis, Missouri, United States

Photographs: Joel Marion

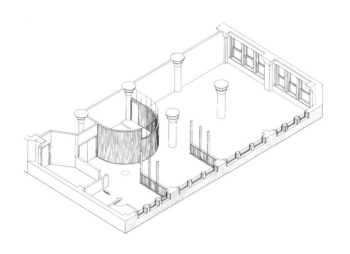

Sophisticated Innovation
Innovación sofisticada / Innovazione sofisticata

Cecconi Simone Inc.

In this apartment, which is a model of the interventions that were designed for the re-conversion of the Sears department store in downtown Toronto, the objective was to conserve the spaciousness characteristic of the spaces while adapting them to the needs of a home.

A symmetrical axis from the entry door to the apartment separates the areas that require enclosure, such as the laundry room, which remain close to the access to the loft, thus allowing the suite to remain as spacious as possible. High ceilings, concrete floors, columns in pilasters and industrial lighting contribute to call up the image and spirit of the building's former life as a department store. A serene bathroom and a modern kitchen give the space a very comfortable appearance. The mixture of juxtaposed materials and finishes, along with the combination of cool and warm atmospheres, converts this loft into a sophisticated, innovative example of the new urban lifestyle in Toronto.

En este apartamento, modelo de las intervenciones que se diseñaron para la reconversión del almacén Sears en el Downtown de Toronto, el objetivo era conservar la amplitud característica de los espacios acomodándolos a las actuales necesidades de una vivienda.

Un eje de simetría planteado desde la puerta de entrada al apartamento distribuye las áreas que requieren separación, como en el caso del lavadero, que quedan cerca del acceso al loft, permitiendo a la suite mantener toda su amplitud. Techos altos, suelos de hormigón, columnas en pilastras e iluminación industrial contribuyen a recordar la imagen y el espíritu de su anterior vida como almacén. Un baño sereno y una cocina moderna dan un aspecto muy confortable al espacio. La mezcla de materiales y acabados yuxtapuestos junto a la combinación de ambientes fríos y cálidos convierten este loft en un sofisticado e innovador ejemplo de la nueva vivienda urbana en Toronto.

Gli interventi del progetto che hanno trasformato l'antico magazzino Sears, nel Downtown di Toronto, nell'attuale appartamento, avevano come obiettivo mantenere la spaziosità caratteristica degli ambienti, adattandoli alle attuali esigenze di un'abitazione.

Un asse simmetrico che parte dalla porta d'ingresso dell'appartamento distribuisce le aree che richiedono una divisione – come nel caso della lavanderia – che rimangono vicine all'accesso al loft, permettendo alla suite di mantenere tutta la sua ampiezza. Soffitti alti, pavimento in cemento, colonne a lesena, e un tipo di illuminazione industriale contribuiscono a rievocare l'immagine e lo spirito dell'antico magazzino. Un bagno sereno e una cucina moderna conferiscono un aspetto molto confortevole allo spazio. L'abbinamento di materiali e finiture giustapposte, assieme all'accostamento di ambienti freddi e accoglienti trasformano questo loft in un sofisticato e innovativo esempio del concetto di nuova abitazione urbana a Toronto.

Architects: Cecconi Simone Inc.

Location: Toronto, Canada

Photographs: Joy von Tiedemann

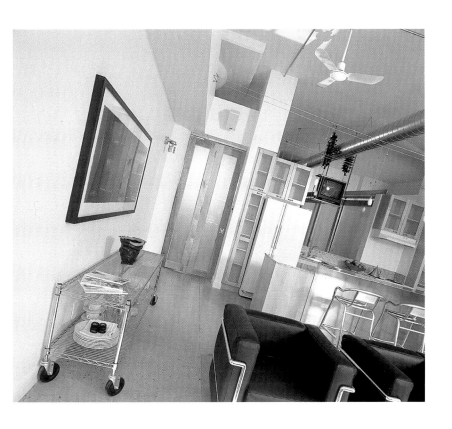

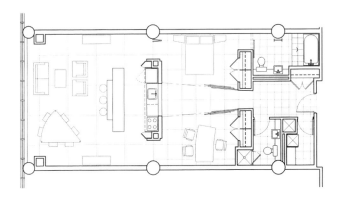

Private Residence
Residencia privada / Residenza privata

Cecconi Simone Inc.

This private residence is located in a promising area in Toronto's East End, an industrial neighborhood that has recently experienced an influx of artists and photographers occupying the old, unused warehouses. The project was to recover and create in an environment in which old and new can coexist.

Many of the components that make up the kitchen were recycled from an old cafeteria or were specially designed by the firm Cecconi Simone Inc., such as the kitchen counter, the bed canopy and the desk that serves as a home office.

The windows were left in their original state, and their exceptional size allows for proper ventilation of the large interior space as well as exceptional views onto Toronto's skyline.

The space was conceived to be absolutely flexible. Throughout the entire floor plan there are curtains that appear not to be hung which are in fact supported by bars suspended from the ceiling whose multiple positions permit the space to be unified or divided at will.

Esta residencia privada está ubicada en una prometedora área del East End de Toronto, un barrio industrial que recientemente ha experimentado una afluencia de artistas y fotógrafos que ocupan los antiguos almacenes en desuso. El proyecto fue un estudio de recuperación y creación de un entorno donde conviven lo viejo y lo nuevo.

Muchos de los componentes que conforman la cocina fueron reciclados de una antigua cafetería o bien especialmente diseñados por la firma Cecconi Simone Inc., como el mostrador de la cocina, el dosel de la cama o el escritorio que hace de oficina doméstica.

Las ventanas se encuentran en su estado original y su excepcional dimensión permite una correcta ventilación del gran espacio interior junto a unas excepcionales vistas del *skyline* de la ciudad de Toronto.

El espacio fue concebido para ser absolutamente flexible. A lo largo de toda la planta se dispone de unas cortinas a modo de telones descolgados que se sujetan a unas barras suspendidas del techo cuyas múltiples posiciones permiten unificar o dividir el espacio a voluntad.

Questa residenza privata si trova in una promettente area dell'East End di Toronto, un quartiere industriale che, di recente, ha fatto registrare un'affluenza di artisti e fotografi che occupano gli antichi magazzini ormai in disuso. Il progetto prevedeva uno studio di recupero e la creazione di un ambiente dove convivessero il vecchio e il nuovo.

Molti dei componenti che formano la cucina sono stati riciclati da una vecchia caffetteria. Altri sono stati appositamente disegnati dalla ditta Cecconi Simone Inc., come per esempio il banco della cucina, il parato del letto, o la scrivania che funge da ufficio domestico.

Le finestre si trovano nel loro stato originale e le loro eccezionali dimensioni permettono un'adeguata ventilazione del grande spazio interno e al contempo offrono viste meravigliose dello *skyline* della città di Toronto.

Lo spazio fu concepito per essere assolutamente flessibile. Lungo tutto il piano, troviamo delle tende simili a sipari calati, agganciate a delle sbarre appese al soffitto, le cui molteplici posizioni permettono di unificare o di dividere lo spazio a proprio piacimento.

Architects: Cecconi Simone Inc.

Location: Toronto, Canada

Photographs: Joy von Tiedemann

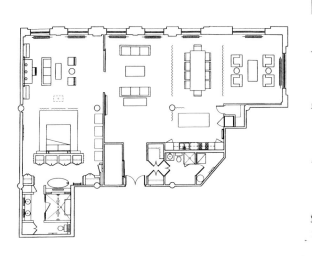

Recycled elements from an old cafeteria and restored food storage compartments give a nostalgic yet functional touch to the kitchen area.

Elementos reciclados de una antigua cafetería y casilleros de comida restaurados dan una nostálgica aunque funcional imagen del ámbito de la cocina.

Gli elementi riciclati da una vecchia caffetteria e le dispense a scaffali restaurate danno un'immagine nostalgica, per quanto funzionale, dell'ambiente della cucina.

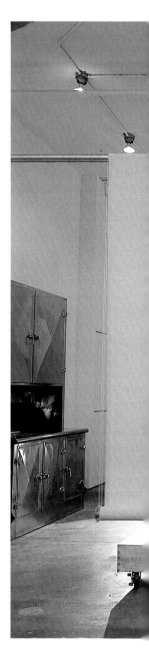

The design of a completely flexible space does not distinguish individually-designed areas. The headboard of the bed is a designby Cecconi Simone Inc. based on a movable canopy that can be manipulated depending on the amount of privacy desired.

El proyecto de un espacio completamente flexible no distingue áreas diseñadas individualmente. La cabecera de la cama es un diseño de Cecconi Simone Inc. según un dosel móvil que puede ser manipulado en función del grado de privacidad deseado.

Il progetto di uno spazio completamente flessibile non distingue aree disegnate individual-mente. La testata del letto è stata disegnata da Cecconi Simone Inc. secondo un parato mobile che può essere manovrato in funzione del grado di privacy desiderato.

Workshop and Living Space
Taller y vivienda / Laboratorio e abitazione

Fernando Campana

This 1940 building, which is located in a residential district in the center of the city of São Paulo, was originally a merchandise warehouse.

The original structure of the old establishment consisted of two concrete bodies, one in front and the other in the back, between which there was another block of bathrooms connecting the two main bodies. The design for the loft eliminated these bathrooms in order to create a 32.45 m² outdoor patio between the two parts. The Campana loft has a studio, an exhibition hall and a living space. On the front building's ground floor we can find the living room and a large exhibition hall, while the back building houses the workshop and the kitchen. Finally, the bedroom and a bathroom are on the lower level. There is a total of 229 m² divided into different levels and depths.

En su origen, este edificio de 1940 ubicado en un tejido residencial del centro de la ciudad de São Paulo era un almacén de mercancías.

La estructura original del viejo establecimiento consistía en dos cuerpos de hormigón, uno frontal y otro posterior, entre los que se encajaba otro bloque de aseos que los comunicaba. El proyecto del loft eliminó estos lavabos para abrir un patio al descubierto, de 32,45 m², entre ambas piezas. El loft Campana dispone de estudio, sala de exposiciones y vivienda. En la planta baja del edificio frontal encontramos la sala de estar junto a un gran salón de exposiciones; mientras que en el edificio posterior hallamos el taller de trabajo y la cocina. Finalmente, en la planta inferior se ubicó el dormitorio y un baño. Un total de 229 m² repartidos en varios niveles y en profundidad.

Inizialmente, questo edificio del 1940, situato in una zona residenziale del centro della città di São Paulo, era un deposito di mercanzia.

La struttura originale del vecchio stabile consisteva in due corpi di cemento, uno frontale e l'altro posteriore, tra i quali si incastrava un altro blocco, riservato ai servizi, che li metteva in comunicazione. Il progetto del loft eliminò questi servizi per aprire un cortile all'aperto, di 32,45 m², tra entrambi gli spazi. Il loft Campana è composto da: studio, sala per esposizioni e abitazione. Al pian terreno dell'edificio frontale troviamo il soggiorno, accanto a un grande salone per esposizioni; mentre in quello posteriore si trova il laboratorio di lavoro e la cucina. In ultimo, al piano inferiore sono stati collocati la stanza da letto e un bagno. Un totale di 229 m² divisi in vari livelli e in profondità.

Architect: Fernando Campana
Location: São Paulo, Brazil
Photographs: Andrés Ortero

The workshop and kitchen on the other end of the patio. Floor of polished, burned and waxed concrete and painted plaster walls emphasize the sturdiness of the construction.

El taller de trabajo y la cocina al otro lado del patio. Suelo de hormigón pulido, quemado y encerado y paredes pintadas sobre grueso enlucido para enfatizar la tosquedad de la construcción.

Il laboratorio e la cucina nell'altro lato del cortile. Pavimento in cemento lisciato, bruciato e incerato, pareti dipinte su un volume intonacato per enfatizzare la ruvidità della costruzione.

The furniture was conceived by the renowned brothers, Fernando and Humberto Campana, and produced by various firms from around the world.

El mobiliario está ideado por los hermanos Fernando y Humberto Campana, de reconocido prestigio, y producido por diversas firmas en todo el mundo.

La mobilia è stata ideata dai fratelli Fernando e Humberto Campana, artisti di riconosciuto prestigio, ed eseguita da ditte di diverse parti del mondo.

Round armchair by Ricardo Fasanello
(1972) and black chair with wheels by
Pedro Schimitd (1954). The rest of the
furniture was designed by Campana.

Sillón redondo de Ricardo Fasanello
(1972) y sillón negro con ruedas de
Pedro Schimitd (1954). El resto del
mobiliario es diseño de Campana. ☞

Poltrona rotonda di Ricardo Fasanello
(1972) e sedia nera con ruote, di Pedro
Schimitd (1954). Il design del resto dei
mobili porta la firma dei fratelli Campana.

Formal Unities
Unidades formales / Unità formali

Knott Architects

The empty shell of a loft can cause panic for many clients. Open spaces with undifferentiated functions and an underestimation of the amount of available space lead to rejection by some purchasers. The consequence of these fears is a desire to divide the space into traditional rooms, a solution that does a disservice to this type of buildings.

Knott Architects faced this dilemma when they had to house two bedrooms, two bathrooms, a kitchen and a living room in a 120 m² space located in this restored building in London's Soho district. Their achievement, which does not compromise the integrity of the space, is due to a rigorous design philosophy which clearly and consistently conceives of a distinction between the inserted areas and the surroundings.

Taming a large space for this project meant the prior definition of materials and finishes that define each zone. Thus, once the materials were set, the adoption of a single compositional language for the entire project was the final step providing formal and organizational criteria to this design.

El caparazón vacío de un loft puede provocar el pánico de muchos clientes. Los ambientes abiertos sin diferenciación de funciones y la subestimación de la cantidad de espacio disponible provoca el rechazo de algunos compradores. El resultado de tales miedos es la voluntad de dividir el ámbito en habitaciones tradicionales, solución que desvirtúa este tipo de edificaciones.

Knott Architects se enfrentaron a este dilema al tener que albergar dos habitaciones, dos baños, una cocina y una sala de estar en una superficie de 120 m² ubicada en un edificio reformado del Soho londinense. Su acierto, sin comprometer la integridad del espacio, se debe a una rigurosa filosofía del diseño, que concibe claramente y en todo momento la distinción entre los elementos insertados y la envolvente.

Domesticar el gran espacio significó para este proyecto la previa definición de unos materiales y acabados que determinan las zonas. De modo que, establecidos los materiales, la adopción de un solo lenguaje compositivo en la intervención fue el paso definitivo que dio un criterio formal y organizativo a este proyecto.

L'armatura vuota di un loft può provocare panico a molti clienti. Gli ambienti aperti senza distinzione tra le varie funzioni e la sottovalutazione della quantità di spazio disponibile causano il rifiuto di alcuni compratori. Alla base di tali paure vi è la volontà di dividere l'ambiente in stanze tradizionali, soluzione che snatura questo tipo di costruzione.

Il personale di Knott Architects si è trovato di fronte a questo dilemma, dovendo includere due stanze, due bagni, una cucina e un soggiorno in una superficie di 120 m² ubicata in un edificio restaurato nel quartiere londinese di Soho. L'ottimo risultato raggiunto, senza compromettere l'integrità dello spazio, è dovuto a una rigorosa filosofia del design, che concepisce chiaramente e in ogni momento la distinzione tra gli elementi inseriti e l'involucro.

Per questo progetto, «addomesticare» il grande spazio a disposizione ha comportato la definizione preliminare dei materiali e delle finiture che contraddistinguono gli ambienti. In maniera tale che, una volta stabiliti i materiali, l'adozione di un solo linguaggio compositivo durante l'intervento, è stato il passo definitivo che ha dato un criterio formale e organizzativo al progetto stesso.

Architects: Knott Architects

Location: London, United Kingdom

Photographs: Jefferson Smith, Laurent Kalfala, Knott Architects

All the interventions are made of wood, steel and glass in order for the new construction to stand out against the existing walls, which are plastered and painted white. The partitions are emphasized through wood boards covering the entire floor which allow the utility installations to remain hidden.

Todas las intervenciones son de madera, acero y vidrio para destacar la nueva construcción ante las paredes existentes, enyesadas y pintadas de blanco. Las particiones se enfatizan mediante una tarima de madera que cubre todo el suelo y permite ubicar las instalaciones sin ser vistas.

Tutti gli interventi prevedevano l'uso di materiali quali il legno, l'acciaio e il vetro, per mettere in risalto la nuova costruzione rispetto ai muri già esistenti, ingessati e dipinti di bianco. Le divisioni vengono sottolineate mediante un parquet in legno che copre l'intero pavimento e consente di sistemare tutti gli impianti senza che quest'ultimi rimangano a vista.

Transparent Floors
Suelos transparentes / Pavimenti trasparenti

Fraser Brown
McKenna Architects

The project consists of remodeling the two top floors of an industrial building located in Bethnal Green. Although the vault that covers part of the old terrace had been constructed prior to the Fraser Brown McKenna Architects renovation, the majority of the spaces were dark, small and excessively compartmentalized.

In the space under the vault, which until now has been a double space, the architects installed a translucent floor and placed the kitchen, the dining room and the living room. The lower floor was completely freed of dividing walls and designed as a single space for working and sleeping, although it is divided by a large, ten-meter long translucent panel that houses the bedroom area and the bathrooms, as well as the small storage area covered on the outside by copper sheeting. One end of the screen can be folded in order to allow the bedroom to considerably increase in size.

The natural daylight entering through the vault, the translucent floors and the walls are the most important values of this project.

El proyecto consiste en la remodelación de las dos últimas plantas de un edificio industrial sito en Bethnal Green. Aunque la bóveda que cubre parte de la antigua terraza había sido construida con anterioridad a la reforma de Fraser Brown McKenna Architects, la mayoría de los espacios eran oscuros, pequeños y excesivamente compartimentados.

Bajo la bóveda, en lo que hasta entonces era un doble espacio, los arquitectos instalaron un suelo translúcido y ubicaron la cocina, el comedor y la sala de estar. La planta inferior fue completamente liberada de tabiques y planteada como un solo espacio para trabajar y dormir, aunque queda dividida por una gran pantalla translúcida de diez metros de longitud que aloja la zona del dormitorio y los baños, y que también cobija el pequeño almacén revestido en su exterior de chapa de cobre. Un extremo final de la pantalla se abate para dejar crecer generosamente las dimensiones del dormitorio.

La transmisión de la luz natural a través de la bóveda, los suelos translúcidos y los paramentos son los valores más importantes de este proyecto.

Il progetto consiste nella ristrutturazione dei due ultimi piani di un edificio industriale sito nel Bethnal Green. Sebbene la volta che copre parte della vecchia terrazza sia stata costruita prima del restauro portato a termine da Fraser Brown Mckenna Architects, la maggior parte degli spazi erano bui, piccoli ed eccessivamente compartimentati.

Sotto la volta, in quello che fino allora era un doppio spazio, gli architetti hanno installato un pavimento traslucido e vi hanno collocato la cucina, il soggiorno e la sala da pranzo. Il piano inferiore è stato completamente liberato da tramezzi e concepito come un unico spazio dove lavorare e dormire, sebbene rimanga diviso da un grande schermo trasparente, lungo dieci metri, dietro il quale si trovano la stanza da letto, i bagni, ed anche il piccolo sgabuzzino rivestito all'esterno da lamiera di rame. Un'estremità finale del suddetto schermo si abbatte per lasciare crescere generosamente le dimensioni della camera da letto.

Il passaggio della luce naturale attraverso la volta, i pavimenti traslucidi e i paramenti sono i valori più importanti di questo progetto.

Architects: Fraser Brown McKenna Architects
Location: London, United Kingdom
Photographs: Nick Hufton/View

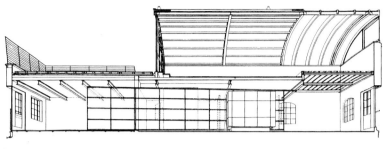

Side view   Sección fugada   Sezione vista dall'alto

Upper floor   Planta superior   Pianta superiore

Elevation   Alzado   Alzato

Lower floor   Planta inferior   Pianta inferiore

1. Study	1. Estudio	1. Studio
2. Storage area	2. Almacén	2. Deposito
3. Bathroom	3. Baño	3. Bagno
4. Balustrade	4. Balaustrada	4. Balaustrata
5. Stairway	5. Escalera	5. Scala
6. Bedroom	6. Dormitorio	6. Camera da letto
7. Kitchen	7. Cocina	7. Cucina
8. Dining room	8. Comedor	8. Sala da pranzo
9. Living room	9. Sala de estar	9. Soggiorno
10. Terrace	10. Terraza	10. Terrazza

Blank and Empty
Blanco y vacío / Bianco e vuoto

Hugh Broughton
Architects

The Hugh Broughton architectural studio converted this old industrial space into an apartment for a married couple. For the 148 m² of surface area, the architects decided on an agenda that would guarantee connections between the different areas and privacy in the areas that required it (bedrooms and bathrooms). They created two differentiated areas, one for day and the other for night: first, the kitchen, the living room and the dining room, located near the entrance; and second, the private area, made up of the bedrooms and one of the bathrooms.

One can best perceive the building's old industrial use in the daytime zone, due to both its diaphanous floor plan and its preserving the exposed brick walls and wrought pillars.

A structural axis, formed by a line of wrought pillars, crosses the apartment lengthwise. In the more private areas, these structural elements disappear as they are converted into a wall into which a closet has been built.

Finally, the curved wall delimiting the bathroom breaks with the verticality of the pillars and becomes the sculptural effect that characterizes this open, airy space.

El estudio de arquitectura de Hugh Broughton convirtió un antiguo espacio industrial en un apartamento para un matrimonio. Para los 148 m² de superficie, los arquitectos plantearon un programa que garantizaba a un tiempo la comunicación entre los distintos ámbitos y la privacidad en las áreas que la requerían (dormitorios y baños). Se crearon dos zonas diferenciadas, una de día y otra de noche: por un lado, la cocina, el salón y el comedor, situados junto a la entrada, y por el otro, la zona privada, constituida por los dormitorios y uno de los baños.

En la zona de día es donde mejor se percibe el antiguo uso industrial del edificio, tanto por su planta diáfana como porque conserva los muros de ladrillo visto y los pilares de fundición.

Un eje estructural, formado por una línea de pilares de fundición, atraviesa el apartamento en toda su longitud. En la zona de mayor privacidad, la estructura desaparece convertida en un muro en el que queda empotrado un armario.

Finalmente, el muro curvo que delimita el baño rompe con la verticalidad de los pilares y se convierte en el efecto escultórico que caracteriza este espacio diáfano.

Lo studio di architettura di Hugh Broughton ha convertito un vecchio spazio industriale in un appartamento per una coppia. Per i 148 m² di superficie, gli architetti pensarono a un programma che garantisse la comunicazione tra i diversi ambienti e al contempo la privacy di alcune zone quali le stanze da letto e i bagni. Furono create due zone differenziate, una zona giorno e una notte; da una parte la cucina, il salone e la sala da pranzo, situati accanto all'ingresso, e dall'altra, la zona privata, formata dal le camere da letto e da uno dei due bagni.

La zona giorno è dove si percepisce meglio l'antico uso industriale dell'edificio, sia per la sua pianta diafana, sia perché conserva i muri di mattone a vista e i pilastri in ghisa.

Un asse strutturale, formato da una fila di pilastri in ghisa, attraversa in lungo l'intero appartamento. Nella zona di maggiore privacy, la struttura scompare per trasformarsi in un muro che alloggia un armadio incassato.

In ultimo, il muro curvo che delimita il bagno spezza la verticalità dei pilastri e si trasforma nell'effetto scultoreo che caratterizza questo spazio diafano.

Architects: Hugh Broughton Architects
Location: London, United Kingdom
Photographs: Carlos Domínguez

The white finish of the walls and ceiling contrast with the original exposed brick walls, the acid-treated glass walls and the African wood used on the floor panels. The lighting combines natural daylight, which enters through the windows, with a series of spotlights built into the hanging ceiling, points of atmospheric lighting along with the light that filters in through the translucent walls.

El acabado blanco de paredes y techos contrasta con los muros originales de obra vista, los paramentos de cristal al ácido y la madera africana de la tarima del solado. La iluminación combina la luz natural que entra por los ventanales con una serie de focos empotrados en el falso techo, los puntos de luz ambiental y la que se filtra por los paramentos translúcidos.

La finitura bianca delle pareti e dei soffitti contrasta con i muri originali, di mattoni a vista, con i paramenti in cristallo inciso all'acido, e il legno africano della pavimentazione. L'illuminazione abbina la luce naturale che entra dai finestroni con una serie di faretti incassati nel controsoffitto, con dei punti di luce ambiente, e con la luce filtrata attraverso i paramenti trasparenti.

General floor plan	Planta general	Pianta generale
1. Living room	1. Sala de estar	1. Soggiorno
2. Dining room	2. Comedor	2. Sala da pranzo
3. Kitchen	3. Cocina	3. Cucina
4. Balcony	4. Balcón	4. Balcone
5. Vestibule	5. Vestíbulo	5. Atrio
6. Half bathroom	6. Aseo	6. Toilette
7. Bedroom	7. Dormitorio	7. Stanza da letto
8. Bathroom	8. Baño	8. Bagno

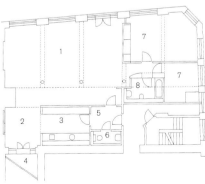

New Concordia Wharf

Mark Guard Architects

The client bought 186 m² on the fifth floor of a warehouse located on the Thames River. The space was made of an irregular shape dominated by circular pillars and beams, a grid of windows, and dark exposed brick walls.

The project proposed a 23-meter long wall to divide the guest bedroom, the utility room, the kitchen, and the bathrooms from the large main space. This wall contains all the utility installations and is interrupted in order to allow light to reach the access area of the apartment. The grid like network traced by the seams of a stone flooring reinforces the presence of the wall as the principal, organizing geometry of the space. From the entrance door of the apartment, this wall creates a false perspective that directs one's vision towards the view of the river.

The end of this wall forms part of the master bedroom, which can be opened or closed at will to the large living room space through a four-meter sliding wall.

El cliente compró 186 m² de la quinta planta de un almacén ubicado junto al río Támesis. Una forma irregular dominada por pilares circulares y vigas, una cuadrícula de ventanas y oscuras paredes de ladrillo visto conformaban el lugar.

El proyecto plantea una pared de 23 metros de largo que divide la habitación de invitados, el cuarto de servicios, la cocina y los baños del gran espacio principal. Este muro contiene todas las instalaciones de servicios y se interrumpe para hacer llegar la luz que asoma por el este hasta el área de acceso al apartamento. La retícula cuadriculada, dibujada por las juntas de un pavimento de piedra, refuerza la presencia del muro como geometría primordial y organizadora del espacio. Desde la puerta de entrada al piso, esta pared crea una falsa perspectiva que dirige la mirada hacia las vistas sobre el río.

El final de esta pared forma parte del dormitorio principal, una habitación que se puede abrir o cerrar a voluntad hacia el gran espacio del salón mediante una pared corredera de cuatro metros.

Il cliente comprò 186 m² del quinto piano di un deposito sito accanto al Tamigi. Il posto era formato da una forma irregolare dominata da pilastri circolari e da travi, finestre a trama quadrettata, e delle oscure pareti in mattone a vista.

Il progetto presenta una parete lunga 23 metri che divide la stanza degli ospiti, la lavanderia, la cucina e i bagni dal grande spazio principale. Questo muro contiene tutte le installazioni delle utenze e si interrompe per fare arrivare la luce che spunta dalla zona a est fino ad arrivare all'area di accesso all'appartamento. La quadrettatura, disegnata dalle fughe di un pavimento in pietra, rafforza la presenza del muro come geometria primordiale e organizzatrice dello spazio. Dalla porta d'ingresso all'appartamento, questa parete crea una falsa prospettiva che volge lo sguardo verso le vedute sul fiume.

La fine di questa parete fa parte della camera da letto principale, una stanza che si può aprire o chiudere a proprio piacimento verso l'ampio spazio del salone mediante una parete scorrevole di quattro metri.

Architects: Mark Guard Architects

Location: London, United Kingdom

Photographs: Allan Mower, John Bennett

1. Entrance	1. Entrada	1. Ingresso
2. Shower	2. Ducha	2. Doccia
3. Utility room	3. Servicio	3. Servizio
4. Fold-away bed	4. Cama abatible	4. Letto ribaltabile
5. Glass counter	5. Mostrador de cristal	5. Banco di vetro
6. Pivoting door	6. Puerta pivotante	6. Porta ruotante
7. Kitchen	7. Cocina	7. Cucina
8. Sliding metal table	8. Mesa deslizante de metal	8. Tavolo scorrevole in metallo
9. Bathroom	9. Lavabo	9. Lavabo
10. Stone bathtub	10. Bañera de piedra	10. Vasca da bagno in pietra
11. Privalite screen	11. Pantalla privalite	11. Schermo Priva-lite
12. Master bedroom	12. Dormitorio principal	12. Stanza da letto principale
13. Closet	13. Guardarropa	13. Guardaroba
14. Balcony	14. Balcón	14. Balcone
15. Sliding glass table	15. Mesa deslizante de cristal	15. Tavolo scorrevole in vetro

A stainless steel rail integrated into the stone flooring allows the tables to slide and their uses to vary.

Un carril de acero inoxidable integrado en el pavimento de piedra permite deslizar las mesas y variar el uso que se pueda hacer de ellas.

Una guida in acciaio inossidabile, integrata nel pavimento in pietra, permette di far scorrere i tavoli e di cambiare l'uso che se ne può fare.

Oliver's Wharf

McDowell + Benedetti
Architects

Oliver's Wharf, a 1870 tea warehouse, was one of the first London port buildings to be re-converted to residential use during the 1970s. The two upper floors, with outstanding views of the city, were originally occupied by the architect who remodeled the building. When the current owner acquired it, it had been abandoned for several years.

It is a double-high space 250 m² large, with wrought iron pillars that support enormous oak lattices and a complex roof. In addition to repairing many existing elements in the construction, the intervention by McDowell + Benedetti Architects led to a total transformation of the space thanks to the installation of intermediate levels and the creation of two rooftop terraces.

The loft's layout revolves around the kitchen on the main level, around which a sequence of spaces is developed: entrance, stairway, gallery, chimney and living room with views. A small bedroom near the entrance with a foldaway bed and a half bathroom is occasionally used as a guest bedroom.

The main division of the space consists of a 20-centimeter thick limestone wall which is located in the middle of the space and reaches three stories high.

Oliver's Wharf, un almacén de té de 1870, fue uno de los primeros locales portuarios londinenses en ser reconvertidos a un uso residencial durante los primeros años de la década de los setenta. El ático de los dos pisos superiores, con unas vistas extraordinarias sobre la ciudad, fue ocupado originalmente por el mismo arquitecto que remodeló el edificio. Cuando lo adquirió el propietario actual, llevaba varios años abandonado.

Se trataba de un doble espacio de 250 m² con pilares de hierro colado que soportaban unas enormes celosías de roble y una cubierta compleja. Además de reparar muchos elementos de la construcción existente, la intervención de McDowell + Benedetti Architects supuso la transformación total del espacio gracias a la instalación de niveles intermedios y a la extensión de dos terrazas en la cubierta.

La distribución del loft gira en torno a la cocina en el nivel principal, alrededor de la cual se desarrolla una secuencia de espacios: recibidor, escalera, galería, chimenea y sala de estar con vistas. Una pequeña habitación junto a la entrada, que dispone de una cama plegable y un aseo, se utiliza ocasionalmente como dormitorio de invitados.

La principal división del espacio consiste en un muro de 20 centímetros de ancho de piedra caliza, situado en el centro del volumen y que alcanza la altura de las tres plantas.

Oliver's Wharf, un magazzino di una fabbrica di tè del 1870, fu uno dei primi locali della zona portuaria londinese ad essere riconvertito ed adibito a uso residenziale, nei primi anni '70. L'attico dei due piani superiori, con delle viste straordinarie sulla città, fu occupato originariamente dallo stesso architetto che ha rimodernato l'edificio. Quando venne acquistato dall'attuale proprietario, l'attico era abbandonato da vari anni.

Si trattava di un doppio spazio di 250 m² con pilastri in ferro colato che reggevano delle enormi travi in rovere e un tetto dalla struttura complessa. Oltre a riparare molti elementi della costruzione esistente, l'intervento di McDowell + Benedetti Architects ha comportato la trasformazione totale dello spazio grazie all'installazione di livelli intermedi e all'estensione, nel tetto, di due terrazze.

La distribuzione del loft, nel livello principale, gira attorno alla cucina, spazio circondato da una sequenza di spazi: ingresso, scala, veranda, caminetto, e soggiorno con vista. Una piccola stanza accanto all'entrata, con un letto pieghevole e con toilette, viene utilizzata a volte come stanza per gli ospiti.

La principale divisione dello spazio consiste in un muro spesso 20 centimetri, in pietra calcare, situato al centro del volume e che raggiunge l'altezza dei tre piani.

Architects: McDowell + Benedetti Architects

Location: London, United Kingdom

Photographs: Tim Soar

For the new elements, which act as articulations that serve to order the space, natural materials have been used to contrast with the ruggedness of the existing construction.

Para los nuevos elementos, que actúan como articulaciones que ordenan el espacio, se han utilizado materiales naturales que contrastan con la aspereza de la construcción existente.

Per i nuovi elementi, che agiscono come articolazioni che ordinano lo spazio, sono stati utilizzati materiali naturali che contrastano con la ruvidità della costruzione esistente.

On the upper level, two mezzanines have been built: one of these is occupied by the master bedroom and bathroom, and the other by a small study with an enormous pivoting window with views of the Thames.

En el nivel superior se han construido dos altillos: uno de ellos está ocupado por el dormitorio y el baño principales, y el otro, por un pequeño estudio con una enorme ventana pivotante con vistas al Támesis.

Nel livello superiore sono stati costruiti due soppalchi: uno di questi è occupato dalla stanza da letto e il bagno principali; l'altro, da un piccolo studio con un'enorme finestra ruotante, con vista sul Tamigi.

Post Office in London
Oficina postal en Londres / Ufficio postale a Londra

Orefelt Associates

The project consisted of re-converting an old post office into a studio and living space for a painter. One of this intervention's major accomplishments was to avoid designing the living space within the conventional framework of a single-family home, as the building might lend itself to at first glance.

Another success is the fact that the feeling of both vertical and horizontal spaciousness is retained inside the house. The changing interior perspective offered by the floor plan is a demonstration of the mastery of space which is the hallmark of this project. The lower level is reserved for the bedrooms and bathrooms on one side, for a generous sized vestibule (including a billiards table) on the other, and for a double-high studio space in the back. In an open space on the upper floor, the living room, kitchen and dining room areas are laid out, lit by large skylights and looking onto the painting studio.

El proyecto consistía en reconvertir una antigua oficina de correos en estudio y residencia de una pintora. Un gran acierto de esta intervención fue no desarrollar la vivienda dentro del marco convencional de casa unifamiliar como, a primera vista, podía sugerir el edificio.

Otro éxito es que se mantiene en el interior la sensación de espacialidad, tanto horizontal como vertical. La perspectiva interior cambiante que ofrece la distribución es una demostración del dominio del espacio de que hace gala este proyecto. La planta baja se reserva para los dormitorios y baños, a un lado; para un vestíbulo generoso (que incluye un billar), al otro, y para un espacio con doble altura que corresponde al estudio, en la parte trasera. En un espacio abierto de la planta superior, se distribuyen las zonas de estar, cocina y comedor, iluminadas por amplias claraboyas y con vistas al estudio de pintura.

Il progetto consisteva nel trasformare un antico ufficio postale in uno studio e dimora di una pittrice. Una decisione alquanto azzeccata di questo intervento fu quella di non sviluppare l'abitazione all'interno della struttura convenzionale di casa unifamiliare come poteva, a prima vista, suggerire l'edificio.

Un altro buon risultato è che all'interno si mantiene la sensazione di spazialità, sia orizzontale che verticale. La prospettiva interna, sempre mutevole, data dalla distribuzione, è la dimostrazione del dominio dello spazio del quale può fare sfoggio questo progetto. Il piano terra viene riservato per le stanze da letto e i bagni, da una parte; per un ampio ingresso (che comprende un biliardo) dall'altra, e per uno spazio a doppia altezza che corrisponde allo studio, nella parte posteriore. In uno spazio aperto del piano superiore, si distribuiscono il soggiorno, la cucina e la sala da pranzo, illuminati da ampi abbaini e con vista sullo studio di pittura.

Architects: Orefelt Associates

Location: London, United Kingdom

Photographs: Alberto Ferrero

Gems in the owner's collections include a sofa with leopard-skin upholstery, a dog by Jeff Koons, a selection of McDonalds gift toys lined up on a shelf in the bathroom, a set of miniature Eiffel Towers, and a Snow White and the Seven Dwarves rug.

Entre las joyas de la colección de la propietaria figuran un sofá con tapicería de leopardo, un perro obra de Jeff Koons, una selección de muñequitos regalo de McDonald's alineados en una estantería del baño, un repertorio de miniaturas de la torre Eiffel y una alfombra de Blancanieves y los siete enanitos.

Tra i gioielli della collezione della proprietaria, figurano un sofà con tappezzeria leopardata, un cane opera di Jeff Koons, una raccolta di pupazzetti regalo di McDonald's allineati su uno scaffale del bagno, un repertorio di miniature della torre Eiffel e un tappeto con un disegno di Biancaneve e i sette nani.

Home for a Painter
Vivienda para una pintora / Abitazione per una pittrice

Simon Conder
Associates

The need for a free space without any type of compartmentalization governed this project located in an old factory. The client, a painter living in Kent, wanted to have an apartment in London as a base of operations in order to explore the capital city's artistic life.

The objective was to maximize a 116 m^2 space, fostering the sense of spaciousness and luminosity that characterized the original property.

Given the small area available, a single access was left, although this would be disassociated by the stairway that visually separates the living room from the bedroom. Three vertical elements define the main environment: the kitchen, which is made of stainless steel, and two cylinders that house the shower and a half bathroom.

The light is manipulated through the use of the different materials covering the surfaces. The walls and ceilings, which are painted white, provide even more light, and the metal sheeting gives off reflections that multiply the interior light effects.

La necesidad de un espacio libre, sin compartimentación alguna, rige este proyecto ubicado en una antigua fábrica. El cliente, una pintora que reside en Kent, deseaba tener un apartamento en Londres como base de operaciones para poder explorar la vida artística de la capital.

El objetivo era rentabilizar una extensión de 116 m^2, potenciando la sensación espacial y la luminosidad que caracterizaban la propiedad original.

Dada la escasez de superficie disponible, se optó por mantener un único ámbito, aunque disociado por la escalera que separa perceptivamente la zona de estar del dormitorio. Tres elementos verticales definen el ambiente principal: la cocina, de acero inoxidable, y dos cilindros, que albergan la ducha y un aseo.

La luz se manipula mediante el uso de diferentes materiales que cubren las superficies: las paredes y techos, pintados de blanco, iluminan aún más, y las chapas metálicas emiten reflejos que multiplican los efectos de luz que se producen en el interior.

Il bisogno di uno spazio libero, senza nessuna compartimentazione, sta alla base di questo progetto di riconversione di una vecchia fabbrica. Il cliente, una pittrice che risiede nel Kent, desiderava avere un appartamento a Londra da utilizzare come base logistica, per poter esplorare la vita artistica della capitale.

Lo scopo era di sfruttare al massimo un'estensione di 116 m^2, potenziando la sensazione spaziale e la luminosità che caratterizzavano l'immobile originario.

Vista la scarsa superficie a disposizione, si decise di mantenere un unico ambiente, sebbene diviso dalla scala che separa in modo evidente la zona soggiorno dalla stanza da letto. Tre elementi verticali definiscono l'ambiente principale: la cucina, di acciaio inossidabile, e due cilindri, che contengono la doccia e un servizio.

La luce si gestisce mediante l'uso di diversi materiali che coprono le superfici: le pareti e i soffitti, dipinti di bianco, illuminano ancora di più, e le lamine di metallo emettono riflessi che moltiplicano gli effetti di luce che si producono all'interno di tutto l'ambiente.

Architects: Simon Conder Associates

Location: London, United Kingdom

Photographs: Simon Archer

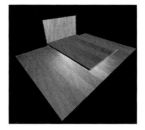

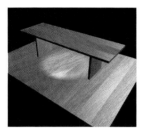

The materials used in the design confer a certain minimalist feeling to the environment. The kitchen, the stairway structure and the frames of the glassed-in gallery are made of stainless steel. The floor is white oak and houses the heating system.

Los materiales utilizados en el proyecto confieren cierto aire minimalista al ambiente. La cocina, la estructura de la escalera y las carpinterías de la galería acristalada son de acero inoxidable. El suelo es de roble blanco y alberga la calefacción.

I materiali utilizzati nel progetto donano una certo aspetto minimalista all'ambiente. La cucina, la struttura della scala, e i serramenti della veranda vetrata sono di acciaio inossidabile. Il pavimento è in legno di rovere bianco, con l'impianto di riscaldamento incorporato.

FOA London

FOA. Foreign
Office Architects

This space, a loft in the London neighborhood of Pimlico, is L-shaped and is 4.8 meter high, and it includes a second space not quite as high with direct access from the street. The main space, which houses the living room and the dining room, opens up to the outside through two large bays and to the interior patio through a large window.

The double-high wall that dominates the living room is the screen onto which all types of images are projected, illuminating the space and filling it with virtual reality. In the mezzanine, which is 60 m² and looks out on this scene, there is a bedroom which is dividable using sliding panels, a bathroom, and a library that opens out onto the main space.

In order to highlight the qualities of the original space, few materials were used repeatedly on all the walls in the apartment.

The furniture, which is exempt from curved, complex geometrical forms, is dressed up with pieces by illustrious designers such as Paulin, Jacobsen and Eames. The indirect lighting from incandescent tubes and halogen spotlights mixes with the light reflected by the walls.

El espacio, un loft en el barrio londinense de Pimlico, tiene forma de L y una altura libre de 4,8 metros a la que se anexa un segundo espacio algo más bajo, con acceso directo desde la calle. La estancia principal, que alberga la sala de estar y el comedor, se abre al exterior a través de dos vanos de largas proporciones y al patio interior mediante un gran ventanal.

El muro a doble altura que preside el salón se convierte en la pantalla donde se proyecta todo tipo de imágenes que iluminan el espacio y lo llenan de realidad virtual. En la entreplanta, de 60 m², que mira abiertamente a este escenario, se ubican un dormitorio divisible mediante paneles corredizos, un baño y una biblioteca que queda al descubierto del espacio principal.

Para resaltar las cualidades del espacio original se utilizaron pocos materiales que se repiten y aplican en todos los paramentos de la vivienda.

El mobiliario, exento de formas geométricas curvas y complejas, se viste con piezas de diseñadores ilustres como Paulin, Jacobsen o Eames. La iluminación indirecta de tubos incandescentes y focos halógenos se une a la luz reflejada por los muros.

Lo spazio, un loft nel quartiere londinese di Pimlico, ha la forma di una L e un'altezza libera di 4,8 metri, alla quale si annette un secondo spazio leggermente più basso, con accesso diretto dalla strada. La stanza principale, che ospita il soggiorno e la sala da pranzo, si apre all'esterno mediante due vani dalle lunghe proporzioni, e al cortile interno mediante un grande finestrone.

Il muro a doppia altezza che presiede il salone si trasforma in uno schermo dove si proiettano vari tipi di immagini che illuminano lo spazio e lo riempiono di realtà virtuale. Nel seminterrato, di 60 m², rivolto apertamente a questo scenario, si trovano una stanza da letto divisibile mediante pannelli scorrevoli, un bagno e una biblioteca che rimane allo scoperto rispetto allo spazio principale.

Per risaltare le qualità dello spazio originario, sono stati utilizzati pochi materiali, che si ripetono e applicano in tutti i paramenti dell'abitazione.

La mobilia, priva di forme geometriche curve e complesse, è formata da pezzi, opera di famosi designer come Paulin, Jacobsen o Eames. L'illuminazione indiretta con tubi incandescenti e faretti alogeni si unisce alla luce riflessa dai muri.

Architects: FOA. Foreign Office Architects

Location: London, United Kingdom

Photographs: Valerie Bennett

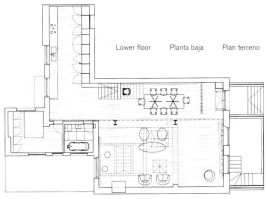

Lower floor   Planta baja   Pian terreno

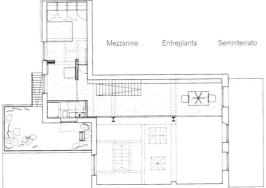

Mezzanine   Entreplanta   Seminterrato

A system of centralized switches allows
the light to be controlled from a
computer, which can be programmed
into various sequences.

Un sistema de interruptores centralizado
permite el control de la iluminación
desde un ordenador programable en
distintas secuencias.

Un impianto di interruttori centralizzato
permette di controllare l'illuminazione
mediante un computer programmabile in
varie sequenze.

217

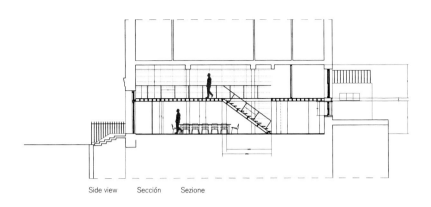

Side view   Sección   Sezione

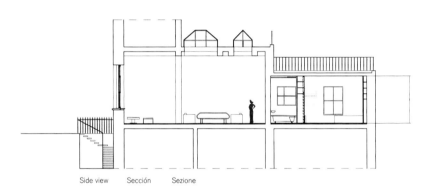

Side view   Sección   Sezione

The back wall of the kitchen is covered with slate.

La pared del fondo de la cocina se revistió de pizarra.

La parete in fondo alla cucina è stata ricoperta di ardesia.

The cupboards are integrated into the wall architecture, playing with the orthogonal rigor of the space.

Los armarios se integran en la arquitectura de paredes jugando con el rigor ortogonal del espacio.

Gli armadi si integrano nell'architettura delle pareti giocando con il rigore ortogonale dello spazio.

Conversion of a Warehouse

Conversión de un almacén / Conversione di un magazzino

Adam Caruso,
Peter St. John

This project constitutes a catalogue of refusals: minimal compartmentalization of the space, minimal relationship to the street, minimal furniture, minimal wall finishes.

The objective was the conversion of an old two-story warehouse located in Islington, in the north of London, into a living space and studio. The warehouse had a rectangular floor plan, 4.6 meters of façade by 9.8 meters of depth (a usable surface era of 45 m² per floor), and it was built with brick walls and wooden beams. The floor plan was totally open with neither divisions nor pillars.

Caruso and St. John decided to substitute the old façade with a glass wall. This screen, made up of double Climalit glass (8+24+6), provides thermal and acoustic insulation. The windows are translucent and are reminiscent of a silk or Japanese paper screen. During the day the façade is totally hermetic, as if it were covered with metal sheeting. At night, it becomes a lamp lighting up the street.

Regarding the composition of the façade, not all the divisions are fixed glass panes; some can be opened, such as the entry door or a window on the first floor, and they are covered with opaque panels similar to Eternit Eflex.

Este proyecto constituye un catálogo de renuncias: mínima compartimentación del espacio, mínima relación con la calle, mínimo mobiliario, mínimo acabado de los paramentos.

El objetivo era la conversión de un antiguo almacén de dos plantas situado en Islington, en el norte de Londres, en vivienda y estudio. El almacén tenía una planta rectangular de 4,7 metros de fachada por 9,8 metros de profundidad (una superficie útil de 45 m² por piso) y estaba construido con muros de ladrillo y viquetas de madera. La planta era completamente libre, sin divisiones ni pilares exentos.

Caruso y St. John decidieron sustituir la antigua fachada por un muro de cristal. Esta pantalla, formada por un doble vidrio Climalit (8+24+6), tiene propiedades aislantes, térmicas y acústicas. Las lunas son translúcidas y funcionan como una pantalla de seda o de papel chino. Durante el día la fachada es completamente hermética, como si estuviese revestida de chapa metálica. Por la noche, se convierte en una lámpara que ilumina la calle.

Respecto a la composición de la fachada, no todas las divisiones corresponden a vidrios fijos, sino que algunas son practicables, como la puerta de entrada o una ventana del primer piso, y están revestidos con un panel opaco del tipo Eternit Eflex.

Questo progetto costituisce un catalogo di rinunce: minima compartimentazione dello spazio, minima relazione con la strada, minime finiture dei paramenti, e minima presenza di mobili.

L'obiettivo era la conversione di un vecchio magazzino di due piani situato a Islington, a nord di Londra, in abitazione e studio. Il magazzino presentava una pianta rettangolare con 4,7 metri di larghezza e 9,8 metri di profondità (una superficie utile di 45 m² per appartamento) ed cra costruito con muri in mattone e travetti in legno. La pianta era completamente libera, senza divisioni né pilastri isolati.

Caruso e St. John decisero di sostituire l'antica facciata con un muro di vetro. Questa superficie, formata da vetro doppio Climalit (8+24+26), possiede proprietà isolanti, termiche e acustiche. Le ante vetro sono traslucide e funzionano come un paralume di seta o di carta cinese. Durante il giorno, la facciata è completamente ermetica, come se fosse ricoperta da lamiera di metallo. Di notte, diventa una lampada che illumina la strada.

Rispetto alla composizione della facciata, non tutte le divisioni corrispondono a vetri fissi, ma alcune sono praticabili, come la porta d'ingresso o una finestra del primo piano, e rivestite di un pannello opaco di tipo Eternit Eflex.

Architects: Adam Caruso, Peter St. John

Location: London, United Kingdom

Photographs: Hélène Binet

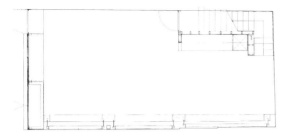

In the back part, the ironwork has been eliminated and a room-sized lantern has been built on the roof, which produces a well of light. The utilities, kitchen, bathroom and stairway are located in this area.

En la parte trasera se han vaciado los forjados y se ha construido una linterna del tamaño de una habitación en la cubierta, lo que da lugar a un pozo de luz. En esta zona se ubican los servicios, la cocina y el baño, así como la escalera.

Attic   Altillo   Soppalco

Nella parte posteriore, sono state svuotate le solette, e nel tetto è stata costruita una lanterna grande quanto una stanza, creando così un pozzo luce. In questa zona, si trovano i servizi, la cucina, il bagno, ed anche la scala.

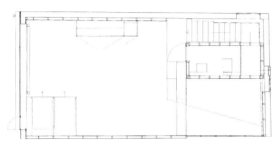

Lower floor   Planta baja   Pian terreno

Lofts on Wall Street
Lofts en Wall Street / Loft a Wall Street

Chroma AD. Alexis Briski + Raquel Sendra

The Chroma team, made up of Alexis Briski and Raquel Sendra, have designed a project of thirteen lofts at 15 Dutch Street, in New York, in the middle of the business district.

Two types of floor plans were created: one L-shaped and the other rectangular with a central line of pillars where the kitchen island is located. The dressing rooms are equipped with industrial equipment and offer privacy and roomy storage spaces. Other important elements are the monumental bathrooms with imported porcelain tile finishes, specially designed lighting, and 1.8 meter high granite counters.

El equipo Chroma, formado por Alexis Briski y Raquel Sendra, ha diseñado un proyecto de trece lofts en el número 15 de Dutch Street, Nueva York, en pleno barrio de negocios.

Se crearon dos tipos de planta, una en forma de L y otra rectangular con una línea central de pilares donde se ubica la isla de la cocina. Los vestidores están equipados con instalaciones industriales y ofrecen privacidad y un amplio espacio de almacenaje. Otros elementos importantes son los baños monumentales con acabados de azulejos de porcelana importados, la iluminación diseñada especialmente y los mostradores de granito de hasta 1,8 metros.

Il gruppo Chroma, formato da Alex Briski e Raquel Sendra, ha disegnato un progetto per tredici loft siti nel numero 15 di Dutch Street, a New York, nel cuore del quartiere degli affari.

Furono creati due tipi di pianta, una a forma di L e l'altra rettangolare con una linea centrale di pilastri dove si trova lo spazio riservato alla cucina. Gli stanzini, dotati di attrezzature di tipo industriale, offrono privacy e un ampio spazio per conservare sia oggetti che indumenti. Altri elementi importanti sono i bagni, dalle dimensioni monumentali e rifiniti con piastrelle di porcellana importate, l'illuminazione appositamente disegnata, e i banchi in granito, lunghi fino a 1,8 metri.

Architects: Chroma AD. Alexis Briski + Raquel Sendra

Location: New York, United States

Photographs: David M. Joseph, Bart Michaels

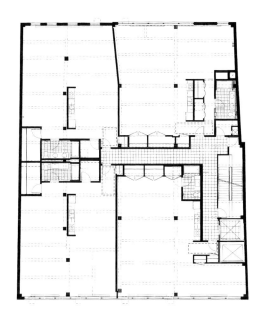

Top Floors on Wardour Street

Áticos en Wardour Street / Attici a Wardour Street

CZWG Architects

The addition of two top floors on an industrial building in London's Soho district was designed as an aesthetic and constructional continuation of the floors immediately below. This time, there is not the usual differentiation between the new and the old that architects always bemoan with interventions in pre-existing structures.

The transformation of this industrial building through this process of superimposing rooftop floors is revealing of how our constructed environment has evolved throughout time. The current trend consists of superimposing or intermingling layers, while in the past substituting or renovating were preferred.

From a technical standpoint, the architects opted for anchoring a system of metallic porticos in the concrete structure of the old building. The use of steel continues along the façades and the frames of the large windows, such that it ends up constituting an element that dominates the exterior image of the two top floors. Similarly, the roof draws a gentle curve made of zinc sheeting.

La adición de dos áticos a un edificio industrial del Soho londinense se diseñó como una continuación estética y constructiva de los pisos inmediatamente inferiores. No se produce, esta vez, la habitual diferenciación entre lo nuevo y lo viejo que siempre reclaman los arquitectos cuando intervienen en construcciones preexistentes.

La transformación de este edificio industrial mediante este proceso de superposición de plantas cubierta es revelador de cómo ha evolucionado nuestro entorno construido a lo largo del tiempo. La tendencia actual consiste en superponer o entremezclar capas, mientras que en el pasado se prefería sustituir o renovar.

Desde el punto de vista técnico, se ha optado por anclar un sistema de pórticos metálicos en la estructura de hormigón del antiguo edificio. El uso del acero se extiende a las fachadas y carpinterías de los grandes ventanales, de manera que acaba constituyéndose en el elemento que domina la imagen exterior de los dos últimos pisos. Paralelamente, la cubierta dibuja una suave curva formada por una chapa de cinc.

L'annessione di due attici a un edificio industriale della zona londinese di Soho, è stata disegnata come una continuazione estetica e costruttiva degli appartamenti immediatamente inferiori. Questa volta, non si produce la consueta differenziazione tra il vecchio e il nuovo, che sempre esigono gli architetti quando intervengono in costruzioni già esistenti.

La trasformazione di questo studio industriale mediante il processo di sovrapposizione di piani coperti rivola come sia cambiato, nel corso del tempo, il modo in cui si costruiscono gli ambienti. La tendenza attuale consiste nel sovrapporre o mischiare i vari strati, mentre in passato si preferiva sostituire o rinnovare.

Dal punto di vista tecnico, si è optato per fissare un sistema di portici metallici nella struttura di cemento del vecchio edificio. L'uso dell'acciaio si estende alle facciate e ai serramenti delle grandi finestre, in modo tale che finisce per costituire l'elemento che domina l'aspetto esterno degli ultimi due piani. Parallelamente, la copertura delinea una leggera curva formata da una lamiera di zinco.

Architects: CZWG Architects

Location: London, United Kingdom

Photographs: Chris Gascoigne

One of the aspects to which CZWG Architects paid most painstaking attention was the lofts' connection with the outside. First, the façades mostly consist of enormous windows running from floor to ceiling. Second, they built large terraces for each apartment.

Uno de los aspectos que más han cuidado CZWG Architects ha sido la conexión de los lofts con el exterior. Por una lado, las fachadas están constituidas por enormes ventanales de suelo a techo. Por otro, se han habilitado amplias terrazas para cada apartamento.

Uno degli aspetti più curati da CZWG Architects è stato il collegamento dei loft con l'esterno. Da un lato, le facciate sono formate da enormi finestre che vanno dal pavimento al soffitto. Dall'altro, per ogni appartamento, sono state recuperate delle ampie terrazze.

Lee House
Casa Lee / Casa Lee

Derek Wylie

Lee House is located in Clerkenwell, west of the City, the financial center of London. It was Derek Wylie himself who found an abandoned apartment building on St. John Street, with a two-story warehouse in the back part that in the past had housed a silver workshop. The building's total surface area is 450 m², but it was a long, narrow plot which was completely surrounded by buildings, making it difficult for natural daylight to enter.

The proposed plan was not simple: in addition to a home for a couple and their two children, the project had to provide for a small office with an entrance from the street and an apartment with a direct street access which was to be sold in order to partially finance the construction.

A small patio separates the adjacent building (which houses the apartment and the office) from the silver workshop, which is occupied by the 250 m² main residence. Light penetrates through the patio and various galleries that have been covered with translucent glass. Likewise, the new architectural elements (stairways, walkways, flooring, walls and doors) and the furniture are used to re-organize the space without radically transforming its appearance.

La casa Lee se encuentra en Clerkenwell, al oeste de la City, el centro financiero de Londres. Fue el propio Derek Wylie quien encontró un edificio de apartamentos abandonado en St. John Street, con un almacén de dos plantas en la parte trasera que en el pasado había albergado un taller de platería. La superficie total del edificio era de 450 m², pero se trataba de un solar estrecho y largo, completamente rodeado de edificaciones que dificultaban la entrada de luz natural.

El programa propuesto no era sencillo: además de una vivienda para una pareja y dos hijos, el proyecto debía prever una pequeña oficina con entrada desde la calle y un apartamento para vender (y así financiar parte de las obras), a su vez con acceso directo.

Un pequeño patio separa el edificio contiguo a la calle (que alberga el apartamento y el despacho) de la platería, ocupada por la vivienda principal, de 250 m² de superficie. La luz penetra por el patio y por varias galerías cubiertas con vidrio translúcido. Paralelamente, los nuevos elementos arquitectónicos (escaleras, pasarelas, pavimentos, tabiques y puertas) y el mobiliario se utilizan para reordenar el espacio, aunque sin transformar radicalmente su aspecto.

La Casa Lee si trova a Clerkenwell, ad ovest della City, il centro finanziario di Londra. Fu lo stesso Derek Wylie che trovò uno stabile di appartamenti abbandonato, nella St. John Street, con un magazzino di due piani nel retro, che in passato aveva ospitato una bottega orafa. La superficie totale dell'edificio era di 450 m², ma si trattava di un'area lunga e stretta, completamente circondata da edifici che impedivano il passaggio della luce naturale.

Il programma proposto non era semplice: oltre a un'abitazione per una coppia con due figli, il progetto doveva prevedere un piccolo ufficio con accesso dalla strada e un appartamento da vendere (e così poter finanziare parte dei lavori), a sua volta con accesso diretto.

Un piccolo cortile interno separa l'edificio prossimo alla strada (dove si trovano l'appartamento e l'ufficio) dalla bottega orafa, occupata dall'abitazione principale, con una superficie di 250 m². La luce penetra attraverso il cortile e varie verande coperte con vetro traslucido. Parallelamente, i nuovi elementi architettonici (scale, passerelle, pavimenti, tramezzi, e porte) e i mobili si utilizzano per riordinare lo spazio, senza però trasformarne radicalmente l'aspetto.

Architect: Derek Wylie

Location: London, United Kingdom

Photographs: Nick Kane, excepto cocina (Mainstream) y detalle del balcón del patio (Derek Wylie

The project's strategy consisted
of exposing the buildings' original
structures and constructing a home
filled with fluid spaces, with special
care taken to maximize natural light.

La estrategia de proyecto consistió en
sacar a la luz la estructura original de
los edificios y construir una vivienda
de espacios fluidos, con un especial
cuidado en maximizar la iluminación
natural.

La strategia progettuale consistette nel
portare alla luce la struttura originaria
degli edifici e costruire un'abitazione
dagli spazi fluidi, cercando specialmente
di massimizzare l'illuminazione naturale.

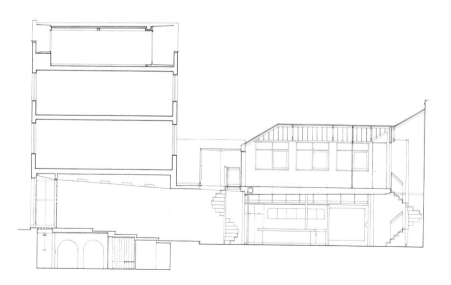

The stairways have been strategically placed in order to separate the different areas within the living room without interrupting the continuity of the space.

La escalera se ha situado estratégicamente para separar las diferentes áreas de la sala de estar sin interrumpir la continuidad del espacio.

Le scale sono state disposte strategicamente, per separare i diversi ambienti del soggiorno, senza interrompere la continuità dello spazio.

Loft in Clerkenwell
Loft en Clerkenwell / Loft a Clerkenwell

Circus Architects

This loft is a result of the re-conversion of two apartments in Clerkenwell, the area with the most spaces of this type within London's Soho district. The building dates from the 1930s, and is an old printing press that Manhattan Loft Corporation (MLC) remodeled for residential use. MLC itself advised its clients (a four-member family) to choose Circus as their architects.

The structure, with large, concrete-edged beams, and the enormous windows with metallic frames give the building an industrial appearance. Circus's intervention is based on building an attic floor and a series of pieces made of metal sheeting and curved contours to house the utilities and visually separate the different areas within the loft.

The children's bedrooms are located on the lower floor, with almost direct access from the entrance, while the couple's bedroom is located in the attic, at the furthest point from the access to the loft.

Circus Architects decided that it would undertake no reforms in the original structure one meter above the attic. Likewise, part of the interior or wall surface on the façade has been left untreated.

El loft resulta de la reconversión de dos apartamentos en Clerkenwell, la zona que cuenta con más espacios de este tipo dentro del Soho londinense. El edificio data de los años treinta y es una antigua imprenta que Manhattan Loft Corporation (MLC) remodeló para darle un uso residencial. Fue la propia empresa MLC quien aconsejó a los clientes (una familia de cuatro miembros) la elección de Circus como arquitectos.

La estructura, con grandes vigas de canto de hormigón, y los enormes ventanales, con carpinterías metálicas, dan al edificio un aspecto industrial. La intervención de Circus se basa en la construcción de una planta altillo y una serie de piezas de chapa metálica y contornos redondeados que albergan los servicios y sirven para separar visualmente las diferentes zonas del loft.

Los dormitorios de los hijos se ubican en la planta baja, con acceso casi directo desde la entrada, mientras que el de la pareja se halla en el altillo, en el punto más alejado del acceso a la vivienda.

Circus Architects decidieron que a partir de un metro por encima del altillo no se llevaría a cabo ningún cambio en la estructura original. Igualmente, parte de la superficie interior del muro de fachada se ha dejado sin tratar.

Il loft è il risultato della riconversione di due appartamenti siti a Clerkenwell, la zona che vanta più spazi di questo tipo, nel quartiere londinese di Soho. L'edificio risale agli anni '30 ed è una vecchia tipografia che Manhattan Loft Corporation (MLC) ha rimodernato per adibirla a uso residenziale. Fu la stessa ditta MLC che consigliò ai clienti (una famiglia di quattro membri) di scegliere Circus come architetti.

La struttura è composta da grandi travi con canti in cemento, enormi finestre, e serramenti in metallo, che danno all'edificio un aspetto industriale. L'intervento di Circus si basa nella costruzione di un piano soppalco e in una serie di spazi in lamiera metallica dai contorni arrotondati che contengono i servizi e servono per separare visualmente le diverse aree del loft.

Le stanze da letto dei figli sono ubicate a piano terra, con accesso quasi diretto dall'ingresso, mentre quella dei genitori si trova nel soppalco, nel punto più lontano dall'accesso all'abitazione.

Circus Architects decise che a partire da un metro al di sopra del soppalco, non si sarebbe apportata nessuna modifica alla struttura originaria. Allo stesso modo, parte della superficie interna del muro della facciata è stata lasciata grezza.

Architects: Circus Architects

Location: London, United Kingdom

Photographs: Martin Levint (collage), Richard Glover

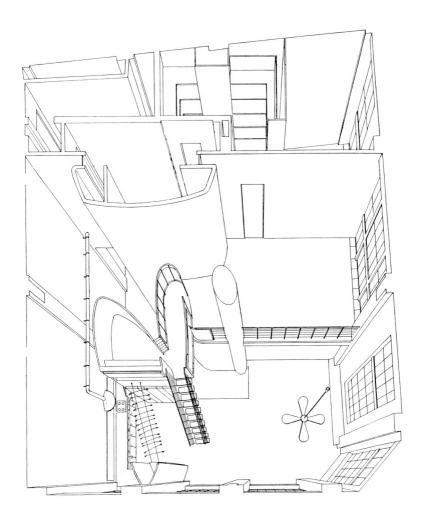

The balcony, which was created to look out onto the double space, is converted into an ideal observatory separating the façade from the inside of the apartment.

El balcón creado para asomarse al doble espacio se convierte en un mirador idóneo que aleja la fachada del interior del apartamento.

Il balcone creato per affacciarsi sul doppio spazio, diventa un belvedere ideale che allontana la facciata dall'interno dell'appartamento.

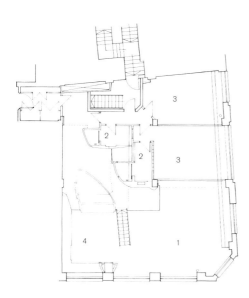

Upper floor

1. Reception
2. Bathroom
3. Bedroom
4. Kitchen

Planta superior

1. Recepción
2. Baño
3. Dormitorio
4. Cocina

Pianta superiore

1. Ingresso
2. Bagno
3. Stanza da letto
4. Cucina

Lower floor

1. Reception
2. Studio
3. Emergency exit
4. Bathroom
5. Bedroom

Planta inferior

1. Recepción
2. Estudio
3. Salida de emergencia
4. Baño
5. Dormitorio

Pianta inferiore

1. Ingresso
2. Studio
3. Uscita di emergenza
4. Bagno
5. Stanza da letto

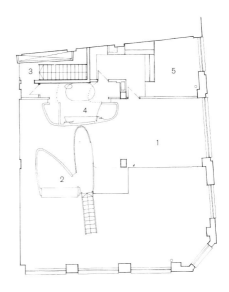

A semi-elliptical metal tower separates the laundry room from the pantry.

Una torre semielíptica de metal aloja la lavadora y la despensa.

Una torre di metallo semiellittica alloggia la lavatrice e la dispensa.

Unit 203

Buschow Henley
& Partners

This 180 m² apartment was designed to be lived in by a single person.

The loft is organized from east to west by four columns that divide the space into five parts. These columns are built using a combination of materials that join together brick and tile elements with pieces of concrete, an example of the mixture of materials that make up the outer walls.

The project's main idea was to describe each space in a different way by placing new walls paired with concrete. These new walls also have to hide the inevitable utilities of daily life, from the shower to the pantry, and generate spaces for living, eating and sleeping.

Este apartamento, de 180 m², se diseñó para ser habitado por una sola persona.

El loft queda estructurado de este a oeste mediante cuatro columnas que dividen el local en cinco partes. Estas columnas se construyen según una combinación de materiales que apareja conjuntamente elementos de ladrillo y baldosa con piezas de hormigón, ejemplo de la mezcla de materiales que conforma las paredes envolventes.

La idea principal del proyecto consiste en describir cada espacio de manera diferente mediante la implantación de nuevos muros aparejados con hormigón. Estas nuevas paredes también deben ocultar las inevitables funciones de la vida doméstica, desde una ducha hasta una despensa, y generar los espacios para estar, comer o dormir.

Questo appartamento, di 180 m², è stato progettato per essere abitato da una sola persona.

Il loft viene strutturato, da est ad ovest, mediante quattro colonne che dividono il locale in cinque parti. Queste colonne, al pari delle pareti avvolgenti, presentano abbinamenti di materiali ed elementi di distinta natura – mattoni, piastrelle, pezzi in

L'idea principale del progetto consiste nel descrivere ogni spazio in maniera diversa mediante l'inserimento di nuovi muri allineati in cemento. Queste nuove pareti devono inoltre occultare le inevitabili funzioni della vita domestica, da una doccia fino a una dispensa, e creare gli spazi riservati alle varie attività: vita diurna, mangiare o dormire.

Architects: Buschow Henley & Partners

Location: London, United Kingdom

Photographs: Nick Kane/Arcaid

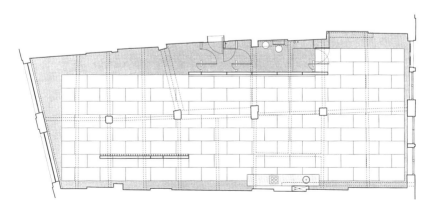

Chromatic Treatment
Tratamiento cromático / Trattamento cromatico

AEM

Glyn Emrys and Pascal Madoc Jones, the two members of AEM, understood perfectly well that the decision to re-convert a loft into a home could not be limited to a merely aesthetic option, but that it also involves the client's having a certain vital attitude and the architect's understanding of this alternative nature.

One of these factors of complicity is the love of empty rooms, the attraction of spare spaces that are barely furnished. Stripping the space of unnecessary elements means reinventing furniture, the limits of this space.

In this London loft, the chromatic treatment of the few pieces of furniture and the modulation of the light through filters not only accommodate the commitment to barely alter the existing construction, they also manage to uncover the lyricism underlying these types of spaces.

Glyn Emrys y Pascal Madoc Jones, los dos componentes de AEM, comprendieron perfectamente que la decisión de reconvertir un loft en vivienda no puede limitarse a una opción estética, sino que implica en el cliente una determinada actitud vital y exige del arquitecto la comprensión de ese carácter alternativo.

Uno de esos factores de complicidad es el amor por las salas vacías, la atracción por los espacios desnudos, apenas amueblados. Despojar el espacio de lo innecesario supone reinventar el mobiliario, los límites de ese espacio.

En este loft londinense, el tratamiento cromático de las escasas piezas de mobiliario y la modulación de la luz a través de filtros no sólo se ajustan al compromiso de no alterar apenas la construcción existente, sino que consiguen desplegar el lirismo subyacente en este tipo de espacios.

Glyn Emrys e Pascal Madoc Jones, i due componenti di AEM, capirono perfettamente che la decisione di riconvertire un loft in un'abitazione non può limitarsi a un'opzione estetica, ma presuppone, da parte del cliente, un determinato stile di vita e un carattere alternativo, che l'architetto ha l'obbligo di comprendere.

Uno dei fattori di complicità che accomuna il cliente e l'architetto, è l'amore per le sale vuote, l'attrazione per gli spazi nudi, scarsamente ammobiliati. Spogliare lo spazio degli elementi superflui presuppone reinventare la mobilia, i limiti del suddetto spazio.

In questo loft londinese, il trattamento cromatico dei pochi mobili inseriti, e la modulazione della luce mediante dei filtri non solo si adattano all'impegno di non alterare quasi la costruzione esistente, ma riescono a dispiegare il lirismo che si cela in questi spazi.

Architects: AEM

Location: London, United Kingdom

Photographs: Alan Williams

254

The architects viewed the existing metallic structure as an artistic element that enriches the space.

With the exception of the most private activities (which are limited to the bathroom and the bedroom), the other occupations are resolved in a single large space. The magic of this room comes from its remaining empty. For this reason, furniture has been reduced to only those pieces that are indispensable.

Los arquitectos valoran la estructura metálica existente como un elemento plástico que enriquece el espacio.

Salvo las actividades más íntimas (aisladas en el baño y el dormitorio), el resto de las ocupaciones se resuelve en un único gran espacio. La magia de esa sala radica en que permanezca vacía. Por eso, el mobiliario se reduce solamente a las piezas indispensables.

Gli architetti valutano la struttura metallica esistente come un elemento plastico che arricchisce lo spazio.

Salvo le attività più intime (isolate nel bagno e nella camera da letto), il resto di occupazioni si risolve in un unico grande spazio. La magia di questa sala risiede proprio nel fatto che rimane vuota. Per questo motivo, la mobilia si riduce soltanto ai pezzi indispensabili.

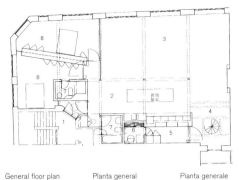

General floor plan

1. Entrance
2. Kitchen
3. Living room
4. Stairway to the terrace
5. Storage area
6. Sauna
7. Bathroom
8. Bedroom

Planta general

1. Entrada
2. Cocina
3. Sala de estar
4. Escalera a la terraza
5. Almacén
6. Sauna
7. Baño
8. Dormitorio

Pianta generale

1. Ingresso
2. Cucina
3. Soggiorno
4. Scala che porta alla terrazza
5. Dispensa
6. Sauna
7. Bagno
8. Stanza da letto

The acid-treated glass is not merely an architectural device; it is also poetic. The figures behind glass become blurred; they become spiritual and fragile, like the levitating woman in the picture, like the one sitting down to read on a chair made of air.

El vidrio tratado al ácido no es un recurso meramente arquitectónico, sino también poético. Las figuras tras el vidrio pierden cuerpo, se vuelven espirituales y frágiles… como la mujer que levita en el cuadro, como la que se sienta a leer sobre un sillón hecho de aire.

Il vetro trattato con acido non è una risorsa meramente architettonica, ma anche poetica. Le figure dietro il vetro perdono corpo, diventano spirituali e fragili… come la donna che lievita nel quadro, come quella che si siede a leggere su una poltrona gonfiabile.

Interior Landscape
Paisaje interior / Paesaggio interno

Florian Beigel
Architects

This apartment is a long, narrow container 8 x 21 meters, on a single floor located in the center of London in a building that had been a shoe factory. The building's structure is made of reinforced concrete, and it was built in the 1930s.

The plan for the loft is conceived as an interior landscape. The new pieces emerge in the apartment like small ships anchored in a bay, floating there. These objects, scattered about liberally, contain spaces that are highly compressed, where one can take a shower or a bath or sleep. Thus, we find the shower between blue walls and floor and a ceiling made of transparent polycarbonate which uncovers the structure made of concrete beams and the apartment's fluorescent lighting. A small room the size of a double bed in which one can sleep is hidden away, as is a large six-meter long envelop made of stainless steel and laminated wood that comprises the kitchen. In contrast with this privacy, the rest of the apartment expands openly for any unexpected uses that could take place in larger spaces.

El apartamento es un contenedor alargado y estrecho, de 8 x 21 metros, de una sola planta que se encuentra en el centro de Londres y había sido una fábrica de zapatos. La estructura del edificio es de hormigón armado y fue construido en los años treinta.

El proyecto del loft se concibe como un paisaje interior. Las nuevas piezas emergen en el piso como pequeños barcos anclados en una bahía, en orden flotante. Estos objetos, dispuestos libremente, contienen unos espacios muy comprimidos donde uno puede ducharse, bañarse o dormir. Así, encontramos la ducha entre paredes y suelo azules y un techo de policarbonato transparente que descubre la estructura de vigas de hormigón y la iluminación fluorescente del piso. También se oculta un pequeño cuarto encerrado del tamaño de una cama de matrimonio donde se puede dormir, o un gran sobre de seis metros de largo de acero inoxidable y madera laminada que conforma la cocina. En contraste con esta privacidad, el resto del piso se expande abierto a usos inesperados que pueden tener lugar en los espacios más grandes.

L'appartamento, che anticamente era stato una fabbrica di scarpe, è un contenitore allungato e stretto, di 8 x 21 metri, che si sviluppa su un unico piano e si trova nel centro di Londra. La struttura dell'edificio è di cemento armato e risale agli anni '30.

Il progetto del loft si concepì come un paesaggio interno. I nuovi elementi emergono nell'appartamento come se fossero piccole imbarcazioni ormeggiate in una baia, in ordine galleggiante. Questi oggetti, disposti liberamente, contengono degli spazi molto compressi dove ci si può fare la doccia, il bagno o dormire. Così vi troviamo, infatti, la doccia, tra un pavimento e delle pareti di colore blu, e un soffitto di policarbonato trasparente che mette in evidenza la struttura di travi di cemento e l'illuminazione fluorescente dell'appartamento. Nascosta vi è anche una stanzetta, grande quanto un letto matrimoniale, dove si può dormire, o un grande piano lungo 6 m, in acciaio inossidabile e legno laminato che conforma la cucina. In contrasto con questa privacy, il resto dell'appartamento si espande, aprendosi a usi inattesi che possono avere luogo negli spazi più grandi.

Architects: Florian Beigel Architects

Location: London, United Kingdom

Photographs: Hélène Binet

High-frequency fluorescent tubes run across connecting joints a few centimeters below the ceiling tiles.

Tubos fluorescentes de alta frecuencia cuelgan dispersos sobre regletas de conexión a pocos centímetros por debajo de la losa del forjado.

Tubi fluorescenti ad alta frequenza pendono sparsi, dalle guide di connessione, pochi centimetri al di sotto della lastra della soletta.

In the bedroom and bathroom, the doors have been covered in plywood boards using cement and transparent matte polyurethane.

En el dormitorio y el baño se han revestido las puertas de tableros de fibras de madera aglomeradas con cemento y poliuretano mate transparente.

Nella stanza da letto e nel bagno, le porte sono state rivestite con pannelli in fibra di legno agglomerata con cemento e poliuretano opaco trasparente.

Top view   Planta   Pianta

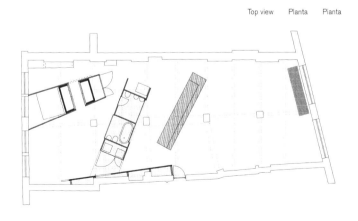

The walls and floor of
the shower are in
Yves Klein blue.

La ducha tiene
paredes y suelo en el
azul de Yves Klein.

Il blu di Yves Klein
riveste il pavimento e
le pareti della doccia.

Neutral Space
Espacio neutral / Spazio neutrale

Felicity Bell

This loft is located in a building from the 1930s that had been used for light industry, but according to the Australian architect, Felicity Bell, its attraction did not lie in its manufacturing past.

The plan for the 76 m² of the apartment was for an absolutely neutral space where different private and working environments could be place arbitrarily.

The layout of the space is divided along a central axis which constitutes the kitchen, a long wall containing the household appliances and hidden wastebaskets. The counter is made of jarrah wood, an indigenous Australian species, with a lovely intense color that contrasts with the other furniture. Finally, we find designer furniture, such as the dining room table and the chairs by Charles and Ray Eames, which suggest the continuation of the ideals of the modern movement in domestic spaces. This loft is a clear example of flexibility and the re-conversion of uses in a single space.

El loft se encuentra en un edificio de los años treinta dedicado a la industria ligera pero, según afirma la arquitecta australiana Felicity Bell, el atractivo no era su carácter fabril.

El ideal planteado para los 76 m² del apartamento fue un espacio absolutamente neutral donde disponer diferentes ambientes privados y de trabajo arbitrariamente.

La distribución del espacio se divide según un eje central que constituye la cocina, una larga pared que contiene los electrodomésticos y cubos de basura ocultos. La encimera es de madera de jarrah, una especie autóctona australiana, de un bonito color intenso que contrasta con el resto del mobiliario. Finalmente, encontramos mobiliario de firma como la mesa de comedor y las sillas de Charles y Ray Eames, que sugieren la continuación de los ideales del movimiento moderno en el espacio doméstico. Este loft es un claro ejemplo de flexibilidad y reconversión de usos en un mismo espacio.

Il loft si trova in un edificio degli anni trenta dedito all'industria leggera anche se, secondo quanto afferma l'architetto australiano Felicity Bell, ciò che l' ha colpita non è stato il suo aspetto industriale.

L'idea pensata per i 76 m² dell'appartamento fu quella di uno spazio assolutamente neutrale dove sistemare arbitrariamente diversi ambienti sia privati che di lavoro.

La distribuzione dello spazio si divide secondo un asse centrale che forma la cucina, una lunga parete che contiene gli elettrodomestici e, nascosti, i contenitori per i rifiuti. Il piano è in legno *jarrah*, una specie autoctona australiana, dal bel colore intenso che contrasta con il resto dei mobili. Troviamo inoltre, mobili di artisti famosi come il tavolo della sala da pranzo e le sedie di Charles e Ray Eames, che suggeriscono la continuazione degli ideali del movimento moderno nello spazio domestico. Questo loft è un esempio chiaro di flessibilità e di riconversione d'usi in uno stesso spazio.

Architect: Felicity Bell

Location: London, United Kingdom

Photographs: Chris Tubbs

A layout option for exclusively domestic use.

Opción de distribución para el uso exclusivamente doméstico.

Opzione di distribuzione per l'uso esclusivamente domestico.

Layout of all the open working areas, with the meeting table for clients in the access area of the apartment.

Distribución de todas las áreas de trabajo abiertas, con la mesa de reuniones para clientes en la zona de acceso a la vivienda.

Distribuzione di tutte le aree di lavoro aperte, con il tavolo per riunioni con i clienti nella zona d'accesso all'abitazione.

Layout of the movable variants along with the studio closet that occupies a large space and the conversion of the access area into a guest bedroom.

Distribución de las variantes móviles con el armario estudio que ocupa el gran espacio y la conversión en dormitorio de invitados de la zona de acceso.

Distribuzione delle varianti mobili con l'armadio studio che occupa lo spazio più grande e la conversione della zona di accesso in camera per gli ospiti.

No Restrictions
Sin restricciones / Senza restrizioni

Blockarchitecture:
Graeme Williamson +
Zoe Smith

Each of the projects carried out by the Blockarchitecture team (previously known as 24/seven) has been governed by a series of parameters or variables that have responded to each idea that has arisen in the design process. Their approach to the project is direct and unrestricted, based on interpretation of and reaction to the needs, the result of a prior imaginative process.

The proposal consisted of maintaining the concrete structure that defines and contains the entire space as intact and open as possible. The size and the shape are emphasized by the force of the wood floor that is laid along the dominant direction in the apartment: toward the balconies located on this building's façade. A nine-meter long wall made of recycled steel panels dominates and organizes the environment. Inside it we have the dressing room, a small storage area, the half bathroom and a dark bedroom. The lighting directed toward the ceiling makes the orthogonal structure of the beams covering the apartment stand out. Over a concrete floor that floats on the surface of the loft, the bathroom pieces are organized just like any other pieces of furniture.

Cada uno de los proyectos llevados a cabo por el equipo Blockarchitecture (antes 24/seven) se ha regido por una serie de parámetros o variables que han dado respuestas a cada idea surgida en el proceso de diseño. Su aproximación al proyecto es directa y sin restricciones, basada en la interpretación y reacción frente a las necesidades, fruto de una imaginación previa.

La propuesta consistió en mantener lo más entera y abierta posible la estructura de hormigón que define y contiene todo el espacio. La medida y la forma se enfatizan por la rotundidad de la tarima de madera que se dispone según la dirección que domina la pieza del apartamento: hacia los balcones dispuestos en la fachada este del edificio. Un largo muro de nueve metros construido con paneles reciclados de acero domina y organiza su entorno. En su interior tenemos el vestíbulo, un pequeño almacén, el aseo y una habitación oscura. La iluminación dirigida al techo resalta la estructura ortogonal de vigas que cubren el piso. Sobre una tarima de hormigón que flota en el pavimento del loft, las piezas del baño se ordenan como cualquier otro mueble más.

Ognuno degli interventi portati a termine dall'equipe di Blockarchitecture (anteriormente 24/seven) è stato condotto in base a una serie di parametri e variabili che hanno dato risposta ad ogni idea, sorta durante la fase progettuale. Il loro approccio al progetto è diretto e senza restrizioni, basato sull'interpretazione e sulla reazione di fronte alle esigenze, frutto di un'immaginazione preliminare.

La proposta consistette nel mantenere quanto più intera ed aperta possibile la struttura di cemento che definisce e contiene tutto lo spazio. La misura e la forma si enfatizzano grazie alla pienezza del parquet di legno che si dispone secondo la direzione che domina il vano dell'appartamento: verso i balconi disposti nella facciata est dell'edificio. Un muro, lungo nove metri, costruito con pannelli riciclati di acciaio domina e organizza l'ambiente. Internamente, trovano spazio l'atrio, una piccola dispensa, la toilette e una stanza buia. L'illuminazione rivolta verso il soffitto risalta la struttura ortogonale delle travi che coprono l'appartamento. Su una pedana di cemento che quasi galleggia sul pavimento del loft, i pezzi del bagno si dispongono come un qualsiasi altro mobile.

Architects: Blockarchitecture: Graeme Williamson + Zoe Smith

Location: London, United Kingdom

Photographs: Chris Tubbs

Both the surface of the stove and the bathtub platform are made of concrete.

Tanto el sobre de la cocina como la plataforma del baño son de hormigón.

Sia il ripiano della cucina che la piattaforma del bagno sono di cemento armato.

Kopf Loft

Buschow Henley

Kopf Loft forms part of the renovation of an entire Victorian-era building located in Shepherdess Walk, which had been used as a warehouse. The entire project was carried out by Buschow Henley architects. The 10,230 m² building has a structure consisting of six floors on the west side and five on the east. In the middle, a patio extends along an elongated axis running from north to south. The building's volume has the shape of a rhomboid.

The urban planning project only included the residential units, leaving aside the commercial units, while it required a parking space for each apartment. Given the building's proportions, this meant limiting the total number of units and the impact that the promotion was going to have on the neighborhood.

Curiously, the units coincide with the original dividing walls. On the east and west of the patio, the asymmetrical houses are divided from two to four, and the others from three to four.

El Kopf Loft forma parte de la reforma de todo un edificio de estilo victoriano, situado en Shepherdess Walk, que estuvo destinado por completo a almacén. La totalidad del proyecto fue llevada a cabo por los arquitectos Buschow Henley. El edificio, de 10.230 m², tiene una estructura de seis pisos al oeste y cinco al este. En el centro, un patio se extiende según un eje alargado que va de norte a sur. En volumen, la construcción describe un romboide.

El proyecto urbano amparaba sólo las unidades residenciales y prescindía de las comerciales, a la vez que exigía una plaza de aparcamiento por cada vivienda. Dadas las proporciones del edificio, esto suponía limitar el número de unidades totales y el impacto que la promoción iba a tener en el barrio.

Las unidades coinciden, curiosamente, con los muros divisorios originales. En el este y oeste del patio, las casas de pisos asimétricas están divididas de dos a cuatro y de tres a cuatro las otras.

Il Kopf Loft fa parte del rinnovamento di tutto un edificio in stile vittoriano, sito a Shepherdess Walk, che anticamente era del tutto adibito a magazzino. La totalità del progetto è stata portata a termine dagli architetti Buschow Henley. L'edificio, di 10.230 m², ha una struttura di sei piani ad ovest e cinque ad est. Al centro, si trova un cortile che si estende secondo un asse allungato che va da nord a sud. In termini di volume, la costruzione descrive un romboide.

Il progetto urbano tutelava solo le unità residenziali e non comprendeva quelle commerciali; al contempo esigeva un posto macchina per ogni abitazione. Viste le proporzioni dell'edificio, questo significava limitare il numero di unità totali e l'impatto che la sua promozione avrebbe avuto nel quartiere.

Le unità coincidono, curiosamente, con i muri divisori originari. Ad est e ad ovest del cortile, i blocchi asimmetrici sono formati da due e quattro appartamenti, i primi, e da tre e quattro appartamenti, gli altri.

Architects: Buschow Henley

Location: London, United Kingdom

Photographs: Nick Kane/Arcaid

278

"With limited means, the transformation was meant to be quite honest." (Buschow Henley)

«Con unos medios limitados, la transformación quería ser bastante honesta.» (Buschow Henley)

«Con dei mezzi limitati, la trasformazione voleva essere abbastanza onesta.» (Buschow Henley)

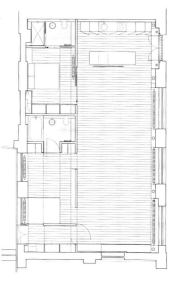

Multidirectional Light
Luz multidireccional / Luce multidirezionale

Buschow Henley

This loft forms part of the London building in Sheperdess Walk that was restored by the architects, Buschow Henley.

The promoter wanted to create a multi-purpose building that combined residences and commercial spaces. Initial studies indicated that the construction could accommodate approximately fifty apartments on the upper floors, with the commercial spaces on the ground floor and the basement used as a parking lot.

Specifically, the plan for this loft consisted of providing the apartment with two bedrooms/studios for a couple that was already tired of living in a typical loft with exposed brick walls and cement floors. Approximately 205 m², the design of the new apartment, which was bought empty, as a container, was centered on making the most of the double high ceilings offered by this part of the building.

Este loft forma parte del edificio londinense de Shepherdess Walk restaurado por los arquitectos Buschow Henley.

El promotor quería crear un edificio de uso mixto combinando unidades residenciales y comerciales. Unos primeros estudios indicaron que la construcción podía acoger unos cincuenta pisos en las plantas superiores, con las unidades comerciales en la planta baja y el sótano para los coches.

Concretamente el proyecto de este loft consistía en proveer de dos habitaciones estudio el apartamento de una pareja que ya estaba cansada de vivir en el típico loft de paredes de ladrillo visto y suelo cementado. De aproximadamente 205 m², el diseño del nuevo apartamento, que fue comprado vacío, como un contenedor, se centró en sacar el máximo partido a la doble altura que le proporcionaba la sección del edificio.

Questo loft fa parte dell'edificio londinese di Shepherdess Walk restaurato dagli architetti Buschow Henley.

Il promotore voleva creare un edificio di uso misto, abbinando unità residenziali e commerciali. Degli studi preliminari indicarono che la costruzione poteva accogliere circa cinquanta appartamenti nei piani superiori, con le unità commerciali a piano terra e il garage per le auto nel piano interrato.

Concretamente, il progetto di questo loft consisteva nel dotare di due stanze/studio l'appartamento di una coppia che era ormai stufa di vivere nel tipico loft, dalle pareti con mattoni a vista e pavimento cementato. L'appartamento, di circa 205 m², fu comprato vuoto, come un contenitore; il progetto prevedeva di sfruttare al massimo la doppia altezza datagli dalla sezione dell'edificio.

Architects: Buschow Henley

Location: London, United Kingdom

Photographs: Nick Kane

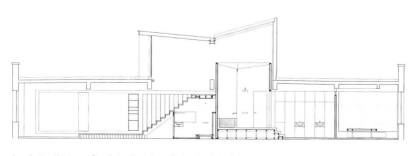

Lengthwise side view   Sección longitudinal   Sezione longitudinale

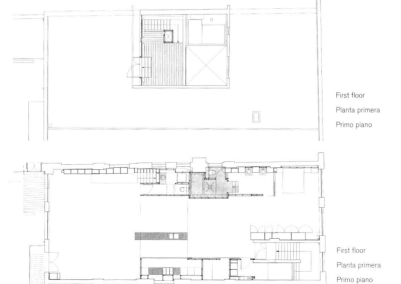

First floor

Planta primera

Primo piano

First floor

Planta primera

Primo piano

The mezzanine defines the lower space and allows light and views to reach the lower level through horizontal slots.

La entreplanta define el espacio de abajo y permite el paso de la iluminación y vistas al nivel inferior mediante ranuras horizontales en la sección.

Il seminterrato definisce lo spazio di sotto e consente il passaggio dell'illuminazione e viste del livello inferiore mediante scanalature orizzontali nella sezione.

Piper Building

Wells Mackereth
Architects

The Piper Building is a concrete office building originally designed by British Gas at the end of the 1950s, whose name is an inheritance from the artist, John Piper, the creator of the murals that decorate the building. In 1997, the Lifschutz Davidson studio rehabilitated the building where later several lofts created by architects including Ron Arad and John Pawson would be located. This loft, designed in 1998 by James Wells and Sally Mackereth for a young business executive, recovers a large volume of open, airy, continuous space in a quite skillful and flexible exercise in layouts.

The entire floor in this apartment is covered by large beech wood covered plywood panels, a material and placement that according to Mackereth was the most appropriate given the proportions of this loft. Tall pivoting doors made of reinforced glass, placed along dividing walls that do not reach the ceiling, allow control and growth of the space at will.

El Piper Building es un bloque de oficinas de estructura de hormigón diseñado originalmente por British Gas a finales de los años cincuenta y cuyo nombre es herencia del artista John Piper, el autor de los murales que decoran el edificio. En 1997, el estudio Lifschutz Davidson rehabilitó el edificio donde más tarde se ubicarían algunos de los lofts creados por arquitectos como Ron Arad o John Pawson. El loft, diseñado en 1998 por James Wells y Sally Mackereth para un joven ejecutivo de negocios, recupera un gran volumen de espacio diáfano y continuo en un ejercicio de distribución de la planta muy diestro y flexible.

Toda la superficie del suelo de este apartamento loft está cubierta de grandes tableros de madera contrachapada de abedul, un material y una disposición que según Mackereth era la adecuada para las proporciones del loft. Unas altas puertas pivotantes de vidrio armado, dispuestas a continuación de unas paredes divisorias que no llegan al techo, permiten el control y crecimiento del espacio a voluntad.

Il Piper Building è un blocco di uffici, con struttura in cemento, disegnato verso la fine degli anni cinquanta e il cui nome si deve all'artista John Piper, autore dei murales che decorano l'edificio. Nel 1997, lo studio Lifschutz Davidson ristrutturò l'edificio che più tardi avrebbe ospitato alcuni dei loft creati da architetti come Ron Arad o John Pawson. Il loft, disegnato nel 1998 da James Wells e Sally Mackereth per un giovane uomo d'affari, recupera un ampio volume di spazio diafano e continuo, in un esercizio di distribuzione della pianta molto accorto e flessibile.

L'intera superficie del pavimento di questo loft è rivestita da pannelli di legno compensato di betulla, un materiale e una disposizione idonei, secondo Mackereth, alle proporzioni dell'appartamento. Porte alte e ruotanti di vetro armato, disposte dopo pareti divisorie che non raggiungono il soffitto, permettono il controllo e la crescita a volontà dello spazio.

Architects: Wells Mackereth Architects

Location: London, United Kingdom

Photographs: Chris Gascoine/View, Dominic Blackmoren/Mitchell Beezley Picture Library

1. Living room, dining room and kitchen
2. Piece of furniture behind a sliding panel
3. Pivoting glass panel
4. Bedrooms
5. Sliding shutter
6. Dressing room
7. Bathroom
8. Bathtub with slate top
9. Engraved glass sliding doors
10. Storage area

1. Sala de estar, comedor y cocina
2. Mueble tras el panel deslizante
3. Panel de cristal pivotante
4. Dormitorios
5. Contraventana corredera
6. Vestidor
7. Baño
8. Bañera con sobre de pizarra
9. Correderas de cristal grabado
10. Almacén

1. Soggiorno, sala da pranzo e cucina
2. Mobile dietro il pannello scorrevole
3. Pannello in vetro ruotante
4. Stanze da letto
5. Controfinestra scorrevole
6. Stanzino
7. Bagno
8. Vasca da bagno con ripiano in ardesia
9. Guide in vetro inciso
10. Dispensa

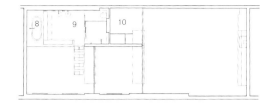

Attic   Altillo   Soppalco

Lower level   Planta baja   Piano terra

The television and music equipment are integrated into the design of the cabinets. The sofas were designed by Terence Woodgate.

La televisión y el equipo de música quedan integrados en el diseño de los armarios. Los sofás son diseño de Terence Woodgate.

La televisione e l'impianto stereo si integrano nel design degli armadi. I sofà portano la firma di Terence Woodgate.

Spatial Contrast
Contraste espacial / Contrasto spaziale

María Rodríguez-
Carreño Villangómez

On the third floor of a building where a gymnasium has been located, this 230 m² living and studio space is placed behind a labyrinthine access. The renovation work began by water-proofing the terrace over the space, which had been altered due to water leakage from the roof. Inside, the old gym equipment was taken out and the entire ceiling was painted white.

The building's structure follows a division based on the number 12: 12 windows, 12 beams, 12 cross-beams in each crossing. The project aimed to make the original structure stand out and avoid compartmentalization in an aim to create a dynamic space. Introducing any volume was viewed as an auxiliary element to the container, such that they are presented as separate pieces that never touch the walls.

The architecture includes great contrasts in the original space through a change of height from the access, which stands at 2.3 meters, and a graffiti on the back wall which serves as a fixed visual referent that dominates the entire environment.

En la tercera planta de un edificio donde había existido un gimnasio, se ubicó esta vivienda estudio de 230 m² tras un acceso laberíntico. La obra de rehabilitación empezó por la impermeabilización de la terraza que cubre el local, afectada por alteraciones debidas a la filtración de agua en la cubierta. En el interior se retiraron los antiguos complementos del gimnasio y se pintó todo el techo de color blanco.

La estructura del edificio sigue una modulación basada en el número 12: 12 ventanas, 12 vigas, 12 viguetas en cada crujía. El proyecto quiso resaltar la estructura original del espacio y evitar la compartimentación para crear un lugar dinámico. La introducción de cualquier volumen se planteó como elemento anexo a la envolvente de forma que se presentan como piezas sueltas que en ningún momento llegan a tocar las paredes.

La arquitectura aportada introduce grandes contrastes en el espacio original mediante un cambio de altura planteado desde el acceso a 2,3 meters o un graffiti en la pared del fondo como referente visual fijo que domina todo el ambiente.

Al terzo piano di un edificio dove prima c'era una palestra, è stata ubicata, dopo un accesso labirintico,questa abitazione studio di 230 m². I lavori di ristrutturazione iniziarono con l'impermeabilizzazione della terrazza che copre il locale, deteriorata per via di infiltrazioni d'acqua nel tetto. All'interno furono rimosse le vecchie attrezzature della palestra e il soffitto venne dipinto di bianco.

La struttura dell'edificio segue una modulazione basata sul numero 12: 12 finestre, 12 travi, 12 travetti in ogni intercapedine. Il progetto ha voluto risaltare la struttura originaria dello spazio ed evitare la compartimentazione per creare un ambiente dinamico. L'introduzione dei singoli volumi è stata concepita come un elemento annesso all'involucro in modo tale che questi si presentano come pezzi sparsi che in nessun momento toccano le pareti.

Il nuovo assetto architettonico introduce grandi contrasti nello spazio originario mediante un cambiamento di altezza progettato dall'accesso a 2,3 metri o un graffiti nella parete di fondo, come un referente visivo fisso, che domina tutto l'ambiente.

Architect: María Rodríguez-Carreño Villangómez

Location: Barcelona, Spain

Photographs: Joan Mundó

The access stairway to the attic consists of T-shaped steps made of steel painted oxiron gray and stamped aluminum sheeting, embedded in the wall. In this space is the bedroom on a lessor scale, more domestic and secluded.

La escalera de acceso al altillo está formada por peldaños hechos de perfiles en T de acero pintado con oxiron gris y chapa embutida de aluminio, empotrados en la pared. En este espacio se dispone el dormitorio a una escala menor, más doméstica y de recogimiento.

La scala di accesso al soppalco è formata da gradini fatti di profilati a forma di T, in acciaio smaltato grigio (con smalto tipo Oxiron) e lamiera imbottita in alluminio, direttamente incassati nella parete. In questo spazio si dispone la stanza da letto, su una scala minore, più domestica e raccolta.

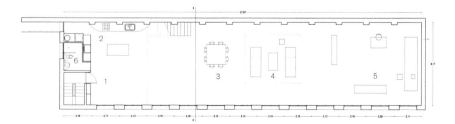

Lower level	Planta baja	Piano terra
1. Entrance	1. Entrada	1. Ingresso
2. Kitchen	2. Cocina	2. Cucina
3. Dining room	3. Comedor	3. Sala da pranzo
4. Living room	4. Salón	4. Salone
5. Studio	5. Estudio	5. Studio
6. Half bathroom	6. Aseo	6. Toilette

Side view Sección Sezione

The studio is presided over by the Julio Rodríguez-Carreño photograph of a graffiti on Virgen street on the island of Ibiza.

El estudio está presidido por la fotografía de Julio Rodríguez-Carreño de un *graffiti* de la calle de la Virgen en la isla de Ibiza.

Lo studio è presieduto dalla fotografia di Julio Rodríguez-Carreño, rappresentante un *graffiti* di una via nell'isola di Ibiza: *la calle de la Virgen.*

The headboard closet in the bedroom, made of varnished iroco wood with metallic edges, has functioning light inside.

El armario cabecero del dormitorio, de madera de iroco barnizada con el canto en chapa metálica, dispone de iluminación practicable desde su interior.

L'armadio posto alla testata del letto, in legno iroco verniciato, con canto in lamiera metallica, è dotato di un dispositivo di illuminazione, regolabile dall'interno.

Leisure and Business
Ocio y negocio / Tempo libero e affari

Ramón Úbeda/
Pepa Reverter

The Barcelona neighborhood of Poblenou, an old industrial zone of the city, is one of the places where artists and professionals in creative fields choose to live or work. Still standing in the area are beautiful structures that used to support buildings that had been used for warehouses or light industry. Today, the recovery of these buildings stands as definitive proof of the authenticity of lofts: making sure that creative work is still being performed in them.

Located on the first of three floors of the building, we find the living space and studio of Ramón Úbeda and Pepa Reverter, creators and inhabitants of this loft, who claim: "Without a doubt, this is the easiest design in the world. The main objective of an interior design project for the renovation of a particular place is always to achieve large spaces and make the most of natural daylight. All of this, so basic yet so difficult to achieve in many places, already existed here. The solid, forceful structure of this old manufacturing building offered more than 300 m² of open, airy floor space in addition to two imposing windows that inundated the space with light streaming in. It is a dream of a space that does not exist in conventional homes."

El barrio barcelonés de Poblenou, antigua zona industrial de la ciudad, es uno de los lugares que artistas y profesionales de la actividad creativa eligen para vivir o trabajar. La zona aún conserva en pie hermosas estructuras que sostuvieron edificios destinados a almacén o industria ligera. La recuperación de estas construcciones confirma, hoy en día, una de las pruebas definitivas de la autenticidad de un loft: cerciorar que en su interior se sigue desarrollando un trabajo creativo.

Ubicada en la primera de las tres plantas del edificio encontramos la vivienda estudio de Ramón Úbeda y Pepa Reverter, creadores y habitantes de este loft, quienes afirman: «Este es, sin duda, el diseño más fácil del mundo. Un proyecto de interiorismo para la reforma de un local tiene siempre el objetivo primordial de conseguir espacios amplios y sacar el máximo partido de la luz natural. Todo eso, tan básico y tan difícil de lograr en muchos lugares, aquí ya existía. La sólida y contundente estructura de esta antigua edificación fabril ofrecía más de 300 m² en planta, limpios y diáfanos, además de dos imponentes ventanales que inundaban el local de luz a raudales. Un lujo de espacio que en las viviendas convencionales no existe».

Il quartiere barcellonese di Poblenou, antica zona industriale della città, è uno dei luoghi prediletti da artisti e professionisti nel campo delle attività creative, sia per vivere che per lavorare. La zona conserva ancora intatte strutture di bella fattura che in passato hanno ospitato edifici adibiti a magazzino o fabbriche dell'industria leggera. Il recupero di queste costruzioni conferma, oggigiorno, una delle prove definitive dell'autenticità di un loft: verificare che all'interno si continui a realizzare un lavoro creativo.

Ubicata al primo dei tre piani dell'edificio, troviamo l'abitazione/studio di Ramón Úbeda e Pepa Reverter, creatori ed inquilini di questo loft, i quali affermano: «Questo è, senza dubbio, il progetto più facile del mondo. Un progetto di arredamento di interni per la ristrutturazione di un locale ha sempre lo scopo primordiale di ottenere ampi spazi e sfruttare al massimo la luce naturale. Tutto questo, così semplice e al contempo difficile da ottenere in molti ambienti, qua già esisteva. La solida e robusta struttura di questa antica costruzione industriale offriva più di 300 m² in pianta, chiari e diafani, oltre a due imponenti finestroni che inondavano il locale di luce naturale. Uno spazio di lusso che non esiste nelle abitazioni convenzionali».

Interior Designers: Ramón Úbeda/Pepa Reverter
Location: Barcelona, Spain
Photographs: Pere Planells

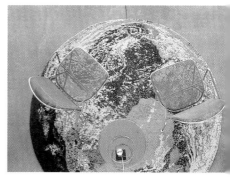

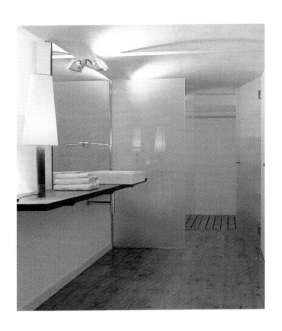

The generous height of the space allowed for the placement of a double high area which enriches the views and accommodates the two most private rooms: the master bedroom and the artist's workshop.

La generosa altura del local permite ubicar un doble espacio destinado a enriquecer las vistas y a acomodar las dos piezas más íntimas: el dormitorio principal y el taller de la artista.

La generosa altezza del locale consente di allestire un doppio spazio destinato ad arricchire le viste e a sistemare le due zone più intime: la stanza da letto principale e il laboratorio dell'artista.

La Nau

Carol Iborra,
Mila Aberasturi

More than 60 years have gone by since the unique building that used to house the industry of a spinning mill arose amidst large buttresses and vaults in the Barcelona neighborhood of Poblenou.

The Catalan name of this loft, La Nau (the factory), which is located on the second floor, makes reference to its industrial past. After finding this architectural gem, with its solid brick and Catalan arches, Mila Aberasturi and Carol Iborra (Forma 7) converted the industrial factory into a home.

The layout of the space provides some spaces, such as the bathroom and the half bathrooms, the kitchen and the home's storage area, with privacy.

The materials chosen for the reform were basic: pinewood floors, light masonry walls, concrete on the walls and floors of the bathrooms, and iron window frames.

Han pasado más de 60 años desde que este singular edificio que antaño albergó la actividad industrial de un taller de hilaturas surgió entre grandes contrafuertes y bóvedas en el barrio barcelonés de Poblenou.

El nombre catalán del loft la Nau (la nave), situado en la segunda planta, hace referencia a su pasado industrial. Tras localizar esta joya arquitectónica a la catalana, Mila Aberasturi y Carol Iborra (Forma 7) convirtieron la nave industrial en vivienda.

La distribución de la nave proporciona privacidad a algunas estancias como los baños y los aseos, la cocina o la zona de almacenaje de la vivienda.

Los materiales elegidos para la reforma son básicos: madera de pino en el pavimento, separaciones ligeras de albañilería en seco, hormigón en las paredes y suelos de los lavabos y estructuras metálicas de hierro.

Sono trascorsi ormai più di 60 anni da quando questo singolare edificio fu costruito, tra grandi contrafforti e volte, nel quartiere barcellonese di Poblenou.

Il nome del loft, («nau», in catalano significa capannone industriale), situato al secondo piano, fa riferimento al suo passato, visto che l'edificio era sede di una bottega di filatura. Dopo aver individuato questo gioiello architettonico di mattone massiccio e volte alla catalana, Mila Aberasturi e Carol Iborra (Forma 7) trasformarono il vecchio capannone industriale in un'abitazione.

La distribuzione del capannone dona privacy ad alcune stanze come i bagni e le toilette, la cucina e la zona dell'abitazione adibita a dispensa.

I materiali scelti per la ristrutturazione sono semplici: legno di pino nel pavimento, separazioni leggere in muratura a secco, cemento nelle pareti e nei pavimenti dei bagni, e strutture metalliche in ferro.

Architects: Carol Iborra, Mila Aberasturi (interiorista)

Location: Barcelona, Spain

Photographs: Xabier Mendiola

An interior enclosure made of fiberglass sheets allows the pearly light that enters from the large windows onto the street to pass through.

Un cerramiento interior de láminas de fibra de vidrio deja pasar la luz nacarada que entra por los grandes ventanales desde la calle.

Un tramezzo interno in lamine di fibra di vetro lascia passare la luce madreperlata che entra dalla strada attraverso gli enormi finestroni.

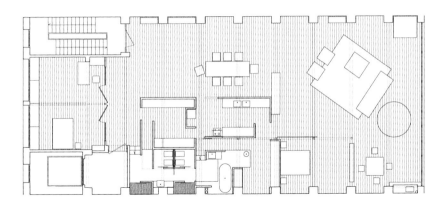

An abstract geometrical composition of blank volumes characterizes the spaces that make up this home.

Una composición geométrica abstracta de volúmenes blancos caracteriza las estancias que conforman la casa.

Una composizione geometrica astratta, dai volumi bianchi, caratterizza gli ambienti che formano la casa.

Urban Panorama
Panorámica urbana / Panoramica urbana

Antoni Arola

The last loft in this old thread factory in Poblenou lies under the roof, on the third floor of the building. A web of metallic struts covers the workshop only to reappear, invading part of the living space. The owner is Antoni Arola, a designer who decided to colonize the place in order to set up his home and work studio, two environments in continuous transformation that generate a laboratory of ideas.

In the domestic privacy of his home, Arola surrounds himself with inspiration: lights, reflections and elements whose interest and promise hidden beauty or emotion are awakened in everyday exchanges with the outside.

In the workshop, the designer has all the tools that allow him to provide the world with his beautiful, ingenious, functional designs. The majority of projects undertaken by his firm are related to industrial manufacturing: lamps, chairs, sofas, and even wrappings or containers, aside from interior architecture for all types of buildings.

The structure of the workshop conserves a large display cabinet construction with the original shapes of the factory that opens the working space up to the outside and brings to mind the urban location of this loft. A small separating wall treated with special chalkboard paint houses a library. The floor is covered with smoothed, polished cement.

El último loft de la vieja fábrica de hilos de Poblenou queda bajo cubierta, en la tercera planta del edificio. Una telaraña de cerchas metálicas cubre el taller y reaparece invadiendo parte de la vivienda. El propietario es Antoni Arola, un diseñador que decidió colonizar el lugar para establecer su vivienda y estudio de trabajo, dos ambientes en continua transformación que generan un laboratorio de ideas.

En la intimidad doméstica de su casa, Arola se rodea de inspiración: luces, reflejos y elementos que en cotidianos intercambios con el exterior despiertan su interés y prometen belleza o emoción oculta.

En el taller, el diseñador dispone de todas las herramientas que le permiten dar al mundo un diseño ingenioso y bello que cumpla con su función. La mayoría de los proyectos que llevan su firma están destinados a la fabricación industrial: lámparas, sillas, sofás, incluso envoltorios o envases, aparte de la arquitectura interior de todo tipo de locales.

La estructura del taller conserva una gran cristalera construida con los perfiles originales de la fábrica que abre el espacio de trabajo hacia el exterior, y recuerda el emplazamiento urbano de este loft. Un pequeño tabique separador tratado con pintura especial para pizarras alberga una biblioteca. El pavimento es de cemento allanado y pulido.

L'ultimo loft di un'antica fabbrica tessile del Poblenou rimane sotto il tetto, al terzo piano dell'edificio. Una ragnatela di centine metalliche copre lo studio e riappare invadendo parte dell'abitazione. Il proprietario è Antoni Arola, un designer che ha deciso di colonizzare il posto per stabilirvi la propria dimora e il proprio studio di lavoro, due ambienti in continua trasformazione che generano un laboratorio di idee.

Nella privacy di casa sua, Arola si circonda di inspirazione: luci, riflessi ed elementi che in un quotidiano scambio con l'esterno, destano il suo interesse, e promettono bellezza o segrete emozioni.

Nello studio, il designer dispone di tutti gli strumenti che gli consentono di dare al mondo un design ingegnoso e bello, che svolga la sua funzione. La maggior parte dei progetti che portano la sua firma si concentra sulla fabbricazione industriale: lampade, sedie, sofà, e persino involucri e confezioni di prodotti, a parte l'architettura di interni per qualsiasi tipo di locale.

Lo studio conserva ancora una grande vetrata costruita sulla base dell'antica intelaiatura, che proietta all'esterno l'ambiente di lavoro, e ricorda l'ubicazione urbana di questo loft. Un piccolo tramezzo separatore, trattato con una pittura speciale per ardesie, ospita una biblioteca. Il pavimento è in cemento spianato e lustrato.

Interiorista y diseñador industrial: Antoni Arola

Location: Barcelona, Spain

Photographs: Pere Planells

Lengthwise side view   Sección longitudinal   Sezione longitudinale

Cross section   Sección transversal   Sezione trasversale

Top view   Planta   Pianta

The bathroom and half bathroom, as well as the
furniture, are integrated into the bedroom space, visually
forming part of the most private patio in the house.

El baño y el aseo, como muebles, se integran en
la estancia del dormitorio formando parte visual
del patio más privado de la casa.

Il bagno e la toilette, come se fossero dei mobili, si
integrano nella stanza da letto, formando una parte
visuale dell'angolo più intimo della casa.

Vapor Llull

Cirici & Bassó, Inés
Rodríguez, Alfonso de
Luna, Norman
Cinamond, Carla Cirici

Cristian Cirici and Carles Bassó transformed an old chemical products factory, made up of a lower floor and two upper floors, into a residential building. The external references to its industrial past are obvious: a large brick chimney that virtually grazes the building and an urban texture that until recently was almost entirely industrial. The exterior brick walls are conserved, as are the hand wrought vaults and the roof made of wooden struts, while three vertical means of connection were added, including a stairway and a freight elevator with views, in order to give independent access to each of the 18 homes. The sophistication of the new elements contrasts with the structures that have been preserved and with the façade, which has been painted orange and blue. Although this was not conceived in order to look good, the intervention resulted in indirectly modern spaces. The exposed metallic structure, the large windows through which natural daylight enters, and an initial layout of open spaces make the typical structural framework of the old factory become a cozy space in which it is appealing to live.

Cristian Cirici y Carles Bassó transformaron una antigua fábrica de productos químicos, de planta baja y dos pisos, en edificio de viviendas. Las referencias externas de su pasado industrial son evidentes: una gran chimenea de obra que casi roza el edificio y un tejido urbano hasta hace pocos años exclusivamente dedicado a la industria. Se conservaron los muros exteriores de ladrillo, los forjados de bovedillas manuales y la cubierta de cerchas de madera, al tiempo que se añadieron tres bloques de comunicación vertical formados por una escalera y un montacargas panorámico, a fin de dar acceso independiente a cada una de las 18 viviendas. La sofisticación de los nuevos elementos contrasta con las estructuras que se han preservado y con la fachada pintada de naranja y azul. A pesar de que no fue concebido para tener buen aspecto, el resultado de la intervención son unos espacios indirectamente modernos. La estructura metálica vista, los grandes ventanales con entradas de luz natural y una configuración inicial de espacios abiertos hacen que el típico armazón estructural de la antigua fábrica se convierta en un lugar acogedor en el que apetece vivir.

Cristian Cirici e Carles Bassó trasformarono una vecchia fabbrica di prodotti chimici, che occupava il piano terra e due piani, in una casa d'abitazione. I riferimenti esterni del suo passato industriale sono evidenti: una grande ciminiera che sfiora quasi l'edificio e un tessuto urbano, fino a pochi anni addietro, prettamente industriale. Si sono mantenuti i muri esterni in mattoni, le solette con volticine fatte a mano, la copertura di centine in legno e al contempo sono stati aggiunti tre blocchi di comunicazione verticale formati da una scala e da un montacarichi panoramico, al fine di dare un accesso indipendente ad ognuna delle 18 abitazioni. La sofisticazione dei nuovi elementi contrasta con le vecchie strutture e con la facciata dipinta di color arancio e blu. Nonostante non fosse stato concepito per avere un bell'aspetto, il risultato dell'intervento sono degli spazi indirettamente moderni. La struttura metallica a vista, i grandi finestroni che lasciano passare la luce naturale e una configurazione iniziale di spazi aperti, fanno in modo che il tipico involucro strutturale della vecchia fabbrica diventi un luogo accogliente nel quale si vive con piacere.

Architects: Cirici & Bassó, Inés Rodríguez, Alfonso de Luna, Norman Cinamond, Carla Cirici

Location: Barcelona, Spain

Photographs: Rafael Vargas

Inés Rodríguez has designed an austere top floor in which the wooden struts acquired a powerful presence.

Inés Rodríguez ha diseñado un ático austero en el que las cerchas de madera adquieren una presencia poderosa.

Inés Rodríguez ha disegnato un attico austero dove le centine in legno acquisiscono una presenza possente.

Norman Cinamond chose a counter to separate the kitchen from the living room which serves as an informal dining room. The Jamaica stools were created by Pepe Cortés.

Norman Cinamond optó por un mostrador que separa la cocina de la sala y que funciona como comedor informal. Los taburetes Jamaica son creación de Pepe Cortés.

Norman Cinamond ha optato per un banco che separa la cucina dalla sala e dove poter consumare dei pasti in modo informale. Gli sgabelli Jamaica sono opera di Pepe Cortés.

The extensive use of wood, the tufa ceramic flooring and the primitive sculptures all give the apartment designed by Alfonso de Luna a misleadingly tropical, decadent appearance.

El uso extensivo de la madera, el pavimento de toba cerámica, las palmeras y las esculturas primitivas transmiten al apartamento diseñado por Alfonso de Luna un aspecto engañosamente tropical y decadente.

L'uso estensivo del legno, il pavimento in tufo ceramico, le palme e le sculture primitive trasmettono all'appartamento, progettato da Alfonso de Luna, un aspetto ingannevolmente tropicale e decadente.

The intervention by Carla Cirici is the one that least modified the original space.

La intervención de Carla Cirici es la que menos modifica el espacio original.

L'intervento di Carla Cirici è quello che meno modifica lo spazio originale.

Apartment for an Actress

Apartamento para una actriz / Appartamento per un'attrice

Franc Fernández

The remodeling of this building transformed into residential use what had previously been a warehouse factory. The industrial feel of this space has been perpetuated by leaving the 4.5 meters height of the original design intact.

Each floor was divided into four 150 m² spaces. The 110 m² apartment described here results from one of these spaces having been divided into two. The owner's profession (actress) conditioned the type of space being sought; the apartment had to be able to be used both to rehearse and to hold performances. Spaciousness, luminosity and versatility thus because the highest priority objectives of the project.

The pre-existing structure was maintained: the metallic main beams and pillars, the undulating ironwork of the ceramic vaults, and even the original large windows. The floor space was divided into two zones: first, in a single space, the kitchen, the dining room and the living room; the other houses the bedroom, the bathroom, the half bathroom and the studio. The first, more public space conserves the high ceilings and enjoys the majority of the light that enters. In the second, however, an intermediate ceiling vertically divides the space into two and provides a feeling of coziness and intimacy in the more private spaces.

La remodelación del edificio transformó en uso residencial lo que había sido antiguamente una fábrica almacén. Al dejar intactos los 4,5 metros de altura del proyecto original se perpetuó el carácter industrial del lugar.

Cada planta fue dividida en cuatro espacios de 150 m². El apartamento descrito a continuación, de 110 m², resulta de haber subdividido en dos uno de ellos. La profesión de la propietaria (actriz) condicionó el tipo de espacio buscado. Así, el apartamento tenía que poder ser utilizado tanto para ensayar como para realizar *performances*. Amplitud, luminosidad y versatilidad pasaron entonces a ser objetivos prioritarios del proyecto.

La estructura preexistente se mantuvo: las jácenas y pilares metálicos, el forjado ondulado de bovedillas cerámicas y hasta los grandes ventanales originales. La planta se dividió en dos zonas: por una parte, y en un único espacio, la cocina, el comedor y la sala de estar; al otro lado, el dormitorio, el baño, el aseo y el estudio. La primera, la más pública, conserva los techos altos y disfruta de gran parte de la entrada de luz. En la segunda, sin embargo, se ha añadido un forjado intermedio que parte en dos el espacio vertical y proporciona una sensación de recogimiento e intimidad en las estancias más privadas.

La ristrutturazione dell'edificio ha trasformato in unità residenziale quella che anticamente era stata una fabbrica magazzino. Lasciando intatti i 4,5 metri di altezza del progetto originale, si è potuto mantenere il carattere industriale del posto.

Ogni piano è stato diviso in quattro spazi di 150 m². L'abitazione di seguito descritta, di 110 m², nasce dall'aver diviso in due uno degli appartamenti. La professione della proprietaria (attrice) ha inciso sulla scelta del tipo di spazio. Infatti, l'appartamento doveva poter essere utilizzato sia per provare che per realizzarvi delle *performance*. Ampiezza, luminosità e versatilità divennero pertanto obiettivi prioritari del progetto.

La struttura preesistente si è mantenuta: le travi maestre e i pilastri in metallo, il solaio ondulato con piccole volte in ceramica, e persino i grandi finestroni originari. La pianta è stata divisa in due zone: da una parte, e in un unico spazio, la cucina, la sala da pranzo e il soggiorno; dall'altra, la stanza da letto, il bagno, la toilette, e lo studio. Nella prima di queste, di uso comune, la luce entra in abbondanza e i soffitti sono rimasti alti. Nella seconda, invece, è stata aggiunta una soletta intermedia che divide in due lo spazio verticale e dà una sensazione di raccoglimento e intimità agli ambienti più intimi.

Architect: Franc Fernández

Location: Barcelona, Spain

Photographs: Joan Mundó

The apartment's floor is entirely covered with solid ipe wood. This wood, which provides a certain feeling of warmth, co-exists simultaneously with a decoration that emphasizes the building's industrial origins.

El suelo del apartamento está revestido en su totalidad con madera maciza de ipé. Esto, que aporta cierta sensación de calidez, convive a su vez con una decoración que enfatiza el origen industrial del edificio.

Il pavimento dell'appartamento è totalmente rivestito in legno massiccio ipé. Ciò dona allo spazio una certa accoglienza e convive al contempo con un arredamento che sottolinea le origini industriali dell'edificio.

The spaces are connected through sliding doors, some of them even made of translucent glass, such that the square meters of the layout are minimal.

Las estancias se conectan a través de puertas correderas, algunas de ellas incluso de vidrio translúcido, con lo que resultan mínimos los metros cuadrados de distribución.

Le stanze si collegano mediante porte scorrevoli, alcune delle quali sono persino in vetro traslucido, pertanto i metri quadrati utilizzati per il disimpegno degli ambienti sono minimi.

Franc Fernández achieves an apartment in which, with somewhat austere resources, a great richness of shapes and a maximum tension in each space is achieved in its final design.

Franc Fernández consigue un apartamento en el que, con cierta austeridad en los recursos, logra en su distribución final una gran riqueza de formas y una máxima tensión en cada espacio.

Franc Fernández ottiene, con delle risorse limitate, un appartamento la cui distribuzione finale presenta una grande ricchezza di forme e una tensione massima in ogni ambiente.

Verticality
Verticalidad / Verticalità

Pere Cortacans

This building is located in Barcelona's Born neighborhood, which is characterized by narrow, irregular and humid streets. An L-shaped building from the turn of the century wrapped around an old tool metal workshop.

This intervention, headed by Pere Cortacans, meant the total reform of the building, including the re-conversion of the workshop into a central garden.

The living space has three levels: the original level, an attic that came from dismantling the lower part of the air ventilation chamber (from the old climate control system), and finally a glassed-in studio that occupies the building's roof and that provides access to the rooftop terrace. It is a home that functions vertically, contrary to the idea of horizontal spaces that usually characterizes lofts. Each level is associated with a series of activities, each with different degrees of privacy and intensity.

El edificio se encuentra en el barrio del Born, de calles estrechas, irregulares y húmedas. Un bloque de principios de siglo con forma de L rodeaba un viejo taller de planchas metálicas rotuladas.

La intervención dirigida por Pere Cortacans supuso la reforma total del edificio, incluida la reconversión del taller en un jardín central.

La vivienda tiene tres niveles: el original, un altillo que resulta de desmantelar la parte inferior de la cámara de aire ventilada (antiguo sistema de control climático) y, finalmente, un estudio acristalado que ocupa la cubierta del edificio y que da acceso a la terraza habilitada en la misma. Se trata de una vivienda que funciona en vertical, contrariamente a la idea de horizontalidad que se tiene cuando se habla de un loft. Cada nivel está asociado a un conjunto de actividades con un grado de privacidad e intensidad diferentes.

L'edificio si trova nel Born, un quartiere dalle strade strette, irregolari ed umide. Uno stabile d'inizio secolo, a forma di L, circondava un'antica bottega per l'incisione di lastre metalliche.

L'intervento, diretto da Pere Cortacans ha comportato la ristrutturazione totale dell'edificio, compresa la riconversione della bottega in un giardino centrale.

L'abitazione presenta tre livelli: quello originario, un soppalco ottenuto dallo smantellamento della parte inferiore della camera d'aria ventilata (antico sistema di controllo climatico) e infine, un monolocale con pareti di vetro. Quest'ultimo e l'adiacente terrazza fungono da copertura dell'edificio. Si tratta di un'abitazione che si sviluppa in verticale, contrariamente all'idea di orizzontalità che viene in mente quando si parla di loft. Ogni livello è associato a un insieme di attività che hanno intensità e livelli di privacy diversi.

Architect: Pere Cortacans
Location: Barcelona, Spain
Photographs: David Cardelús

Austerity or Design
Austeridad o diseño / Austerità o design

These two apartments, remodeled by the same architect and located in the same building, nevertheless represent two different options for a loft home. The materials, finishes and furniture chosen give each one of the spaces very different characteristics: one is more industrial, the other more palatial.

In the first one, the majority of the structural elements have been left exposed (ceiling vaults, façade wall, lattice beams) and for the flooring a single material was chosen: polished concrete. Its appearance is deliberately industrial and, to some degree, austere and harsh.

In the second loft, the walls have been painted a yellowish tone. In this case, the loft is made up of a large double high living room which includes an open kitchen and a lateral area divided into three levels. The dining room, staircase, and a half bathroom are located on the lower level; the master bedroom and two other rooms, the dressing room and the full bathroom, are located on the mezzanine. Finally, three is an independent third level exclusively for the children, with two bedrooms, a bathroom, and a game room or shared study.

Estos dos apartamentos, remodelados por el mismo arquitecto y ubicados en el mismo edificio, representan, sin embargo, dos opciones diferentes de vivienda loft. Los materiales, los acabados y los muebles seleccionados aportan a cada uno de los espacios características muy distintas: el uno es más industrial; el otro, más palaciego.

En el primero de ellos, la mayoría de los elementos estructurales se ha dejado sin revestir (las bovedillas del techo, el muro de fachada, las vigas de celosía) y para el pavimento se escogió un material en masa: el hormigón pulido. Su aspecto es voluntariamente industrial y, en cierto modo, austero y duro.

En el segundo loft se ha optado por pintar los muros de un tono amarillo. En este caso, el loft está formado por una gran sala de estar a doble altura que incluye una cocina abierta y una zona lateral dividida en tres niveles. En la planta baja se ubican el comedor, la escalera y un aseo; el altillo está ocupado por el dormitorio principal y dos habitaciones auxiliares: el vestidor y el baño. Finalmente, existe un tercer nivel independiente destinado a los niños, con dos dormitorios, un baño, y una sala de juego o de estudio compartida.

Questi due appartamenti, ristrutturati dallo stesso architetto e ubicati nello stesso edificio, rappresentano, tuttavia, due opzioni diverse di un alloggio tipo loft. I materiali, le finiture e i mobili scelti conferiscono a ognuno degli spazi caratteristiche molto diverse tra loro: uno è più industriale, l'altro è più raffinato.

Nel primo di questi, la maggior parte degli elementi strutturali non sono stati rivestiti (le volticine del soffitto, il muro della facciata, il reticolato delle travi) e per il pavimento si è scelto un materiale impastato: il cemento levigato. Il suo aspetto è volutamente industriale e, in certo modo, austero e duro.

Nel secondo, l'architetto ha scelto di dipingere i muri in un tono giallo. Il loft è formato da un soggiorno spazioso a doppia altezza che comprende una cucina aperta e una zona laterale divisa in tre livelli. Al piano terra si trovano la sala da pranzo, la scala e una toilette; il soppalco è occupato dalla camera da letto principale e due stanze ausiliari: lo stanzino e il bagno. Infine, esiste un terzo livello indipendente, riservato ai bambini, con due camere da letto, un bagno, una sala comune dove poter studiare o giocare.

Architect: Joan Bach

Location: Barcelona, Spain

Photographs: Jordi Miralles

The walls do not touch the ceiling and thus transmit a feeling of uninterrupted space. The exposed brick pillar is not a load-bearing element (since the structure is metallic); it houses the drainage tubes.

Los tabiques no llegan al techo y transmiten así la sensación de espacio ininterrumpido. El pilar de obra vista no es un elemento portante (pues la estructura es metálica), sino que alberga el paso de las tuberías de desagüe.

I tramezzi non arrivano al soffitto, dando quindi la sensazione di uno spazio non interrotto. Il pilastro in mattoni a vista non è un elemento portante (visto che la struttura è di metallo), ma nasconde all'interno il passaggio dei tubi di scarico.

A visual connection between the bedroom and the living room has been maintained despite the fact that they are on different levels. The master bedroom is reached through the bathroom. Just as in Islamic mosques, the access to this bedroom requires prior ablutions.

Se ha mantenido una comunicación visual entre el dormitorio y la sala pese a que se encuentran a diferentes niveles. Al dormitorio principal se accede a través del baño. Como en las mezquitas del Islam, el acceso a esta habitación requiere un aseo previo.

Si è mantenuta una comunicazione visiva tra la stanza da letto e il salone, nonostante si trovino su due livelli diversi. Alla camera da letto principale, si accede attraverso il bagno; come se ci si trovasse in una moschea islamica, per accedere a questa stanza occorre prima lavarsi.

Working at Home
Trabajar en casa / Lavorare a casa

Helena Mateu Pomar

The building was an old electrical supply factory in the Barcelona neighborhood of Gracia. The loft occupies the top floor of the factory, a privileged location that has direct, private access to the rooftop terrace.

The client wanted to renovate the apartment and convert it into a living and working space. When planning the reform, it was essential to maintain the airiness and openness that had captivated the owner. It was also important that the more private and utilitarian spaces could each be closed off separately without interrupting the continuity of space. Freestanding boxes were designed to contain the utilities, and the different spaces—the living room, the office, and the bedrooms—would be generated around it.

Large sliding doors have been placed in the boxes to allow privacy to be controlled at the client's will while at the same time shaping the loft area as a continuous, diaphanous space.

El edificio era una antigua fábrica de material eléctrico en el barrio de Gracia de Barcelona. El loft en cuestión ocupa la última planta de la fábrica, un lugar privilegiado que tiene acceso directo y privado a la terraza de cubierta.

El cliente quiso rehabilitar el piso y convertirlo en vivienda y despacho. En el planteamiento de la reforma resultaba esencial mantener el espacio diáfano, abierto, que originalmente había cautivado a su propietario. Igualmente era importante que las estancias más privadas y de servicio se pudieran clausurar independientemente unas de otras pero manteniendo siempre la continuidad del espacio. Se proyectaron unas cajas exentas que contienen el programa de servicios y a cuyo alrededor se generan las diferentes estancias, el salón, el despacho y las habitaciones.

Se han dispuesto unas grandes puertas correderas situadas en las cajas que permiten el control de la privacidad a voluntad del cliente, y que a un mismo tiempo conforman la superficie del loft como un espacio continuo y diáfano.

L'edificio era una vecchia fabbrica di materiale elettrico sita nel quartiere barcellonese di Gracia. Il loft in questione occupa l'ultimo piano della fabbrica, un luogo privilegiato, con accesso diretto e privato alla terrazza di copertura.

Il cliente ha voluto ristrutturare l'appartamento e trasformarlo contemporaneamente in abitazione e ufficio. Nel progetto di restauro era essenziale mantenere lo spazio diafano, aperto, che aveva originariamente colpito il suo nuovo proprietario. Allo stesso modo, era importante che le stanze più intime e di servizio si potessero chiudere indipendentemente una dall'altra, mantenendo sempre però la continuità dello spazio. Furono proiettati dei vani isolati che contengono il blocco delle stanze di servizio, attorno al quale si sviluppano le altre stanze: il salone, l'ufficio e le stanze da letto.

I vani isolati presentano grandi porte scorrevoli che permettono di controllare la privacy secondo il gusto del cliente, e che allo stesso tempo strutturano la superficie del loft come uno spazio continuo e diafano.

Architect: Helena Mateu Pomar

Location: Barcelona, Spain

Photographs: Jordi Miralles

The uni-directional texture of the beams and the Catalan vault on the ceiling contrast with the continuous, polished surface of the wood floor.

La textura unidireccional de viguetas y bovedilla catalana del techo contrasta con la superficie continua y pulida de la madera del suelo.

La disposizione unidirezionale dei travetti e delle piccole volte alla catalana del soffitto contrasta con la superficie continua e liscia del legno del pavimento.

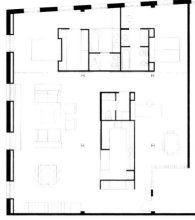

Each bedroom has its own bathroom, allowing privacy to always be maintained.

Cada dormitorio dispone de un baño independiente que permite mantener la privacidad en cada momento.

Tutte le stanze da letto dispongono di un bagno indipendente che consente di mantenere in ogni momento la propria privacy.

353

Effective Layout
Distribución eficaz / Distribuzione efficace

This design occupies the ground floor of a building in the picturesque Barcelona neighborhood of Gracia. The entire construction was subject to a remodeling by the architect Joan Bach, who claimed the first few floors for his own living and office space.

The loft has four different levels, allowing the different functional areas to be delimited without the need to raise walls. The lower level includes the entryway, a small reception area for the office, and a half bathroom.

From the access level, three steps lead down to the living room, which has double-high ceilings, and a small patio that thanks to its low outer walls provides the residence with plenty of natural daylight. The double-high space in the living room houses a small mezzanine where the office is located with views to the outside.

The construction details were painstakingly designed in order to achieve perfect finishes and solutions that made the housing space more comfortable. A good example of this savoir faire are the skylights, which have an electrical mechanism that allows them to be opened and closed in order to increase the complex's ventilation.

El proyecto ocupa los bajos de un edificio en el pintoresco barrio de Gracia, en Barcelona. Toda la construcción fue objeto de una remodelación por parte del arquitecto Joan Bach, que se apropió de las primeras plantas para colocar su vivienda y su despacho.

El loft consta de cuatro niveles diferenciados que permiten delimitar las distintas zonas funcionales sin necesidad de levantar paredes. La planta baja acoge la entrada, una pequeña recepción del despacho y un aseo.

Desde el nivel de acceso, tres peldaños bajan a la sala de estar, que tiene doble altura, y a un patio de dimensiones reducidas pero que gracias a los muros bajos que lo limitan proporciona abundante luz natural a la vivienda. El doble espacio de la sala alberga un pequeño altillo donde se ubica el despacho, que tiene vistas al exterior.

Los detalles constructivos se diseñaron cuidadosamente para ofrecer acabados perfectos y soluciones que hicieran más confortable la estancia en la casa. Un buen ejemplo de este savoir faire son las claraboyas, que están dotadas de un mecanismo eléctrico que permite mover sus cerramientos para aumentar la ventilación del conjunto.

Il progetto occupa un locale a piano terra di un edificio sito nel pittoresco quartiere di Gracia, a Barcellona. Tutta la costruzione è stata oggetto di una ristrutturazione da parte dell'architetto Joan Bach, che si appropriò dei primi piani per stabilirvi la sua dimora e il suo ufficio.

Il loft consta di quattro livelli differenziati che consentono di delimitare le diverse zone funzionali senza bisogno di erigere pareti. Il piano terra ospita l'ingresso, una saletta dell'ufficio, e una toilette.

Dal livello di accesso, partono tre gradini che conducono al soggiorno, ad altezza doppia, e a un cortile di dimensioni ridotte ma che, grazie ai muri bassi che lo delimitano, dona all'abitazione luce naturale in abbondanza. Il doppio spazio del soggiorno comprende un piccolo soppalco dove si trova l'ufficio, con vista sull'esterno.

I particolari costruttivi sono stati progettati con molta cura, al fine di offrire finiture perfette e soluzioni che rendessero più confortevole il soggiorno nella casa. Un buon esempio di questo savoir-faire sono gli abbaini, dotati di un meccanismo elettrico che consente di muovere le loro chiusure in modo tale da aumentare la ventilazione di tutto l'ambiente.

Location: Barcelona, Spain

Photographs: Jordi Miralles

Both the floor and the pillar are finished in a synthetic resin, which is used quite frequently in industrial factory spaces.

Tanto el suelo como el acabado del pilar son de resina sintética, un material muy utilizado en naves industriales.

Sia il pavimento che la finitura della colonna sono di resina sintetica, un materiale molto utilizzato nei capannoni industriali.

All the spaces, with the exception of
the bathrooms, have views to the rest
of the house, emphasizing the perceived
inter-relationship between the spaces.

Todos los espacios, a excepción
de los baños, tienen vistas al resto
de la casa, lo que enfatiza la relación
perceptiva de las estancias.

Da tutti gli spazi, tranne dai bagni,
si ha una vista sul resto della casa,
cosa che sottolinea la relazione
percettiva delle stanze.

Camden Lofts

Cecconi Simone Inc.

Camden Lofts is a new loft-style residential building located in the center of the city of Toronto. It used to be an apartment building, but this building now houses approximately 55 housing units (between 55 m^2 and 112 m^2) and an underground parking lot.

Cecconi Simone Inc. came up with the conception of the loft units that were to be used as housing, as well as the design of the common areas, hallways and the building's pre-existing entrance. The design project for these living suites brings together the best elements that exemplify the loft lifestyle, especially regarding the size of spaces devoted to living and dining rooms, with high ceilings and large windows that open out onto the city.

Camden Lofts es un nuevo edificio residencial *loft style* situado en el centro de la ciudad de Toronto. Antiguamente era un bloque de apartamentos; ahora, este edificio alberga unas 55 unidades de vivienda (entre los 55 m^2 y los 112 m$^{2)}$ y un aparcamiento subterráneo.

Cecconi Simone Inc. llevó a cabo la concepción de las unidades loft destinadas a vivienda, así como el diseño de las zonas comunes, distribuidores y vestíbulo del edificio preexistente. El proyecto que componen estas *suites* vivienda reúne los mejores elementos que encarnan el estilo de vida loft, en cuanto a amplitud de espacios destinados a zonas de estar o comedor, debido a los altos techos y ventanales que se abren a la ciudad.

Camden Lofts è un nuovo edificio residenziale, in stile loft, sito nel centro della città di Toronto. Anticamente era un condominio; adesso l'edificio ospita 55 unità d'abitazione (tra i 55 m^2 e i 112 m^2) e un sotterraneo adibito a garage.

Cecconi Simone Inc. ha ideato le unità loft adibite ad abitazione, così come il design delle zone comuni, dei disimpegni, e dell'atrio dell'edificio preesistente. Il progetto formato da queste abitazioni tipo *suite* riunisce i migliori elementi che incarnano lo stile di vita tipico del loft, in termini di ampiezza di spazi adibiti a zone soggiorno o sala da pranzo, grazie ai soffitti alti e ai finestroni che si aprono sulla città.

Architects: Cecconi Simone Inc.

Location: Toronto, Canada

Photographs: Joy von Tiedemann

The coolness of concrete is counterbalanced by the use of warm materials such as wood, soft fabrics or candles, whose complex juxtaposition attempts to re-create the hustle and bustle that characterizes the neighborhood.

La frialdad del hormigón queda contrarrestada por el uso de materiales cálidos como la madera, telas suaves o cirios, cuya compleja yuxtaposición quiere ser un retrato del bullicio reinante en el vecindario.

La freddezza del cemento viene compensata dall'uso di materiali caldi come il legno, le stoffe leggere, o i ceri, la cui complessa giustapposizione vuole essere un riflesso della chiassosa animazione regnante nel vicinato.

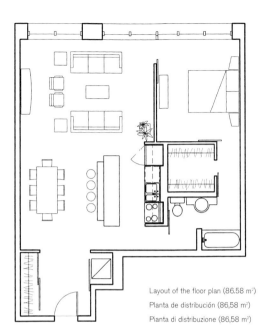

Layout of the floor plan (86.58 m²)
Planta de distribución (86,58 m²)
Pianta di distribuzione (86,58 m²)

House in Igualada
Casa en Igualada / Casa a Igualada

Pep Zazurca i Codolà

Pep Zazurca experiments with structures, materials and finishes that are more often found in industrial buildings than in domestic architecture. This house is organized as a main rectangular space with a structure of metallic pillars and a vaulted ceiling of galvanized steel sheeting supported by struts made of curved latticework which open up to approximately ten meters, encouraging open, airy interiors. The side walls enclosing the house were built with hand-laid bricks and have been left exposed on the inside, while on the outside they have been covered with steel siding.

On the first floor, a large space facing the main façade contains all the house's daytime functions: living room, dining room, kitchen, and library. A hallway located along the longitudinal axis of the large space leads to the bedrooms, which take up the entire depth of the floor.

Pep Zazurca experimenta con estructuras, materiales y acabados más cercanos a los edificios industriales que a la arquitectura doméstica. La vivienda se organiza en una nave de planta rectangular, con una estructura de pilares metálicos y una cubierta abovedada de chapa de acero galvanizado soportada por cerchas de celosía curva, que salvan una luz de aproximadamente diez metros para propiciar interiores amplios y diáfanos. Los muros laterales que cierran la casa se construyeron con ladrillo manual, que se ha dejado visto en el interior, mientras que en el exterior se ha revestido de acero cortén.

En la planta primera, un gran espacio que da a la fachada principal alberga todas las funciones diurnas de la casa: sala de estar, comedor, cocina, biblioteca. Un pasillo situado en el eje longitudinal de la nave conduce a las habitaciones, que ocupan toda la profundidad de la planta.

Pep Zazurca sperimenta con strutture, materiali e finiture più vicini agli edifici industriali che all'architettura domestica. L'abitazione si organizza in un capannone industriale a pianta rettangolare, con una struttura di pilastri metallici e una copertura a volta in lamiera d'acciaio galvanizzato sorretta da una travatura di centine curve; la volta abbraccia una zona luminosa di circa dieci metri che delinea interni spaziosi e diafani. I muri laterali che chiudono la casa sono stati costruiti con mattoni grezzi, che all'interno sono rimasti con faccia a vista, mentre fuori sono stati rivestiti di acciaio corten.

A piano terra, un grande spazio che dà sulla facciata principale è sede di tutte le attività diurne della casa e comprende: il soggiorno, la sala da pranzo, la cucina e la biblioteca. Un corridoio situato nell'asse longitudinale del capannone conduce alle stanze, che occupano tutta la profondità del piano.

Architect: Pep Zazurca i Codolà

Location: Igualada, Spain

Photographs: Eugeni Pons

366

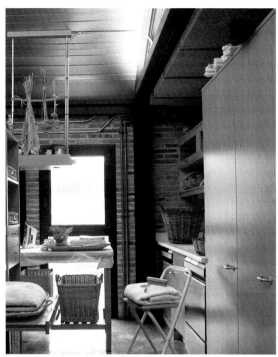

There is parquet flooring throughout the house, except in the kitchen, where the floor is polished concrete. A hanging ceiling made of glued shavings has been installed in order to provide thermal and acoustic insulation.

En toda la casa el pavimento es de parqué, salvo en la cocina, que es de hormigón pulido. En los dormitorios se ha instalado un falso techo de virutas encoladas que aísla térmica y acústicamente.

In tutta la casa il pavimento è di parquet, tranne nella cucina, che è di cemento levigato. Nelle stanze da letto è stato collocato un controsoffitto di trucioli incollati, che isola sia termicamente che acusticamente.

First floor:

1. Library
2. Dining room
3. Living room
4. Kitchen
5. Pantry
6. Dressing room
7. Master bedroom
8. Bathroom
9. Bedroom

Planta primera

1. Biblioteca
2. Comedor
3. Sala de estar
4. Cocina
5. Despensa
6. Vestidor
7. Dormitorio principal
8. Baño
9. Dormitorio

Primo piano

1. Biblioteca
2. Sala da pranzo
3. Soggiorno
4. Cucina
5. Dispensa
6. Stanzino
7. Stanza da letto
   principale
8. Bagno
9. Stanza da letto

The dividers between the bedrooms
are made of DM panels.

Las divisiones entre las habitaciones
están realizadas con paneles de DM.

Le divisioni tra le stanze sono state
realizzate con pannelli di DM.

All utilities have been left exposed.
Todas las instalaciones se han dejado vistas.
Tutti gli impianti sono stati lasciati a vista.

Renovation of a Top Floor
Reforma de un ático / Restauro di un attico

A-cero estudio
de arquitectura y
urbanismo SL

In this top floor there was a true obsession: capturing light in an irregularly-shaped space about 80 m² large. The first view of the apartment unveiled an narrow entry into an overly compartmentalized space with little light. The walls were torn down in order to let the light reach more spaces, and the entire apartment was painted white and divided as little as possible in order to let the light flow through the entire space. Demolishing all the partitions and installing new windows brought light and views back to this top floor apartment.

The existing mezzanine was supported on a pillar that was substituted by a strut anchored in the ceiling, an element that fosters a sense of weightlessness. The plan allows the enclosed spaces to be reduced to a minimum, and the area containing the kitchen, the dining room, the living room, and the bedroom was unified through the use of partitions. In this entire open, airy continuum there was only one issue yet to be resolved: the owner's admitted disorganization along with his enjoyment at having guests. To this end, the built-in closets were designed and placed throughout the entire apartment so that everything could be easily hidden.

En el ático había realmente una obsesión: la captura de luz en un local de forma irregular con una superficie aproximada de 80 m². La primera visita al piso descubrió una entrada angosta a un espacio excesivamente dividido y con poca luz. Se abrieron los muros para conseguir una mayor superficie de iluminación, se pintó todo de blanco y se compartimentó lo mínimo para que la luz fluyera en todo el espacio. La demolición de todas las particiones y la instalación de nuevas carpinterías devolvió la claridad y las vistas al ático.

La entreplanta existente se apoyaba sobre un pilar que fue sustituido por un tirante anclado al techo, elemento que favorace el efecto de ingravidez. El programa permitió reducir al mínimo los espacios cerrados, e intentó mediante sus particiones unificar el área que contiene la cocina, el comedor, el salón y el dormitorio. En todo este continuo diáfano sólo quedaba por resolver una cuestión: el desorden que, según admite el propietario, se apodera de él unido al placer que siente por recibir visitas. A este efecto, los armarios se diseñaron empotrados y dispuestos por todas partes para que todo quedara escondido.

Una vera ossessione ha caratterizzato il restauro di questo loft: la cattura della luce in un locale di forma irregolare con una superficie di circa 80 m². Il primo sopralluogo all'appartamento evidenziò un ingresso stretto a uno spazio eccessivamente diviso e dove entrava poca luce. Si aprirono i muri per ingrandire la superficie di illuminazione, si dipinse tutto di bianco e si usarono pochissime compartimentazioni in modo tale che la luce circolasse in tutto lo spazio. La demolizione di tutte le separazioni e l'installazione di nuovi serramenti restituirono chiarore e vedute all'attico.

Il seminterrato preesistente si appoggiava su un pilastro che è stato sostituto con un tirante fissato al soffitto, elemento che favorisce l'effetto di leggerezza. Il progetto permise di ridurre al minimo gli spazi chiusi, e cercò, mediante le sue divisioni, di unificare l'area che contiene la cucina, la sala da pranzo, il salone e la camera da letto. In tutto questo spazio continuo e diafano rimaneva soltanto una questione da risolvere: il disordine che, secondo quanto ammette lo stesso proprietario, lo assale unito però al piacere che prova quando riceve delle visite. All'uopo, sono stati disegnati degli armadi a muro sparsi un po' ovunque affinché tutto rimanesse nascosto.

Architects: A-cero estudio de arquitectura y urbanismo SL

Location: La Coruña, Spain

Photographs: Juan Rodríguez

Lower level	Planta baja	Piano terra
1. Vestibule	1. Vestíbulo	1. Atrio
2. Half bathroom	2. Aseo	2. Toilette
3. Kitchen/dining room	3. Cocina comedor	3. Cucina sala da pranzo
4. Living room	4. Salón	4. Salone
Upper level	Planta alta	Piano rialzato
1. Bedroom	1. Dormitorio	1. Stanza da letto
2. Dressing room	2. Vestidor	2. Stanzino
3. Bathroom	3. Cuarto de baño	3. Bagno

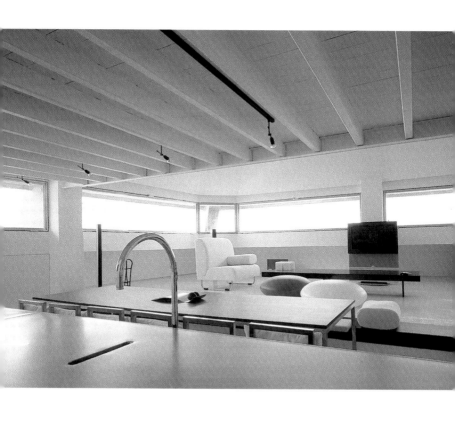

In the highly austere finishes, white paint is used on the walls, floors and ceiling. This is not true in the bathrooms, where glass walls were installed, providing waterproof surfaces with few seams.

En los acabados, de gran austeridad, se emplea pintura blanca en las paredes, suelos y techos. No es así en los baños, donde se han instalado paramentos de vidrio que logran superficies impermeables y con pocas juntas.

Per le finiture, molto austere, è stata utilizzata pittura bianca nelle pareti, nei pavimenti e nei soffitti. Nel bagno, invece, sono stati istallati dei paramenti in vetro con i quali si ottengono superfici impermeabili e con poche giunture.

377

Interior Garden
Jardín interior / Giardino interno

Alain Salomon

This 300 m² loft is located in a small private alley near Stalingrad Square in the north-east of Paris, in the middle of an industrial complex characteristic of the 19th century. For this reason, the designer decided to create an interior landscape that would protect the home from aggressive views of its environments.

The original structure of this old electrical engine factory consisted of a two-floor building, a shed, and a garage. On the back side there is a spiral staircase which brings in a shaft of light that illuminates the gallery, which in turn leads to the dining room. On the lower level, a series of new spaces constructed in the old garage include the library, the guest bedroom, and a bathroom with sauna. On the same floor, the kitchen acts as a hinge to bring together the entrance, the living room, the dining room, and the gallery.

From the lower level, slim, slanted metallic columns hold up the portico, which allows the main bedroom to extend as far as the first floor.

Este loft, de 300 m², está situado en un pequeño callejón privado cercano a la plaza Stalingrad, al nordeste de París, en medio de un complejo industrial típico del siglo XIX. Por este motivo, el diseñador decidió crear un paisaje interior que protegiera la vivienda de las agresivas vistas de su entorno.

La estructura original de este antiguo taller de motores eléctricos consistía en un edificio de dos plantas, un cobertizo y un garaje. En la parte trasera se situó una escalera de caracol, que abre un cañón de luz para iluminar la galería, que desemboca en el comedor. En la planta baja, una serie de nuevas estancias construidas en el antiguo garaje conforman la biblioteca, la habitación de invitados y un baño con sauna. En la misma planta, la cocina, desde su posición de bisagra, articula la entrada, la sala de estar, el comedor y la galería.

Desde la planta baja unas finas columnas metálicas inclinadas sostienen el pórtico, que permite agrandar la habitación principal del primer piso.

Questo loft, di 300 m², si trova in una stradina privata vicino alla piazza Stalingrad, a nordest di Parigi, nel cuore di un tipico complesso industriale del XIX secolo. Per questo motivo, il progettista decise di creare un paesaggio interno che proteggesse l'abitazione dal panorama tutt'altro che disteso dell'ambiente circostante.

La struttura originaria di questa vecchia officina di motori elettrici consisteva in un edificio a due piani, una tettoia e un garage. Nella parte posteriore si collocò una scala a chiocciola, che dà inizio a un tunnel di luce che illumina tutto il ballatoio, che a sua volta sbocca nella sala da pranzo. A piano terra, una serie di nuove stanze costruite nel vecchio garage formano la biblioteca, la stanza degli ospiti, e un bagno con sauna. Sullo stesso piano, a partire dalla cucina, posta a guisa di cerniera, si aprono l'ingresso, il soggiorno, la sala da pranzo e il ballatoio.

Dal piano terra, delle sottili colonne metalliche inclinate sorreggono il portico che permette di allargare la stanza principale del primo piano.

Architect: Alain Salomon
Location: Paris, France
Photographs: Chris Tubbs, Gilles Trillard, Alain Salomon

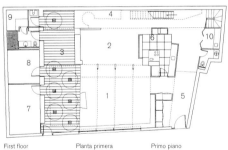

First floor	Planta primera	Primo piano
1. Living room	1. Sala de estar	1. Soggiorno
2. Dining room	2. Comedor	2. Sala da pranzo
3. Interior garden	3. Jardín interior	3. Giardino interno
4. Gallery	4. Galería	4. Ballatoio
5. Entrance	5. Entrada	5. Ingresso
6. Kitchen	6. Cocina	6. Cucina
7. Library	7. Biblioteca	7. Biblioteca
8. Guest bedroom	8. Habitación de invitados	8. Stanza degli ospiti
9. Bathroom and sauna	9. Baño y sauna	9. Bagno e sauna
10. Eat-in kitchen	10. Office	10. Office

Second floor	Planta segunda	Secondo piano
11. Master bedroom and dressing room	11. Habitación principal y vestidor	11. Stanza da letto principale e stanzino
12. Bathroom	12. Baño	12. Bagno
13. Child's bedroom	13. Habitación para niño	13. Stanzetta per bambir
14. Child's bedroom	14. Habitación para niño	14. Stanzetta per bambir
15. Children's bathroom	15. Baño de los niños	15. Bagno dei bambini
16. Stairway to the terrace	16. Escaleras de la terraza	16. Scala della terrazza
17. Gallery	17. Galería	17. Ballatoio

The trees, under which a automatic sprinkler system for fires was installed, grow over alquorques made of metallic grilles which give a certain urban feeling to the garden.

Los árboles, bajo los cuales se ha instalado un sistema de extinción de incendios por rociadura automática, crecen sobre alcorques de rejilla metálica, que dan un cierto aire urbano al jardín.

Gli alberi, sotto i quali è stato installato un sistema antincendio automatico, crescono su un sottofondo di rete metallica, che dona un certo aspetto urbano al giardino.

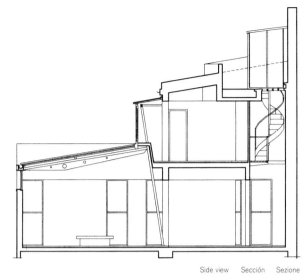

Side view   Sección   Sezione

A metallic spiral staircase connects the living space with the rooftop terrace. A view of the garden can be had from the hallway.

Una escalera metálica de caracol conecta la vivienda con una terraza ubicada en el tejado. Desde el pasadizo se obtienen vistas del jardín interior.

Una scala metallica a chiocciola collega l'abitazione con una terrazza sita nel tetto. Dall'andito è possibile vedere il giardino interno.

The master bedroom receives light from above through a portico made of slanted columns which allow windows in both the ceiling and the façade.

El dormitorio principal recibe luz cenital mediante el pórtico de columnas inclinadas, que permite abrir ventanas tanto en el techo como en la fachada.

La stanza da letto principale riceve la luce zenitale mediante il portico di colonne inclinate, con finestre apribili sia nel soffitto che nella facciata.

Visual Connection
Conexión visual / Connessione visuale

Christophe Pillet

This loft's client is an expert in design who works as a professional contractor and decided to set up his center of operations in his own house.

The two floors allow the different spaces to be organized on two levels: the daytime zone (kitchen, dining room, half bathroom, studio, and living room) is located on the lower level, while on the upper floor the bedroom with its own bathroom is located. The spiral stairway connecting the two floors is made of iron, and the steps, which are soldered to the banister, are petal-shaped.

In order to increase the feeling of spaciousness in a small house, all the spaces are visually connected. Following this proposition, the vertical partitions separating the bathroom and the kitchen have a circular glass window. Likewise, the floor in the mezzanine is transparent, such that a good perceptual relationship between all the spaces is achieved.

Given the client's interest in art work and furniture by renowned designers, Christophe Pillet came up with the idea of a neutral space in which the functional elements and those meant for viewing could stand out. In order to do this, simple, natural finishes such as stone flooring and plaster walls painted in light colors such as gray, white and blue were chosen.

El cliente de este loft es un experto en diseño que trabaja como autónomo y que decidió establecer el centro de operaciones en su propia casa.

Las dos plantas permiten organizar las distintas estancias en dos niveles: la zona de día (cocina, comedor, aseo, estudio y sala de estar) se sitúa en la planta baja, mientras que en el piso superior se dispone el dormitorio con su correspondiente baño. La escalera que comunica ambas plantas es de caracol, está construida en hierro y los peldaños, a los que va soldada la barandilla, tienen forma de pétalos.

Para favorecer la sensación de amplitud en una casa de dimensiones reducidas, todos los espacios quedan conectados visualmente. Siguiendo este propósito, las particiones verticales que cierran el baño y la cocina disponen de una ventana circular de cristal. Igualmente, parte del suelo del altillo es transparente, con lo que se logra una buena relación perceptiva entre todas las estancias.

Dado el interés del cliente por las obras de arte y las piezas de mobiliario de reconocido diseño, Christophe Pillet ideó un espacio neutro donde los elementos funcionales y los de pura contemplación adoptan un protagonismo especial. Para ello, se eligieron acabados sencillos y naturales como piedra en el pavimento o el enyesado y paredes de tonos claros, grises, blancos y azulados.

Il cliente di questo loft è un esperto di design che lavora in proprio e ha deciso di stabilire il proprio centro operativo nella stessa abitazione.

I due piani permettono di organizzare i vari ambienti su due livelli: la zona giorno (cucina, sala da pranzo, toilette, studio e soggiorno) occupa il piano terra, mentre la zona notte quello superiore, dove si trovano la stanza da letto ed il bagno. La scala a chiocciola che comunica i due piani è di ferro; i gradini, ai quali è saldata la ringhiera, sono a forma di petali.

Al fine di favorire la sensazione di spaziosità in una casa dalle dimensioni ridotte, tutti gli spazi sono collegati visualmente. Seguendo questo proposito, le divisioni verticali che delimitano il bagno e la cucina dispongono di un oblò di vetro. Allo stesso modo, parte del pavimento del piano rialzato è trasparente, ottenendo così un'ottima relazione percettiva tra tutte le stanze.

Visto l'interesse del cliente per le opere d'arte e per i mobili dal prestigioso design, Christophe Pillet ideò uno spazio neutro dove gli elementi funzionali e quelli di mera contemplazione assumono un protagonismo speciale. Per questo motivo, sono state scelte finiture semplici e naturali: la pietra per il pavimento e l'ingessatura, pareti dai toni chiari, grigi, bianchi ed azzurrati.

Interior Designer: Christophe Pillet
Location: Paris, France
Photographs: Jean François Jaussaud

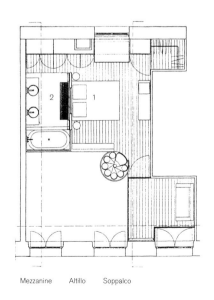

Mezzanine   Altillo   Soppalco

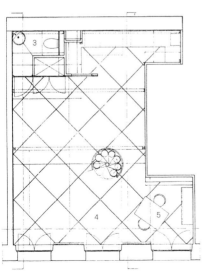

Lower floor   Planta baja   Piano terra

1. Bedroom
2. Bathroom
3. Half bathroom
4. Living room
5. Studio

1. Habitación
2. Baño
3. Aseo
4. Sala de estar
5. Estudio

1. Camera da letto
2. Bagno
3. Toilette
4. Soggiorno
5. Studio

This loft, which is functional while having an ingenious layout, easily combines the domestic and professional activities of its users.

El loft, funcional pero de distribución ingeniosa, combina cómodamente las actividades domésticas y profesionales de los usuarios.

Il loft, funzionale, sebbene dalla distribuzione alquanto ingegnosa, riesce a far coesistere armoniosamente le attività domestiche e professionali dei propri utenti.

Living Space and Studio
Vivienda y estudio / Abitazione e studio

Christophe Pillet

The French designer, Christophe Pillet, works for prestigious international furniture firms as a designer and interior designer for shops, hotels, and homes. His residence in Paris is a 125 m² apartment located near the historic Père Lachaise cemetery, and it also houses his studio, the reform of which he planned himself.

The intervention in this top floor, a minor project, was limited to eliminating the walls as much as possible in order to gain spaciousness in the living area, repairing and cleaning the structure, and painting the entire house white. The result is an austere environment featuring both emptiness and light, which inundates the house through numerous windows and two large skylights located over the central space.

The house is designed around two main spaces: a living area which includes the living room and the dining room, and the studio, which occupies two separate rooms. In the first part, the original lattice of wooden beams was left exposed and was painted the same color as the walls.

The design studio was resolved using the same simplicity that Pillet has used throughout the rest of the house.

El diseñador francés Christophe Pillet trabaja para prestigiosas firmas internacionales de mobiliario como diseñador e interiorista proyectando tiendas, hoteles y viviendas. Su residencia en París es un piso de 125 m² situado junto al histórico cementerio Père Lachaise, y acoge también su estudio, cuya reforma fue planteada por él mismo.

La intervención en este ático, de obra menor, se limitó a eliminar en lo posible todos los tabiques para ganar amplitud en la zona de estar, sanear y limpiar la estructura y pintar toda la casa de blanco. El resultado es un ambiente austero que otorga protagonismo al vacío y a la luz, que inunda la casa atravesando numerosos ventanales y dos grandes lucernarios situados sobre el ambiente central.

La vivienda se articula en torno a dos espacios principales: una zona de estar, que acoge el salón y el comedor, y el estudio, que ocupa dos habitaciones separadas. En la primera se ha dejado a la vista parte del entramado original de vigas de madera, pintado del mismo color que las paredes.

El estudio de diseño se ha resuelto con la misma sencillez que Pillet ha impreso al resto de la vivienda.

Il disegnatore francese Christophe Pillet lavora come designer e architetto d'interni per delle prestigiose ditte internazionali di mobili, progettando negozi, alberghi e abitazioni. A Parigi vive in un appartamento di 125 m² – sito accanto allo storico cimitero Père Lachaise – da lui stesso ristrutturato, e che comprende anche lo studio dove svolge la propria attività.

Nell'attico in questione, l'intervento è stato minimo; Pillet si è limitato ad eliminare, per quanto possibile, tutti i tramezzi al fine di guadagnare spazio nella zona soggiorno, a risanare e pulire la struttura, e dipingere di bianco tutta la casa. Il risultato è un ambiente austero che dà protagonismo al vuoto e alla luce che inonda la casa attraversando numerose finestre e due grandi lucernari situati sulla zona centrale.

L'abitazione si articola attorno a due spazi principali: una zona soggiorno, che comprende il salone e la sala da pranzo, e lo studio, che occupa due stanze separate. Nella prima di queste, parte dell'impalcato originale formato da travi in legno è stato lasciato a vista e dipinto dello stesso colore delle pareti.

Lo studio di design è stato realizzato con la stessa semplicità che Pillet ha impresso al resto dell'abitazione.

Interior Designer: Christophe Pillet

Location: Paris, France

Photographs: Agence Omnia

With the exception of the RAR chairs
by Charles and Ray Eames, the table by
Jacobsen and a lamp by Sotsass, the rest
of the furniture are actually the original
design prototypes.

Salvo las sillas RAR de Charles y Ray Eames,
la mesa de Jacobsen y una lámpara de
Sotsass, el resto del mobiliario lo forman los
prototipos de sus propios diseños.

Tranne le sedie RAR di Charles e Ray Eames,
il tavolo di Jacobsen e una lampada di
Sotsass, il resto dei mobili è formato dai
prototipi dei suoi progetti.

While this report was being made, the furniture came
from xO, Domeau & Péres, Ceccoto, Cappellini and
Toutlemonde Bouchard.

En el momento de hacer este reportaje, los muebles
procedían de xO, Domeau & Péres, Ceccoto, Cappellini
y Toutlemonde Bouchard.

All'epoca di questo reportage, i mobili erano di:
xO, Domeau & Péres, Ceccoto, Cappellini e
Toutlemonde Bouchard.

A Cluster of Lofts
Agrupación de lofts / Gruppo di loft

Alain Salomon

Near the Porte de Pantin in Paris, this 150 m² loft belongs to a film actor and his wife. The spaces form part of a cluster of thirty lofts created for an artists' colony in this 19th century warehouse. The loft is organized on three levels: the street level with a garage, the entry level, and a mezzanine.

The owner's office can be directly accessed from the outside, but the loft's private entrance is reached through the building's patio. An internal staircase connects the office and the garage with the home on the upper level.

The floor plan has a double-high space in the living and dining rooms, an open kitchen, an extra bathroom, and a guest bedroom. The space reserved for the latter is used as a breakfast nook on a daily basis, and it has sliding glass doors which open out onto the corridor, a solution that allows outdoor meals to be held in the summer time.

The curved mezzanine follows the contour of a grand piano. The loft's owner decided to use it as a rehearsal space, and this is where the master bedroom and bathroom are located.

Cercano a la Puerta de Pantin de París, este loft de 150 m² pertenece a un actor de cine y a su mujer. El espacio forma parte de un grupo de treinta lofts creado para una comunidad de artistas en este almacén del siglo XIX. El loft se organiza en función de tres niveles: el de la calle —con un garaje—, el de la entrada y un altillo.

La oficina del propietario tiene acceso directo desde el exterior, pero a la entrada privada del loft se llega por la patio del edificio. Una escalera interior conecta la oficina y el garaje con la vivienda de la planta superior.

Esta planta dispone de un doble espacio en la sala estar y el comedor, una cocina abierta, un baño complementario y una habitación de invitados. La estancia reservada a éstos últimos se usa a diario como sala para el desayuno, y está provista de puertas correderas de cristal que se abren al corredor, solución que permite celebrar comidas al aire libre durante el verano.

El altillo curvo imita el contorno de un piano de cola. El dueño de la casa lo utiliza como lugar de ensayo y es donde se ubican el dormitorio y el baño principal.

Vicino alla Porta di Pantin di Parigi, troviamo questo loft di 150 m², di proprietà di un attore cinematografico e di sua moglie. Lo spazio fa parte di un gruppo di trenta loft creato per una comunità di artisti in un magazzino del XIX secolo. Il loft si organizza in base a tre livelli: quello della strada – con un garage –, quello dell'ingresso e un soppalco.

All'ufficio del proprietario si accede direttamente dall'esterno, mentre all'entrata privata del loft si arriva dal cortile dell'edificio. Una scala interna collega l'ufficio e il garage all'abitazione del piano superiore.

Quest'ultimo dispone di un doppio spazio nel soggiorno e nella sala da pranzo, di una cucina aperta, un doppio servizio e una stanza per gli ospiti. Quest'ultima si utilizza ogni giorno come sala dove fare colazione, ed è dotata di porte scorrevoli in vetro che si aprono sulla veranda, soluzione questa che permette di consumare dei pasti all'aperto durante i mesi estivi.

Il soppalco ondulato imita il profilo di un pianoforte a coda. Il proprietario della casa utilizza questo spazio, che comprende anche la camera da letto e il bagno principale, per provare.

Architect: Alain Salomon

Location: Paris, France

Photographs: Chris Tubbs, Alain Salomon

1. Garage	1. Garaje	1. Garage
2. Office	2. Oficina	2. Ufficio
3. Entrance	3. Entrada	3. Ingresso
4. Guest bedroom	4. Habitación de Invitados	4. Stanza degli ospiti
5. Kitchen	5. Cocina	5. Cucina
6. Living and dining room	6. Comedor y sala de estar	6. Sala da pranzo e soggiorno
7. Master bedroom	7. Dormitorio principal	7. Stanza da letto principale
8. Master bathroom	8. Baño principal	8. Bagno principale
9. Mezzanine	9. Altillo	9. Soppalco

Lower level   Planta baja   Piano terra

First floor   Planta primera   Primo piano

Mezzanine   Altillo   Soppalco

The guest bathroom is illuminated by the translucent concrete and glass-brick wall through which the shape of the stairway leading to the mezzanine can be seen.

El baño de invitados se ilumina por la pared de hormigón translúcido o pavés que transparenta el perfil de la escalera de acceso al altillo.

Il bagno degli ospiti viene illuminato grazie alla parete in vetro traslucido che lascia trasparire la sagoma della scala che dà accesso al soppalco.

Spaciousness
Espacialidad / Spazialità

Patrizia Sbalchiero

Located in the Old Navigli neighborhood in Milan, the almost 200 m² loft was formerly a woodworking shop made up of two large spaces, one of them with a roof made of wood and the other of decorated sheeting.

The first part of the reform, carried out by the BAUQ studio, was devoted to restoring the entire roof, conserving the old framework and inserting a large window to illuminate the central area. The reform also included dividing the space into three different units which later have been reformed by each owner's architects.

The main requirement was to provide a large amount of light to the studio area, which is equipped with desks and computers and was independent from the functioning of the rest of the house despite the fact that it formed part of it.

Characterized by the roof, the project fosters the feeling of spaciousness in this studio-home. The use of floor-to-ceiling doors highlights the size of the new space.

The stairway leading to the studio is a linear structure whose presence becomes a central element in the house.

The decoration, conceived by the owner, mixes designer objects with other pieces collected from flea markets and antiques shops.

Ubicado en el viejo barrio del Navigli de Milán, este loft de casi 200 m² fue en otro tiempo una ebanistería que contaba con dos grandes naves, una de ellas con tejado de madera y la otra cubierta con chapa grecada.

La primera parte de la reforma, ejecutada por el estudio BAUQ, se dedicó a la restauración de toda la cubierta, conservando el viejo armazón e insertando una gran vidriera para iluminar la zona central. La reforma también planteó la división en tres unidades distintas que posteriormente han sido reformadas por arquitectos asignados por cada propietario.

La exigencia principal era proporcionar gran cantidad de luz a la zona de estudio, equipada con mesas y ordenadores e independiente del funcionamiento de la casa aunque integrada en ella.

Caracterizado por la cubierta, el proyecto potencia la sensación de espacialidad en esta casa estudio. El empleo de puertas de suelo a techo marca la dimensión del nuevo espacio.

La escalera que sube al estudio es una estructura lineal, cuya presencia se convierte en el elemento central de la casa. Construida con perfiles metálicos y madera canadiense, presenta dos grandes descansillos entre los que se ubica una chimenea, también metálica, abierta hacia el salón y la cocina.

Situato nel vecchio quartiere dei Navigli di Milano, questo loft di quasi 200 m², fu anticamente un'ebanisteria che disponeva di due grandi capannoni, uno con un tetto di legno e l'altro rivestito di lamiera grecata.

La prima fase del restauro, eseguita dallo studio BAUQ, si concentrò sulla ristrutturazione di tutta la zona di copertura, conservando la vecchia struttura di sostegno e inserendo una grande vetrata per illuminare la zona centrale. Il progetto prevedeva inoltre la divisione dell'ambiente in tre diverse unità abitative, ristrutturate successivamente da architetti assunti dai relativi proprietari.

L'esigenza principale era di dare quanta più luce possibile alla zona studio, dotata di scrivanie e computer, e integrata nella casa, sebbene fosse indipendente dal funzionamento di quest'ultima.

Caratterizzato dalla copertura, il progetto potenzia la sensazione di spazialità all'interno di questa casa studio. L'utilizzo di porte che vanno dal pavimento al soffitto segna la dimensione del nuovo spazio.

La scala che sale allo studio ha una struttura lineare; la sua presenza si trasforma nell'elemento centrale della casa. Costruita con profili metallici e legno canadese, comprende due grandi pianerottoli tra i quali si trova un camino, anch'esso in metallo, rivolto verso il salone e la cucina.

Architect: Patrizia Sbalchiero

Location: Milan, Italy

Photographs: Andrea Martiradonna

Lengthwise view   Sección longitudinal   Sezione longitudinale

An old piece of furniture for lead typography characters dominates the studio, which is lit by two old urban-style ceiling lamps.

Un viejo mueble de tipografía para caracteres de plomo preside el estudio, iluminado por dos viejas lámparas de estilo urbano colgadas del techo.

Un vecchio mobile di tipografia per i caratteri in piombo presiede lo studio, illuminato da due vecchie lampade, di stile urbano, appese al soffitto.

First floor   Planta primera   Primo piano

Lower floor   Planta baja   Piano terra

House for a Painter
Casa para una pintora / Casa per una pittrice

Antonio Zanuso

Artist Anna Muzi Falcone's home occupies the third floor of an old industrial building from the turn of the century located in a picturesque Milan neighborhood. The 250 m² loft is divided into two bodies that form an L-shape. One of the volumes opens onto the building's interior patio, while the other enjoys views of the city. The complex is filled with light thanks to the large pre-existing windows. The tall five-meter ceilings allowed for the creation of an intermediate floor covering part of the apartment that houses the more private spaces: the master bedroom with its won bathroom and dressing room.

The entrance opens onto a large, industrial-style kitchen where a large hallway leading to the living room and the two work studies begins. In the opposite zone there are two bedrooms and a bathroom. The work spaces have no doors and are interconnected; the floor is uniformly covered in gray resin in order to emphasize the relationship between the different spaces.

La vivienda de la artista Anna Muzi Falcone ocupa la tercera planta de un antiguo edificio industrial de principios de siglo ubicado en un pintoresco barrio de Milán. El loft tiene una superficie de 250 m² repartidos en dos cuerpos dispuestos en forma de L. Uno de los volúmenes se abre hacia el patio interior del edificio, mientras que el otro disfruta de vistas a la ciudad. El conjunto es muy luminoso gracias a los grandes ventanales preexistentes. La considerable altura entre plantas, cinco metros, permitió crear una planta intermedia que cubre parte del piso y alberga las estancias más privadas: la habitación principal con baño y vestidor.

La entrada se abre a una enorme cocina tipo industrial donde nace un largo pasillo que conduce a la sala de estar y a los dos estudios. En la zona opuesta se ubican dos habitaciones y un baño. Las estancias de trabajo no tienen puertas y se comunican entre ellas; para enfatizar la relación entre los distintos espacios se unificó el suelo, de resina gris.

L'abitazione dell'artista Anna Muzi Falcone occupa il terzo piano di un vecchio edificio industriale di inizio secolo, sito in un pittoresco quartiere di Milano. Il loft ha una superficie di 250 m² distribuiti su due volumi disposti a forma di L. Il primo di questi si apre verso il cortile interno dell'edificio, mentre dall'altro si gode un'ottima vista della città. Il complesso riceve molta luce grazie alle grandi finestre già esistenti. La notevole altezza tra i piani, cinque metri, ha permesso di crearne uno intermedio che copre parte dell'appartamento e ospita le stanze più private: la camera da letto principale con il bagno e lo stanzino.

Dall'entrata si accede a un'enorme cucina di tipo industriale dove nasce un lungo corridoio che conduce al soggiorno e ai due studi. Nella zona opposta si trovano due stanze e un bagno. Gli spazi riservati al lavoro non hanno porte e sono comunicanti; per sottolineare il rapporto tra i diversi spazi, il pavimento, in resina grigia, è stato unificato.

Architect: Antonio Zanuso

Location: Milan, Italy

Photographs: Henry Bourne/Speranza

The decoration, which envisioned by the owner, mixes designer objectives with other pieces gathered from flea markets and antiques shops.

La decoración, ideada por la propietaria, mezcla objetos de firma con otras piezas recogidas en mercadillos y anticuarios.

L'arredamento ideato dalla proprietaria, mescola oggetti firmati con altri pezzi provenienti da mercatini e negozi di antiquariato.

House in San Giorgio
Casa en San Giorgio / Casa a San Giorgio

Studio Archea

The original building is Renaissance-style and was characterized by large wooden beams that imposed a certain majesty on the spaces. The challenge was to design a residential space that took advantage of the exceptional characteristics of this Quattrocento design while making a comfortable, contemporary environment.

Given the small size of the design, the architects were able to design all the elements in detail, avoiding prefabricated elements and creating unique, almost sculptural elements.

La edificación original es renacentista y estaba marcada por grandes vigas de madera que imponían cierta majestuosidad a los espacios. El reto era diseñar un ámbito residencial que aprovechase las características excepcionales del Quattrocento y que a la vez conformara un ambiente funcional y contemporáneo.

Dadas la reducidas dimensiones del proyecto, los arquitectos tuvieron la posibilidad de diseñar detalladamente todos los elementos, huyendo de la prefabricación y creando objetos únicos, casi escultóricos.

L'edificio originale, in stile rinascimentale, era caratterizzato da grandi travi in legno che imponevano una certa maestosità agli spazi. La sfida dell'intervento consisteva nel progettare uno spazio residenziale che sfruttasse le eccezionali caratteristiche del Quattrocento e che al contempo desse vita a un ambiente funzionale e contemporaneo.

Viste le dimensioni ridotte del progetto, gli architetti hanno avuto la possibilità di progettare minuziosamente tutti gli elementi, evitando la prefabbricazione e creando oggetti unici, quasi scultorei.

Architects: Studio Archea

Location: Florence, Italy

Photographs: Alessandro Ciampi

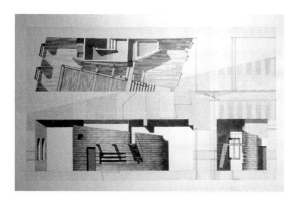

The space is divided around a curved stone wall that organizes the house's different functions and constitutes the foundation for the metallic beams that hold up the mezzanine, which is used as a nighttime zone. A small pool with views can be reached from this horizontal platform via a bridge.

El espacio está distribuido en torno a un muro de piedra curvilíneo que organiza las diversas funciones de la vivienda y constituye el soporte de las vigas metálicas que aguantan el altillo, destinado a la zona de noche. Desde esta plataforma horizontal, y mediante un puente, se llega a una pequeña piscina panorámica.

Lo spazio si distribuisce attorno a un muro di pietra curvilineo che divide le varie funzioni dell'abitazione e forma il supporto delle travi in metallo che reggono il soppalco, adibito a zona notte. Da questa piattaforma orizzontale, e mediante un ponte, si arriva a una piccola piscina panoramica.

The iron stairway that leads to the mezzanine was designed by Studio Archea and was installed by Módulo Laser, the firm that is also responsible for the kitchen, the stone wall and the wooden floors.

El diseño de la escalera de hierro que permite el acceso al altillo es de Studio Archea y ha sido ejecutado por Módulo Laser, firma que también es responsable de la realización de la cocina, el muro pétreo y el pavimento de madera.

Il design della scala in ferro che consente l'accesso al soppalco è di Studio Archea ed è opera di Módulo Laser, ditta che è anche responsabile della realizzazione della cucina, del muro in pietra e del pavimento in legno.

Transparencies
Transparencias / Trasparenze

In one of the city's main reinforced concrete apartment buildings, the architect Rüdiger Lainer has designed a two-story space that takes the place of the old slanted roof. It is a transparent body conceived as a house on top of another house that contains living units.

The agenda required five units which were to be used either as living or office spaces. In the central area, laminated glass is used to form a roof that disrupts the plane and divides the intervention into two interrelated yet distinct zones. The ironwork frames made of metallic sheeting supported by a steel structure create an open, flexible space that makes different layouts possible.

The building's façade, built in 1911, imitates the predominant style of the age, despite the fact that it is a reinforced concrete structure. For the newly-added body, the architect employs a modern language.

En uno de los primeros bloques de viviendas de la ciudad construidos con hormigón armado, el arquitecto Rüdiger Lainer ha proyectado un espacio de dos plantas que sustituye la antigua cubierta a dos aguas. Se trata de un cuerpo transparente concebido como una casa sobre otra casa y que contiene unidades habitables.

El programa exigía cinco unidades para utilizar bien como espacios de vivienda o de oficina, bien como combinación de ambos. En el área central se emplea vidrio laminado para formar una cubierta que rompe el plano y divide la intervención en dos zonas correlacionadas pero distintas. Los forjados de encofrado perdido de chapa metálica soportados por una estructura de acero crean un espacio abierto y flexible que hace posible plantear diferentes distribuciones.

La fachada del edificio, construido en 1911, imita el estilo predominante de la época, a pesar de tratarse de una construcción de hormigón armado. Para el cuerpo añadido, el arquitecto emplea un lenguaje moderno.

In uno dei primi condomini della città, costruiti in cemento armato, l'architetto Rüdiger Lainer ha progettato uno spazio a due piani che sostituisce l'antico tetto a due falde. Si tratta di un corpo trasparente, concepito come una casa posta sopra un'altra, contenente unità abitabili.

Il progetto prevedeva cinque unità da adibire ad abitazioni o uffici, oppure ad una combinazione di entrambi gli ambienti. Nell'area centrale è stato utilizzato del vetro laminato per formare una copertura che rompe il piano e divide l'intervento in due zone correlate ma diverse. Le casseforme a perdere in lamiera metallica, rette da una struttura di acciaio creano uno spazio aperto e flessibile che si presta a diverse distribuzioni.

La facciata dell'edificio, costruito nel 1911, imita lo stile predominante dell'epoca, nonostante si tratti di una costruzione in cemento armato. Per il corpo aggiunto, l'architetto ha usato un linguaggio moderno.

Architect: Rüdiger Lainer

Location: Vienna, Austria

Photographs: Margherita Spiluttini

The building is located two minutes from the historic district and has views over Saint Steven's cathedral. One of the exception aspects of this project is that it was granted a construction permit despite the strict urban planning regulations that govern renovations on any part of the urban fabric in historic Vienna.

El inmueble está ubicado a dos minutos del centro histórico vienés y tiene vistas sobre la catedral de San Esteban. Uno de los aspectos excepcionales de este proyecto es que obtuvo el permiso de obra a pesar de las estrictas normas urbanísticas que rigen las reformas realizadas en cualquier parte del tejido urbano histórico de Viena.

L'immobile si trova a due minuti dal centro storico di Vienna, con vedute panoramiche sulla cattedrale di Santo Stefano. Uno degli aspetti più straordinari di questo progetto è l'aver ottenuto il permesso per i lavori nonostante le rigide norme urbanistiche che regolano i restauri realizzati in qualsiasi parte del tessuto urbano storico della città.

Ecological Apartment
Apartamento ecológico / Appartamento ecologico

Lichtblau & Wagner

This loft has a definition for this space directly under the roof that we call an attic that, due to its particular architecture, has always sparked our interest.

The re-conversion of this attic located in Vienna re-creates this typical attic architecture under whose roof, which is also an exterior wall, there does not have to be anything.

In this work we can see the application of various techniques of sustainability and energy efficiency that until now have been applied in other specific architectural domains. The design by the Lichtblau & Wagner team of architects is based on concepts of energy efficiency in a flexible, creative architecture of versatility.

The floor plan's layout is organized into four basic 50 m² units which are paired off, which share a central zone that both homes can use. Given that lack of greater space in each apartment, the design proposes an area of common spaces that houses a storage area, a laundry room and a multi-purpose space for other activities (meetings, parties and other events).

El loft tiene atribuida una definición que se acerca a ese espacio bajo cubierta que denominamos desván y que, por su particular arquitectura, siempre ha despertado nuestro interés.

La reconversión de este ático situado en Viena recrea este tipo de arquitectura desván bajo cuya cubierta, que hace las veces de pared exterior, no tiene por qué haber nada.

En esta obra podemos ver la aplicación de diversas técnicas de sostenibilidad y ahorro energético que hasta la fecha han sido más empleadas en otros dominios específicos de la arquitectura. El proyecto del equipo de arquitectos Lichtblau & Wagner se basa en conceptos de rentabilidad energética, en una arquitectura flexible y artífice de versatilidad.

La distribución en planta se organiza en cuatro unidades básicas de 50 m², agrupadas en parejas, que comparten una zona central de la cual pueden apropiarse ambas viviendas. Ante la falta de mayor espacio contenido en cada apartamento, el proyecto propone una zona de ambientes comunes que alberga un almacén, una lavandería y una estancia polivalente para otras actividades (reuniones, fiestas u otros quehaceres).

La definizione del loft si avvicina a quella dello spazio posto al disotto del tetto che denominiamo soffitta e che, per la sua particolare architettura, ha sempre destato il nostro interesse.

La riconversione di questo attico, sito a Vienna, ricrea l'architettura tipica delle soffitte, sotto il cui tetto, che fa le veci di parete esterna, non deve necessariamente esserci qualcosa.

In questo intervento possiamo vedere l'applicazione di diverse tecniche di sostenibilità e di risparmio energetico che fino ad oggi sono state usate più comunemente in altri ambiti specifici dell'architettura. Il progetto dell'equipe di architetti Lichtblau & Wagner si basa su concetti di ottimizzazione energetica, su una architettura flessibile e creatrice di versatilità.

La distribuzione planimetrica è strutturata in quattro unità fondamentali di 50 m², raggruppate in due coppie, che condividono una zona centrale che può far parte indistintamente dell'una o dell'altra abitazione. Dinanzi alla mancanza di ulteriore spazio in ogni appartamento, il progetto propone una zona di ambienti comuni che include una dispensa, una lavanderia, e un ambiente polivalente per altre attività (riunioni, feste e altro).

Architects: Lichtblau & Wagner

Location: Vienna, Austria

Photographs: Andreas Wagner, Margherita Spiluttini

Energy-saving elements, such as solar panels that supply warm water to eight apartments in the building and central heating, simultaneously lead to a savings in livable space.

Elementos de ahorro energético, tales como paneles solares que abastecen de agua caliente ocho apartamentos del edificio y la centralización de la calefacción, suponen, a un mismo tiempo, un ahorro a favor del espacio habitable.

Gli elementi di risparmio energetico, quali i pannelli solari che riforniscono di acqua calda otto appartamenti dell'edificio, e l'impianto di riscaldamento centralizzato, presuppongono, allo stesso tempo, un risparmio a favore dello spazio abitabile.

Some utilities have been installed in the flooring in order to leave the inside walls free. The kitchen and bathroom modules can be disassembled and are connected to drains through holes in the floor. In this way, their placement can be changed without leaving marks on the connections.

Algunas instalaciones se han integrado en el suelo para evitar hacer regatas en los paramentos interiores. Los módulos de la cocina y el baño son desmontables y se conectan a los desagües mediante agujeros en el pavimento. De este modo, su ubicación puede ser variable y no dejar rastro en las conexiones.

Alcuni impianti sono stati integrati nel pavimento per evitare incassature nei paramenti interni. I moduli della cucina e del bagno sono smontabili e sono collegati ai tubi di scarico mediante dei fori nel pavimento. In questo modo, la loro ubicazione può variare, non lasciando nessuna traccia negli allacciamenti.

Loft in Bruges
Loft en Brujas / Loft a Bruges

Non Kitch Group

The most decisive operation in the re-conversion of this old tin can factory in the Belgian city of Bruges was certainly the remodeling of the roof, made of a sawtooth-shaped lattice structure which held up the traditional floor.

William Sweetlove and Linda Arschoot, the designers of Non Kitch Group, decided to replace the northern face of each of the parallel strips of the roof with a glassed-in surface. The result is not only an extraordinary increase in the natural daylight entering the home, but also, due to the considerable height of the space (six meters), the interior's virtually becoming an indoor square. On the lower level, the living room opens onto a small garden with a covered pool on one side, such that there are views toward the outside in all corners of the home.

The loft is organized onto three floors. A large triple-high living room occupies the center of the space. Around it a mezzanine has been installed in which the kitchen, the dining room, the bar, and the TV room have been placed. Under the mezzanine and three steps down from the living room are the billiards room, the bedroom, the dressing room, the gymnasium, and the bathroom, which leads directly to the pool.

Seguramente la operación más decisiva en la reconversión de esta antigua fábrica de latas de conserva de la ciudad belga de Brujas fue la remodelación de la cubierta, formada por una estructura de celosías con perfil en diente de sierra que soportaba un tejado tradicional.

William Sweetlove y Linda Arschoot, los diseñadores de Non Kitch Group, decidieron sustituir la vertiente norte de cada una de las franjas paralelas del tejado por una superficie vidriada. El resultado no sólo supone un incremento extraordinario de la iluminación natural de la vivienda, sino que, debido a la considerable altura del espacio (seis metros), el interior se convierte prácticamente en una plaza exterior. En la planta baja, la sala de estar se abre a su vez a un pequeño jardín con una piscina cubierta en uno de sus lados, por lo que las vistas escapan hacia el exterior por todos los rincones de la vivienda.

El loft está organizado en tres niveles. Una gran sala a triple espacio ocupa el centro de la estancia. A su alrededor se ha instalado un altillo en el que se sitúan la cocina, el comedor, el bar y la sala de televisión. Bajo el altillo y a un nivel tres escalones inferior al de la sala de estar, se hallan la sala de billar, el dormitorio, el vestidor, el gimnasio y el baño, que conecta directamente con la piscina cubierta.

Sicuramente l'operazione più decisiva nella riconversione di questa vecchia fabbrica di scatolette per conserve della città di Bruges, in Belgio, è stata la ristrutturazione del tetto, formato da una struttura aperta di tubi metallici con profilo a denti di sega, che reggeva un soffitto tradizionale.

William Sweetlove e Linda Arschoot, i designer di Non Kitch Group, decisero di sostituire lo spiovente nord di ognuna delle strisce parallele del tetto con una superficie vetrata. Di conseguenza, si ottiene un incremento straordinario dell'illuminazione naturale dell'abitazione, e inoltre, per via della considerevole altezza dello spazio (sei metri) l'interno è come se fosse una piazza all'aperto. A piano terra, il soggiorno dà a sua volta su un piccolo giardino con piscina coperta in uno dei suoi lati, pertanto da tutti gli angoli dell'abitazione si dispone di ottime viste sull'esterno.

Il loft è disposto su tre livelli. Una grande sala a spazio triple occupa il centro dell'ambiente. Attorno a questa si trova un soppalco che include la cucina, la sala da pranzo, il bar e la sala TV. Sotto il soppalco e tre gradini più in basso rispetto al livello del soggiorno, troviamo la sala da biliardo, la camera da letto, lo stanzino, la palestra e il bagno, direttamente collegato alla piscina al coperto.

Architects: Non Kitch Group

Location: Bruges, Belgium

Photographs: Jan Verlinde

Given the asceticism of the minimalist interiors, Non Kitch Group feel to be the heirs of the humor and colorful aesthetic of the Memphis group.

Frente al ascetismo de los interiores minimalistas, en Non Kitch Group se sienten herederos del humor y la estética colorista del grupo de Memphis.

Di fronte all'ascetismo degli interni minimalisti, al Non Kitch Group si sentono eredi dell'umore e dell'estetica coloristica del gruppo di Memphis.

Old Spinning Mill
Antigua nave de hilatura / Un vecchio capannone per la filatura

Ernst & Niklaus
Architekten ETH/SIA

In the city of Suhr, in the north of Switzerland, the architects Bertram Ernst and Erich Niklaus have renovated an old spinning mill.

When the architects were given the task of updating the building, the owners had already divided the factory into eight parts. The intervention has consisted of a minimal intervention in what was already constructed in order to allow the newly-built elements to let the intrinsic qualities that had always defined the old building to shine through.

The second floor home is laid out in a Z-shape, following the location of the new staircase and the existing freight elevator. A crosswise varnished oak flooring covers the entire surface of the space.

The fourth and fifth floor homes integrate the structure supporting the roof into their space, bringing luminosity as the daylight comes through.

En la ciudad de Suhr, al norte de Suiza, los arquitectos Bertram Ernst y Erich Niklaus han rehabilitado una vieja nave de hilatura.

Cuando los arquitectos recibieron la tarea de adecuación del edificio, los propietarios ya habían dividido la nave en ocho partes. La intervención ha consistido en una mínima actuación sobre lo construido con el propósito de potenciar con la obra nueva las cualidades intrínsecas que siempre han definido el viejo edificio.

La vivienda de la segunda planta esta distribuida en forma de Z, según la ubicación de la nueva escalera y el espacio del montacargas existente. Un pavimento transversal de roble barnizado ocupa toda la extensión de la pieza.

La vivienda de la cuarta y quinta planta integra la estructura de soporte de la cubierta en el espacio, aportando luminosidad mediante pasos de luz cenital practicados en la misma.

Nella città di Suhr, nel nord della Svizzera, gli architetti Bertram Ernst ed Erich Niklaus hanno ristrutturato un vecchio capannone per la filatura.

Quando gli è stato affidato l'incarico di ristrutturare l'edificio, i proprietari avevano già diviso il capannone in otto parti. Si è trattato di un intervento minimo sulla costruzione preesistente, volto a potenziare con degli elementi nuovi, le qualità intrinseche che avevano da sempre contraddistinto l'edificio.

L'abitazione del secondo piano è dictribuita a forma di 7, secondo l'ubicazione della nuova scala e dello spazio del montacarichi già esistente. Un pavimento trasversale in rovere verniciato occupa tutta l'estensione del locale.

L'abitazione del quarto e del quinto piano integra nello spazio la struttura di sostegno del tetto, apportando luminosità mediante delle entrate di luce zenitale eseguite nello stesso tetto.

Architects: Ernst & Niklaus Architekten ETH/SIA

Location: Suhr, Switzerland

Photographs: Hannes Henz

444

Crosswise view   Sección transversal Sezione trasversale

Lengthwise view. Fourth and fifth floor lofts
Sección longitudinal. Loft plantas cuarta y quinta
Sezione longitudinale. Loft del quarto e del quinto piano

Sopanen / Sarlin Loft
Sopanen/Sarli Loft / Loft di Sopanen/Sarlin

Marja Sopanen +
Olli Sarlin

The young architects Marja Sopanen and Olli Sarlin have designed a loft apartment on the ground floor of an old brick textile factory that was built in 1928, whose upper floor had already been converted into a home.

The Sopanen/Sarlin loft is located on the ground floor of the building, in a large 85 m² L-shaped space. The architects of this renovation decided to completely reclaim the original interior appearance of the building, which had been masked by much additional building during its almost 70 years as a textile factory. In order to do this, they had to eliminate infinite hanging ceilings and dividing walls that made up the offices that had been located there.

While clearing out these constructional elements that did not come with the original building, they discovered a structure made of concrete beams. In any case, some stretches of the wall leave the building's original red bricks exposed.

Los jóvenes arquitectos Marja Sopanen y Olli Sarlin han diseñado un apartamento loft en la planta baja de una antigua fábrica textil de ladrillo rojo construida en 1928, cuyas plantas superiores ya fueron convertidas en vivienda con anterioridad.

El Sopanen/Sarli Loft se encuentra ubicado en la planta baja del edificio, en un amplio espacio en forma de L de 85 m². Los arquitectos de esta reforma decidieron recuperar por completo el aspecto interior del edificio, enmascarado por tanta obra añadida durante los casi 70 años de existencia de la antigua fábrica textil. Para ello tuvieron que librarlo de infinidad de falsos techos y paredes divisorias que conformaban las oficinas allí instaladas.

Durante la limpieza de elementos constructivos que no pertenecían en su origen al edificio, se descubrió una estructura de vigas de hormigón. De todas formas, algunos tramos de pared dejan al descubierto el ladrillo rojo original de los paramentos del edificio.

I giovani architetti Marja Sopanen e Olli Sarlin hanno progettato un loft ad uso abitazione al piano terra di una vecchia fabbrica tessile di mattoni rossi costruita nel 1928, i cui piani superiori erano già stati convertiti in precedenza in abitazioni.

Il loft di Sopanen/Sarlin si trova al piano terra dell'edificio, in un ampio spazio a forma di L di 85 m². Gli architetti di questa ristrutturazione decisero di riportare l'edificio al suo aspetto interno originario, mascherato da tanti lavori aggiunti nel corso di quasi 70 anni di esistenza della vecchia fabbrica tessile. Per questo hanno dovuto eliminare un'infinità di controsoffitti e pareti divisorie che formavano i vari uffici.

Durante la pulizia degli elementi costruttivi, che non appartenevano originariamente all'edificio, è stata scoperta una struttura di travi di cemento. In ogni modo, alcune parti delle pareti sono caratterizzate dai mattoni rossi a vista originali dell'edificio.

Architects: Marja Sopanen + Olli Sarlin

Location: Helsinki, Finland

Photographs: Marja Sopanen, Olli Sarlin

The use of recycled materials, even in basic pieces, for the functioning of utilities such as heating pipes, is one of the values that add authenticity to the conception and realization of this project.

La utilización de materiales reciclados, incluso en piezas básicas, para el funcionamiento de instalaciones tales como las tuberías de la calefacción, es uno de valores que añaden autenticidad a la concepción y realización de este proyecto.

L'utilizzo di materiali riciclati, anche in pezzi di base, per impianti come le tubature del riscaldamento, è uno dei valori che aggiungono autenticità alla concezione e alla realizzazione di questo progetto.

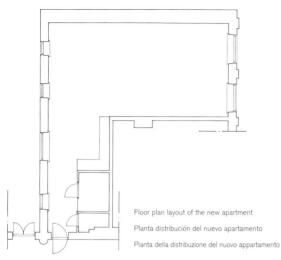

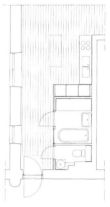

Floor plan layout of the new apartment

Planta distribución del nuevo apartamento

Pianta della distribuzione del nuovo appartamento

Detailed layout of the access

Planta detalle acceso

Pianta dettaglio dell'entrata

The loft's L-shaped layout allows the half bathroom, bathroom, and kitchen to remain separate in the first access wing of the apartment.

La distribución del loft en forma de L permite independizar, en la primera ala de acceso al apartamento, los servicios de aseo, baño y cocina.

La distribuzione del loft a forma di L consente di separare nella prima ala di accesso all'appartamento la toilette, il bagno e la cucina.

"For any type of work that requires space, a loft is the ideal place. When setting up a business, the initial costs are enormous. A loft offers a starting point."

James Soane and Christopher Ash, of Project Orange

«Para cualquier tipo de trabajo que requiera espacio, el loft es el lugar ideal. Cuando se quiere establecer un negocio, los costos iniciales son enormes. El loft ofrece el espacio para empezar.»

James Soane y Christopher Ash, de Project Orange

«Il loft è il luogo ideale per qualsiasi tipo di lavoro che richieda spazio. Quando si inizia un'attività, i costi iniziali sono enormi. Il loft offre lo spazio per iniziare.»

James Soane e Christopher di Project Orange

working
in a loft

trabajar
en un loft

lavorare
in un loft

@radical.media

Rockwell Group

The president of @radical.media, Jon Kamen, chose an industrial building located on the banks of Manhattan for the new offices. This is the most open and spacious loft possible, which encourages communication among the members of a dynamic, flexible, and egalitarian team. Such was the vision that David Rockwell had to convert into reality.

The Rockwell team incorporated the idea of keeping this space in line with its original industrial past through a new layout and finishing materials that would be more similar to those of an old warehouse from the middle of the last century.

Continuity and spaciousness were sought for the entire building, and the structure of large spaces and open rooms was preserved. The different working zones were organized through the placement of waist-high plywood panels around the perimeter of the façade.

El presidente de @radical. media, Jon Kamen, eligió para las nuevas oficinas un edificio industrial situado en la orilla de Manhattan. Un loft lo más abierto y espacioso posible capaz de fomentar la comunicación entre los miembros de un equipo dinámico, flexible e igualitario. Tal fue la tarea que David Rockwell tenía que convertir en realidad.

El equipo Rockwell incorporó la idea de mantener este espacio conforme a su pasado original de carácter industrial mediante una nueva distribución y un material en los acabados que resultara más cercano a los de un viejo almacén de mediados del siglo pasado.

Se persiguió la continuidad y espacialidad de todo el edificio, y se preservó la estructura de espacios amplios y habitaciones abiertas. Las diferentes zonas de trabajo se organizaron mediante paneles de madera contrachapada a media altura, en torno al perímetro de la fachada.

Il presidente di @radical.media, Jon Kamen, ha scelto per i suoi nuovi uffici un edificio industriale situato nei dintorni di Manhattan. Un loft il più aperto e il più spazioso possibile capace di promuovere la comunicazione tra i membri di un team dinamico, flessibile ed egualitario. Questa era la sfida che David Rockwell doveva trasformare in realtà.

Il team di Rockwell ha incorporato l'idea di mantenere questo spazio conforme al suo passato di carattere industriale mediante una nuova distribuzione e un materiale delle rifiniture che fossero simili a quelle di un vecchio magazzino di metà del secolo scorso.

Si voleva creare una continuità e una spaziosità in tutto l'edificio ed è stata conservata la struttura di spazi ampi e stanze aperte. Le diverse zone di lavoro sono state organizzate tramite pannelli di compensato di legno a mezz'altezza intorno al perimetro della facciata.

Architects: Rockwell Group

Location: Manhattan, New York, United States

Photographs: Paul Warchol

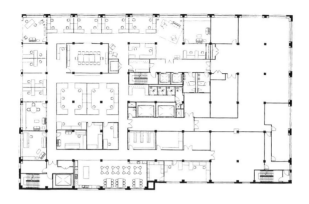

Some partitions, though few, are surrounded by sliding doors, which echo the windows that envelop the old warehouse, and other metallic doors that have been recovered from the 1950s, just like the majority of the furniture.

Algunas particiones, pocas, se rodean con puertas correderas, que son eco de las ventanas que envuelven el viejo almacén, y otras metálicas que, como la mayoría del mobiliario, se han recuperado de 1950.

Alcune partizioni, poche, sono delimitate da porte scorrevoli, che richiamano le finestre che circondano il vecchio magazzino e altre metalliche che, come la maggior parte dell'arredamento, sono state recuperate dal 1950.

Connors Communications

Lee H. Skolnick
Architecture + Design

The transformation of this New York loft into the offices of a renowned public relations and communications agency involved a quite interesting reflection on the type of spaces needed to encourage dialog, versatility, and teamwork.

Lee H. Skolnick and Paul Alter have designed spaces that combine private offices separated from shared working areas, and traditional meeting rooms with areas that are more apt to encourage informal exchanges.

The existing structure consisted of an open layout with six ironwork pillars in the middle. The perimeter walls were left white except in the areas that are used for a specific function, where they have been highlighted using vivid colors. The rest of the walls, such as those in the bathrooms and the production room and the curved wall containing the kitchen have been built with varnished plywood panels that contrast with the warmth of the other furniture.

La transformación de este loft neoyorquino en oficinas de una destacada agencia de relaciones públicas y comunicación de la ciudad lleva implícita una muy interesante reflexión sobre el tipo de espacios necesarios para fomentar el diálogo, la versatilidad y el trabajo en equipo.

Lee H. Skolnick y Paul Alter han diseñado espacios que combinan los despachos privados e independientes con zonas de trabajo compartido, y salas de reuniones tradicionales con áreas que propicien encuentros informales.

La estructura existente consiste en una planta libre, con seis pilares de fundición en el centro. Los muros perimetrales se han dejado blancos salvo en las zonas que cumplen una función específica, donde se han destacado con colores vivos. El resto de paramentos verticales, como las paredes de los aseos y de la sala de producción, y el muro curvo que contiene la cocina, se han construido con paneles de contrachapado de madera lacada que contrastan con la calidez del resto del mobiliario.

La trasformazione di questo loft newyorkese nella sede di una celebre agenzia di relazioni pubbliche e comunicazioni della città possiede implicitamente una riflessione molto interessante sul tipo di spazi necessari per promuovere il dialogo, la versatilità e il lavoro di gruppo.

Lee H. Skolnick e Paul Alter hanno progettato spazi che combinano uffici privati e indipendenti con aree di lavoro comuni, e sale riunioni tradizionali con aree che favoriscano gli incontri informali.

La struttura esistente consiste di uno spazio aperto con sei pilastri di ghisa al centro. I muri perimetrali sono stati lasciati bianchi, eccetto nelle zone in cui svolgono una funzione specifica dove spiccano colori vivaci. Il resto dei tramezzi, come le pareti dei servizi e della sala di produzione e il muro curvo che contiene la cucina, sono stati costruiti con pannelli di legno compensato laccato che contrastano con il calore apportato dal resto degli arredi.

Architects: Lee H. Skolnick Architecture + Design (Lee H. Skolnick, Paul Alter)

Location: New York, United States

Photographs: Andrew Garn

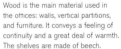

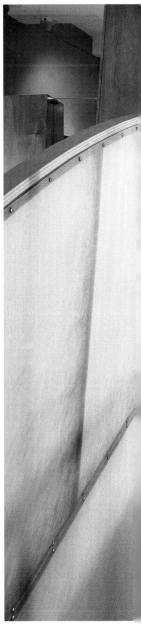

Wood is the main material used in
the offices: walls, vertical partitions,
and furniture. It conveys a feeling of
continuity and a great deal of warmth.
The shelves are made of beech.

La madera es el principal material de
las oficinas: pavimento, particiones
verticales, mobiliario. Transmite
sensación de continuidad y una gran
calidez. Las estanterías son de haya.

Il legno è il materiale principale degli
uffici: pavimento, ripartizioni verticali,
arredi. Trasmette una sensazione di
continuità e di calore. Gli scaffali
sono di faggio.

On the right, the meeting room is integrated with the rest of the space through movable, transformable enclosures.

A la derecha, la sala de reuniones se integra con el resto de la nave mediante cerramientos móviles y transformables.

A destra, la sala riunioni si integra con il resto degli spazi con tramezzi mobili e trasformabili.

1. Entrance
2. Reception and waiting area
3. Conference room
4. President's office
5. Operations room
6. Open office area
7. Production room
8. Bathrooms
9. Kitchen
10. Meeting and rest area

1. Entrada
2. Recepción y zona de espera
3. Sala de conferencias
4. Oficina del presidente
5. Oficina de operaciones
6. Zona de oficinas abiertas
7. Aula de producción
8. Aseos
9. Cocina
10. Zona para reuniones y descanso

1. Entrata
2. Reception e sala d'aspetto
3. Sala conferenze
4. Ufficio del presidente
5. Ufficio operativo
6. Area di uffici aperti
7. Aula di produzione
8. Servizi
9. Cucina
10. Area per riunioni e i momenti di pausa

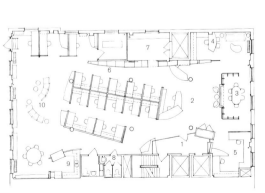

Design Studio in Tribeca
Estudio de diseño en Tribeca / Studio di design a Tribeca

Parsons + Fernández-Casteleiro

The streets in the New York neighborhood of Tribeca is famous for its buildings containing some of the best lofts in New York City. The offices of Parkson + Fernández-Casteleiro were designed by the occupants themselves on one of the five stories in a building that underwent a complete remodeling.

The L-shaped layout is divided on its longer, lengthwise axis by a metallic shelf that is the main theme in the design and in many ways forms its backbone. From one end of the room to the other extend all the utilities and electrical cabling, contained in this shelving, at either end of which the private offices have been located.

The lighting distribution combines suspended fluorescent lamps with other lights installed within frames that run from floor to ceiling. This swath of lights not only illuminates the work tables and the models and plans hanging on the walls; it also confers a unique rhythm on the office.

The floor is made of polished concrete; the walls are white; the shelving and rails are metallic, erector-set fashion. Parsons + Fernández-Casteleiro used an industrial language and low-budget materials.

El barrio neoyorquino de Tribeca es famoso por tener ubicados entre sus calles los edificios que contienen algunos de los mejores lofts de la ciudad de Nueva York. Las oficinas de Parsons + Fernández-Casteleiro fueron diseñadas por ellos mismos en una de las cinco plantas de un edificio que sufrió una remodelación total.

La planta, en forma de L, queda dividida en su eje longitudinal mayor por una estantería metálica que es el tema principal del proyecto y, por así decirlo, su espina dorsal. De punta a punta de la sala se despliegan todas las instalaciones y el cableado eléctrico, que están contenidos en esta estantería a cuyos extremos se encuentran los despachos privados.

La distribución lumínica combina fluorescentes suspendidos con otros colocados entre perfiles que los llevan de suelo a techo. Esta trama de luces no sólo permite iluminar simultáneamente las mesas de trabajo y las maquetas y planos suspendidos de la pared, sino que también confiere a la oficina un ritmo singular.

El suelo es de hormigón pulido; las paredes son blancas; las estanterías y las guías, metálicas, tipo mecano: Parsons + Fernández-Casteleiro emplean un lenguaje industrial y materiales de bajo presupuesto.

Il quartiere newyorkese di Tribeca è famoso per i suoi edifici che contengono alcuni dei migliori loft della città di New York. Gli uffici di Parsons + Fernández-Casteleiro sono stati progettati da loro stessi in uno dei cinque piani di un edificio che è stato completamente ristrutturato.

Il piano a forma di L è diviso lungo l'asse longitudinale maggiore da una scaffalatura metallica che è il tema principale del progetto e, per così dire, la sua spina dorsale. Da una punta all'altra della sala si snodano tutti gli impianti e i cavi elettrici, che sono contenuti in questa scaffalatura alle cui estremità si trovano gli uffici privati.

La distribuzione della luce combina tubi al neon sospesi con altri sistemati in strutture verticali che vanno dal soffitto al pavimento. Questo sistema di luci non solo permette di illuminare contemporaneamente i tavoli da lavoro, i modelli e i progetti appesi alla parete, ma conferisce all'ufficio un ritmo singolare.

Il pavimento di cemento lisciato; le pareti sono bianche; gli scaffali e le scanalature sono metalliche, tipo meccano: Parsons + Fernández Casteleiro utilizzano un linguaggio industriale e materiali economici.

Architects: Parsons + Fernández-Casteleiro

Location: New York, United States

Photographs: Paul Warchol

General layout
1. Reception area
2. Drafting room
3. Office
4. Meeting room

Planta general
1. Recepción
2. Sala de dibujo
3. Despacho
4. Sala de reuniones

Pianta generale
1. Reception
2. Sala progetti
3. Ufficio
4. Sala riunioni

In some ways, the placement of the
fluorescent lights transcends their
strictly functional look and become a
unique piece reminiscent of installations
by James Turrell.

En cierto modo, el trabajo con los
fluorescentes trasciende de su estricto
aspecto funcional para convertirse en
una obra singular que recuerda las
instalaciones de James Turrell.

In un certo modo, il sistema di tubi
al neon trascende il puro aspetto
funzionale per convertirsi in un'opera
singolare che ricorda le installazioni
di James Turrell.

Sunshine Interactive Network

Gates Merkulova
Architects

The space that houses the new offices of Sunshine Interactive Network (SIN) was an empty loft almost 1000 m² in Manhattan. The architects' strategy consisted of introducing elements into the space that would increase its density. The center is occupied by three unique pieces that house functions that are shared by the company's different sectors: a conical volume for audio and video presentations and small meetings; a long, warped piece for larger meetings, movies and video; and a small blue room for slide presentations. These elements are used in a parallel way to separate the different spaces. In one corner there is a recording studio and a video editing room, which are completely isolated. The rest of the office space is open, with the work tables lined up along the façades and fiberglass screens acting as dividers.

El local que alberga las nuevas oficinas de Sunshine Interactive Network (SIN) era un loft vacío situado en Manhattan de casi mil metros cuadrados. La estrategia de los arquitectos consistió en introducir en el espacio elementos que incrementasen su densidad. El centro está ocupado por tres piezas singulares que albergan funciones compartidas por los diferentes sectores de la empresa: un volumen cónico para presentaciones de audio y vídeo y reuniones de poca gente, una pieza alabeada y larga para reuniones multitudinarias, cine y vídeo, y una pequeña sala azul para pases de diapositivas. Estos elementos sirven paralelamente para separar unas áreas de otras. En una esquina y completamente aislados, se hallan un estudio de grabación y una sala de edición de vídeo. El resto de la oficina está abierta, con las mesas de trabajo alineadas a las fachadas y pantallas de fibra de vidrio como elementos divisorios.

Il locale che ospita i nuovi uffici di Sunshine Interactive Network (SIN) era un loft vuoto di quasi mille metri quadrati situato a Manhattan. La strategia degli architetti è stata quella di introdurre nello spazio elementi che aumentassero la sua densità. Il centro è occupato da tre locali singolari che svolgono funzioni condivise dai diversi reparti dell'impresa: un volume conico per presentazioni audiovisive e per riunioni di poche persone, una stanza arcuata e allungata per grandi riunioni, cinema e video e una sala piccola azzurra per la proiezione di diapositive. Questi elementi servono parallelamente per separare alcune aree dalle altre. In un angolo e completamente isolati, si trovano uno studio di registrazione e una sala di montaggio video. Il resto degli uffici sono aperti, con i tavoli da lavoro allineati alle facciate e pannelli di fibra di vetro come elementi divisori.

Architects: Gates Merkulova Architects

Location: Manhattan, New York, United States

Photographs: J.B. Grant Photographs

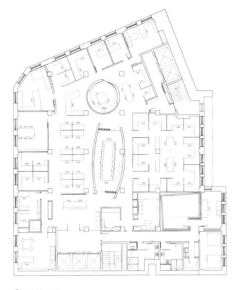

The type of orders received by the company leads to a constant flow of workers. The new offices had to be capable of accommodating both permanent employees (each with his or her own working table) as well as temporary workers, each with his or her own requirements. The space had to be both territorial and non-territorial at the same time, and flexible enough to adapt to the changes in the company.

El tipo de encargos que recibe la compañía provoca un constante flujo de trabajadores. Las nuevas oficinas deben tener la capacidad de acomodar tanto a los empleados fijos (con una mesa de trabajo particular), como a los colaboradores temporales y sus distintas necesidades. El espacio debe ser a la vez territorial y no territorial, común y privado, y lo suficientemente flexible como para adaptarse a los cambios de la empresa.

Il tipo di lavori commissionati alla ditta crea un flusso costante di lavoratori. I nuovi uffici devono avere la capacità di accogliere sia i dipendenti fissi (con un proprio tavolo da lavoro) che quelli temporanei e di soddisfare le diverse necessità. Lo spazio deve essere allo stesso tempo territoriale e non territoriale, comune e privato e sufficientemente flessibile da poter adattarsi all'evoluzione dell'impresa.

General layout
Planta general
Pianta generale

Miller-Jones Studio
Estudio Miller-Jones / Studio Miller-Jones

LOT / EK

Located in the middle of Manhattan, the Miller-Jones Studio, a living and working space for a couple made up of a fashion photographer and a designer, occupies a surface area of 186 m² on the 14th floor of a skyscraper.

The loft enjoys excellent views and a great deal of natural daylight thanks to its southern orientation. The plan by the LOT / EK architect couple consisted of a single wall built with metal panels that presides over the largest area of the interior of this apartment. In addition to giving back the original industrial appearance to the space (high ceilings, exposed tubes, concrete flooring and white walls), the large deteriorated aluminum surface separates the floor into two spaces and divides the space into a private and a working zone. The wall houses the majority of the home's utilities—the bathroom, the kitchen and the closets—some of which are built in and others which are located on the far side. A system of rotating panels permits access to each of these spaces, where the bedroom is also located.

Situado en pleno corazón de Manhattan, el estudio Miller-Jones, lugar de trabajo y residencia de una pareja formada por un fotógrafo de moda y una diseñadora, ocupa una superficie de 186 m² en la planta 14.ª de un rascacielos.

El loft disfruta de unas vistas excelentes y de mucha luz natural gracias a su orientación sur. El proyecto de la pareja de arquitectos de LOT/EK consiste en una sola pared construida con paneles de metal que preside la máxima dimensión del espacio interior de este apartamento. Además de devolver al espacio su aspecto industrial originario (techo alto, instalaciones vistas, solera de hormigón y blanco en las paredes), este gran plano de aluminio deteriorado divide la planta en dos y distribuye el espacio según una zona privada y otra de trabajo. El muro alberga la mayoría de los servicios de la casa –el baño, la cocina o los armarios–, algunos de los cuales están encastrados en su propia superficie y otros, situados al otro lado. Un sistema de paneles que rotan sobre sí mismos permite acceder a cada una de las estancias, donde también se ubica el dormitorio.

Situato nel cuore di Manhattan, lo studio Miller-Jones, luogo di lavoro e abitazione di una coppia formata da un fotografo di moda e una disegnatrice, occupa una superficie di 186 m² al 14° piano di un grattacielo.

Il loft gode di ottime viste e di molta luce essendo orientato a sud. Il progetto della coppia di architetti di LOT/EK consiste di una sola parete costruita con pannelli di metallo che copre la dimensione massima dello spazio interno di questo appartamento. Oltre a riportare lo spazio al suo aspetto industriale originario (soffitto alto, impianti lasciati a vista, pavimento di cemento e pareti bianche), questo grande pannello di alluminio deteriorato divide il piano in due e distribuisce lo spazio in una zona privata e una di lavoro. Il muro contiene la maggior parte dei servizi della casa (il bagno, la cucina e gli armadi), alcuni dei quali sono incassati nella sua superficie e altri sono situati sull'altro lato. Un sistema di pannelli che ruotano su se stessi consentono di accedere a ciascuna delle stanze, tra cui la camera da letto.

Architects: LOT/EK

Location: Manhattan, New York, United States

Photographs: Paul Warchol

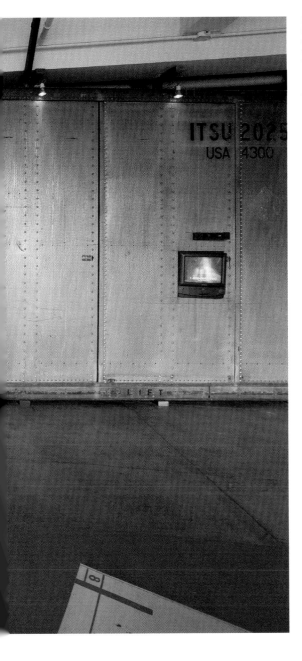

In the center of the studio, four refrigerators laid on the floor are used as working surfaces and as additional storage space. The computer is built into one of the refrigerators, and the scanner and printer form part of the freezer.

En el centro del estudio, cuatro neveras tumbadas sobre el suelo sirven de superficie de trabajo y como espacio adicional de almacenaje. El ordenador se encuentra empotrado en una nevera, el escáner y la impresora forman parte del congelador.

Al centro dello studio, quattro frigoriferi adagiati sul pavimento servono da superficie di lavoro e da ripostiglio. Il computer è incassato in un frigorifero, mentre lo scanner e la stampante fanno parte del congelatore.

Stingel Studio

Cha & Innerhofer

Amid the hustle and bustle and artistic movement in the center of New York City's Chelsea neighborhood lies the Starrett-Lehigh building with this 273 m² loft studio on its top floor. The building was the subject of a study and was shown in a 1932 exhibition at the Museum of Modern Art (Modern Architecture: International Exhibition), and it constitutes an early example of the International Style in the United States. The outer glass façade wall that surrounds the studio is the perfect frame for the dramatic views of Manhattan.

Entre el bullicio y el movimiento artístico del centro de Chelsea, en Nueva York, se encuentra el edificio Starrett-Lehigh con este estudio loft de 372 m² en su planta más elevada. El edificio fue objeto de estudio y mostrado en la exposición del Museo de Arte Moderno del año 1932 (Modern architecture: international exhibition), y constituye un temprano ejemplo del international style en Estados Unidos. La envolvente de la fachada acristalada que rodea el estudio constituye un marco perfecto del panorama dramático que puede ofrecer Manhattan.

Tra la confusione e il viavai di artisti del centro di Chelsea, a New York, si trova l'edificio Starrett-Lehigh con questo loft convertito in studio di 372 m² al suo piano più alto. L'edificio fu oggetto di studio ed esposto nella mostra del Museo di Arte Moderna del 1932 (Modern architecture: international exhibition) e rappresenta un esempio precoce dello Stile Internazionale (International Style) negli Stati Uniti. Le vetrate che circondano lo studio costituiscono una cornice perfetta dello spettacolare panorama di Manhattan.

Architects: Cha & Innerhofer
Location: New York, United States
Photographs: Dao-Lou Zha

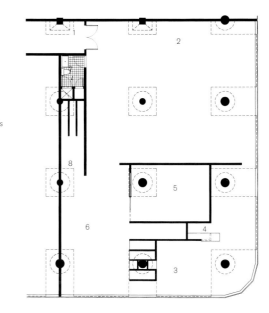

1. Access vestibule
2. Exhibition gallery
3 Reception area
4. Bar
5. Spray room
6. Working area
7. Bathroom
8. Storage area

1. Vestíbulo de acceso
2. Galería de exposiciones
3. Recepción
4. Bar
5. Habitación del *spray*
6. Área de trabajo
7. Baño
8. Almacén

1. Atrio d'ingresso
2. Area espositiva
3. Reception
4. Bar
5. Stanza dello *spray*
6. Area di lavoro
7. Bagno
8 Ripostiglio

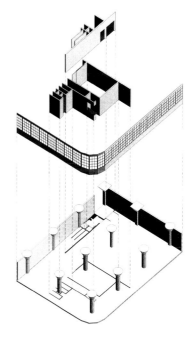

Triple Space
Triple espacio / Triplo spazio

Tow Studios Architecture

This 279 m² office loft located in New York's Chelsea neighborhood boasts a row of northern-facing windows and views of the Empire State Building. The plan had to meet the needs of an office and studio for two designers yet retain at all times the sense of open space inherent in a loft.

The layout distinguishes three very different areas. The creative area is comprised of the design studios lined up along the building's northern façade. The intermediate area houses the access to the space on the east and the office's administrative area in the central and western part of the entire floor. The third and last zone contains the pantry, a small kitchen and the meeting room. The translucent arched wall distinguishes the meeting room from the rest of the offices.

With the objective of maintaining the uniform and homogeneous flow of light coming from the northern façade, the partitions dividing the three areas have been made of sliding translucent panels.

Este loft de oficinas, de 279 m² y situado en Chelsea, alardea de tener una hilera de ventanas de orientación norte y vistas al Empire State Building. El programa debía desarrollar las necesidades de oficina y estudio de dos diseñadores y mantener en todo momento la sensación de espacio abierto inherente al loft.

El proyecto de distribución distingue tres zonas muy diferenciadas. La zona creativa comprende los estudios de diseño alineados a la fachada norte del edificio. La zona intermedia alberga el área de acceso al local por el este y la zona de administración de las oficinas en la parte central y oeste de toda la superficie. La tercera y última zona contiene la despensa, una pequeña cocina y la sala de reuniones. El muro translúcido en forma de arco distingue el lugar de reuniones del resto de las oficinas.

Con la idea de mantener el flujo de la luz uniforme y homogénea de la cara norte de la fachada, las particiones que dividen las tres zonas se han materializado con paneles deslizantes translúcidos.

Questo loft di uffici di 279 m² situato a Chelsea, vanta una fila di finestre orientate a nord e con vista sull'Empire State Building. Il progetto doveva comprendere un ufficio e uno studio per due disegnatori grafici senza perdere la sensazione di spazio aperto propria del loft.

Lo spazio è stato suddiviso in tre zone molto diverse. L'area creativa include gli studi di progettazione disposti lungo il fronte nord dell'edificio. La zona intermedia contiene l'area di accesso al locale a est e la zona di amministrazione degli uffici nelle parti centrale e ovest di tutta la superficie. La terza e ultima zona comprende la dispensa, una piccola cucina e la sala riunioni. Il muro translucido a forma d'arco separa la zona riunioni dal resto degli uffici.

Al fine di mantenere la luce uniforme e omogenea del fronte nord, le tre zone sono state suddivise con pannelli scorrevoli translucidi.

Architects: Tow Studios Architecture
Location: New York, United States
Photographs: Björg/Photography

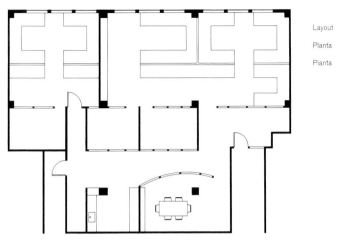

Layout

Planta

Planta

WMA Engineers

Valerio Dewalt
Train Architects

The new offices of WMA Engineers were designed based on the repetition of a model of individual working units. Each of the cells has all the working tools needed (computer, drafting table, catalogues, handbooks, etc.) and all the cells together form an orthogonal web. The client's objective was to achieve the greatest density of working places possible within the space available. The floor's entire space was maximized to the extent possible. In the interior layout no closed offices are conceived; the different working units are separated by low shelves that facilitate communication among workers.

This swath of tables and dividing shelves covers a large central area, on the side of which one finds closed towers containing the different utilities (such as offices, meeting rooms, a storage area, archives, a kitchen, printers and photocopiers).

Las nuevas oficinas de WMA Engineers se diseñaron a partir de la repetición de un modelo de unidad de trabajo individual. Cada una de las células dispone de todas las herramientas de trabajo necesarias (ordenador, mesa de dibujo, catálogos, prontuarios, etc.) y el conjunto de todas las células se dispone regularmente según una malla ortogonal. El objetivo del cliente era alcanzar la mayor densidad posible de lugares de trabajo en el espacio disponible. Se trataba de optimizar al máximo toda la superficie en planta. En la distribución interior no se concibe el despacho cerrado, las diferentes unidades de trabajo están separadas por estanterías bajas que facilitan las consultas entre los trabajadores.

Esta trama de mesas y estantes divisorios cubre una gran área central, en cuyos laterales se disponen unas torres cerradas que contienen los diferentes servicios auxiliares (tales como despachos, salas de reuniones, almacén, archivos, cocina, impresoras y fotocopiadoras).

Il progetto dei nuovi uffici di WMA Engineers è improntato sulla ripetizione di un modello di unità di lavoro individuale. Ciascuna delle cellule dispone di tutti gli strumenti di lavoro necessari (computer, tavolo da disegno, cataloghi, prontuari, etc.) e l'insieme di tutte le cellule è disposto in modo regolare secondo una maglia ortogonale. L'obiettivo del cliente era ottenere il maggior numero possibile di posti di lavoro nello spazio disponibile. Si trattava di sfruttare al massimo tutta la superficie del piano. Nella distribuzione interna non sono stati progettati uffici chiusi, le diverse unità di lavoro sono separate da scaffali bassi che consentono ai dipendenti di consultarsi tra loro.

Questa rete di tavoli e scaffali divisori copre una grande area centrale, ai cui lati si dispongono torri chiuse che contengono i diversi servizi ausiliari (come uffici, sale riunioni, archivi, cucina, stampanti e fotocopiatrici).

Architects: Valerio Dewalt Train Architects

Location: Chicago, Illinois, United States

Photographs: Karant + Associates/Barbara Karant; Neil Sheehan (outside view)

494

The vertical space extends beyond the zigzagging lines that make up the lights, beams and pillars. Other shafts of indirect light are place over the high perimeter walls between the windows.

El espacio vertical crece más allá del zigzag de líneas que conforman luces, vigas y pilares. Otros tramos de luz indirecta están dispuestos sobre las altas paredes perimetrales, entre los ventanales.

Lo spazio verticale si estende oltre il zigzag di linee creato da luci, travi e pilastri. Altri punti di luce indiretta sono disposti sopra le alte pareti perimetrali, tra i finestroni.

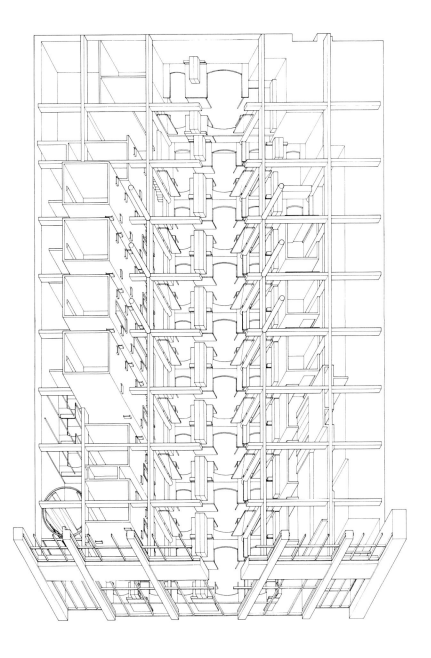

BBDO West

Beckson Design
Associates

The old offices were completely demolished. Three floors became two. The strategy consisted of creating a more condensed, active and dynamic working space.

The architectural design ran parallel to a corporate reorganization: the former hierarchical organization, based on independent departments and closed offices, was replaced by open spaces and flexible teams of associates grouped according to client. In the new order, even the Chairman occupies a working place the same size as the other employees. He himself claims that in the old offices, people wasted too much time in meetings: "They talked a lot about what they were going to do, but they worked little. I asked Beckson if there was any way to bring people together as if they were always in a meeting. Thus, communication would come about by osmosis, by the very fact that they would see and hear the work being done by the others."

In line with the new spirit of BBDO, the architects created an image that would evoke not an office, but an idea factory, with a somewhat industrial appearance: no hanging ceilings, exposed structure and installations, finishes that were apparently dashed together, collage-like.

Las antiguas oficinas fueron totalmente demolidas. De tres plantas se pasó a dos. La estrategia consistía en crear un espacio de trabajo más condensado, activo y dinámico.

El proyecto arquitectónico se desarrolló de forma paralela a la reestructuración de la empresa: la antigua organización jerárquica, basada en departamentos independientes y oficinas cerradas, fue sustituida por espacios abiertos y equipos flexibles de colaboradores, agrupados por clientes. En la nueva ordenación, incluso el presidente ocupa un lugar de trabajo de las mismas dimensiones que el resto de empleados. Él mismo afirma que en las antiguas oficinas, la gente perdía demasiado tiempo en reuniones. «Hablaban mucho de lo que iban a hacer, pero trabajaban poco. Le pregunté a Beckson si había alguna manera de juntar a la gente como si siempre estuviesen reunidos. Así, la comunicación se produciría por osmosis, por el propio hecho de que verían y oirían el trabajo de los demás.»

Según el nuevo espíritu de BBDO, los arquitectos se propusieron crear una imagen que evocase no una oficina, sino una fábrica de ideas, y que tuviera un aspecto industrial: ausencia de falsos techos, estructura e instalaciones vistas, acabados de una aparente inmediatez próxima al colaje.

I vecchi uffici sono stati completamente demoliti. Tre piani sono diventati due. La strategia consisteva nel creare uno spazio di lavoro più concentrato, attivo e dinamico.

Il progetto architettonico si sviluppò parallelamente alla ristrutturazione dell'impresa: la vecchia organizzazione gerarchica, basata su dipartimenti indipendenti e uffici chiusi, fu sostituita con spazi aperti e team flessibili di collaboratori, raggruppati per clienti. Nella nuova distribuzione, perfino il presidente occupa un posto di lavoro che ha le stesse dimensioni di quello del resto dei dipendenti. Lui stesso afferma che nei vecchi uffici la gente perdeva troppo tempo in riunioni. «Parlavano troppo delle cose che avrebbero fatto, ma lavoravano poco. Chiesi a Beckson se c'era un modo di disporre la gente come se fosse sempre in riunione, in modo che la comunicazione avvenisse per osmosi, per il solo fatto che vedevano e sentivano che facevano tutti gli altri.»

Secondo il nuovo spirito di BBDO, gli architetti si proposero di creare un'immagine che non ricordasse un ufficio, ma una fabbrica di idee e che avesse un aspetto industriale: assenza di controsoffitti, struttura e impianti lasciati a vista, rifiniture di un'immediatezza apparente simile al collage.

Architects: Beckson Design Associates

Location: Los Angeles, United States

Photographs: Tom Bonner

The most characteristic element is the modular system with which tables and dividers are easily assembled and disassembled. Different types of surfaces made of simple, economical materials are screwed onto an erector-set like galvanized steel structure.

El elemento más característico es el sistema modular con el que muy fácilmente se montan y desmontan las mesas y las mamparas. En una estructura de acero galvanizado tipo mecano se atornillan diferentes tipos de superficies de materiales sencillos y económicos.

L'elemento più caratteristico è il sistema modulare, che consente di montare e smontare con molta facilità tavoli e paraventi. In una struttura di acciaio zincato tipo meccano si avvitano tipi diversi di superfici fatte di materiali semplici ed economici.

Rhino Entertainment

Beckson Design
Associates

The new headquarters of Rhino Entertainment, located on Santa Monica Boulevard, occupies a surface area of 3,350 m² in a modern office building organized around three atriums. Despite the fact that the renovation had to be carried out in little time (60 days) and a low budget (around 360 euros/m²), and the fact that the building itself (with a speculative spatial organization) encouraged the typical layout based on dividing screens, straight halls and square offices, Michael Beckson, Ed Gabor and Steve Heisler challenged themselves to re-create the young, lively spirit of the company.

The absence of hanging ceilings along with the intensive, risky use of bright colors on both the walls and the carpet evoke the pop aesthetic. The hallways are full of bends, curves and anecdotes that enliven the transitional spaces. Oblique surfaces, angled shapes and the edges of the walls are echoed in the design of the carpet.

La nueva sede de Rhino Entertainment, situada en el Santa Monica Boulevard, ocupa una superficie de 3.350 m² en un edificio moderno de oficinas organizado alrededor de tres atrios. Pese a que el tiempo disponible para realizar las obras (60 días), el presupuesto (alrededor de 360 euros/m²) y el propio edificio (con una organización especulativa del espacio) aconsejaban la típica distribución a base de mamparas, pasillos rectos y despachos cuadrados, Michael Beckson, Ed Gabor y Steven Heisler se propusieron recrear el espíritu juvenil y alegre de la compañía.

La ausencia de falso techo junto al uso intensivo y azaroso de colores vivos tanto en las paredes como en la moqueta evoca la estética pop. Los pasillos de circulación están llenos de giros, curvas y anécdotas que amenizan los espacios de transición. Los planos oblicuos, las formas angulosas y las aristas de los muros se repiten en los dibujos de la moqueta.

La nuova sede di Rhino Entertainment, situata in Santa Monica Boulevard, occupa una superficie di 3.350 m² in un edificio moderno di uffici organizzato attorno a tre atri. Nonostante il tempo disponibile per realizzare i lavori (60 giorni), il preventivo (circa 360 euro/m²) e l'edificio (con una organizzazione speculativa dello spazio) consigliassero l'adozione della tipica distribuzione basata su paraventi, corridoi dritti e uffici quadrati, Michael Beckson, Ed Gabor e Steven Heisler si proposero di ricreare lo spirito giovane e allegro dell'impresa.

L'assenza di un controsoffitto e l'uso intenso e audace di colori vivaci sia per le pareti che per la moquette ricorda l'estetica pop. I corridoi sono pieni di giri, curve e aneddoti che rendono piacevoli gli spazi di transizione. I piani obliqui, le forme angolose e gli spigoli dei muri si ripetono nei disegni della moquette.

Architects: Beckson Design Associates

Location: Los Angeles, United States

Photographs: Tom Bonner

There is no continuous hanging ceiling for all the offices. Nevertheless, in certain places uniquely shaped acoustic ceilings have been placed to help define the spaces.

No existe un falso techo continuo para todas las oficinas. Sin embargo, en determinadas zonas se han colocado techos acústicos de formas originales que ayudan a definir los espacios.

Non esiste un unico controsoffitto per tutti gli uffici. Tuttavia, in determinate aree sono stati costruiti soffitti acustici con forme originali che aiutano a modellare gli spazi.

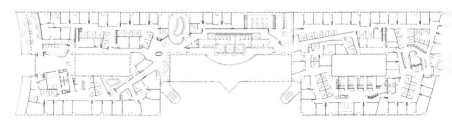

MTV Networks

Felderman + Keatinge
Associates

The team charged with designing this famous American TV channel's new headquarters on the California coast (Felderman + Keatinge Associates) was led by the architect Stanley Felderman. A peculiar sense of humor and innovation in each of his designs have distinguished all of his creations. Currently, this spirit has been conferred on each of the five floors (10,200 m²) located inside a banal office building.

The objective was to project the image of Santa Monica in the middle of the Pacific Ocean: dreamy wharves, beach bungalows, neighborhoods filled with bohemian lofts and art galleries—an avant-garde architecture.

An enormous ship anchored in the square, made of shiny red steel, distinguishes the entrance. An oval-shaped vestibule in which a 1957 polished aluminum Airstream is parked serves as a waiting room. Two gigantic 4 m high steel structures act as the "talking heads," whose eyes and mouths serve as monitors witnessing what is happening around them. A triangular wood envelope marks the reception area and Santa Monica's colorful urban scene is evoked in the hallways. Colored carpets cover the floor, and the white walls contrast with the more lively tones.

El equipo encargado de diseñar la nueva sede en la costa oeste californiana de esta importante emisora de televisión americana (Felderman + Keatinge Associates) está liderado por el arquitecto Stanley Felderman. Un peculiar sentido del humor y la innovación de cada uno de sus diseños han distinguido todas sus creaciones. Actualmente, este espíritu se ha transmitido a cada una de las cinco plantas (10.200 m²) de un banal edificio de oficinas.

El objetivo fue proyectar la imagen de Santa Mónica en pleno océano Pacífico: embarcaderos de ensueño, bungalós de playa, barrios de lofts bohemios y galerías de arte, una arquitectura de vanguardia.

Un enorme barco anclado en la plaza, de acero rojo y brillante, distingue la entrada. Un vestíbulo oval, donde está aparcado un remolque Airstream de 1957 fabricado en aluminio pulido, hace de sala de espera. Dos gigantescas estructuras de acero de 4 m de altura son las «cabezas parlantes» cuyos ojos y bocas actúan como monitores testigos de lo que pasa. Un sobre triangular de madera marca la recepción y en los pasillos se desarrolla la colorista escena urbana de Santa Mónica. Moquetas de colores visten el suelo y el blanco de las paredes contrasta con tonos más vivos.

Il team incaricato del progetto della nuova sede di quest'importante rete televisiva americana (Felderman + Keatinge Associates) è diretto dall'architetto Stanley Felderman. Innovazione e un singolare senso dell'umorismo caratterizzano tutte le sue creazioni. Attualmente, questo spirito è stato trasmesso in ognuno dei cinque piani (10.200 m²) di quello che era un banale edificio di uffici.

L'obiettivo era proiettare l'immagine di Santa Monica in pieno Oceano Pacifico: imbarcaderi da sogno, bungalow sulla spiaggia, quartieri di loft bohémien e gallerie d'arte, un'architettura d'avanguardia.

L'entrata dell'edificio è contraddistinta da un'enorme barca di acciaio rosso e brillante. L'ingresso ovale, in cui è parcheggiato un rimorchio Airstream del 1957 di alluminio lucidato, fa da sala d'aspetto. Due strutture gigantesche di acciaio di 4 m d'altezza sono le «teste parlanti» con dei televisori al posto degli occhi e dalla bocca che mostrano quello che succede. Una busta triangolare di legno indica la reception e per i corridoi è rappresentato lo scenario urbano di Santa Monica. Il pavimento è rivestito di moquette colorate e il bianco delle pareti contrasta con toni più vivi.

Architects: Felderman + Keatinge Associates

Location: Santa Monica, California, United States

Photographs: Toshi Yoshimi

Praxair Distribution Inc.

Herbert Lewis Kruse
Blunck Architecture

Herbert Lewis Kruse Architecture received the assignment of transforming a 5,400 m² warehouse located in an industrial park into a processing and distribution center for soldered pieces. One third of the area was remodeled for the offices and training areas, while the other two-thirds of the premises were left as the workshop and warehouse.

All the design elements (office layout, furniture, lighting, installations) were designed according to a clear linear organization that allows for future extensions. The meeting and training areas were placed near the entrance along with the few existing windows.

The interdependence between the workshop and the offices was likewise reinforced by choosing the same construction materials and adopting a shared aesthetic.

One of the most serious problems that the architects had to resolve was the amount of lighting in the offices, which is quite different from that needed in the warehouse or workshop. Since opening more windows in the building's prefabricated panels would prove to be impossible, they chose to let natural daylight enter through skylights in the roof, under which a continuous, wavy fiberglass panel was placed to diffuse the light throughout the entire office area.

Herbert Lewis Kruse Blunck Architecture recibió el encargo de transformar un almacén de 5.400 m², situado en un parque industrial, en un centro de procesamiento y distribución de piezas soldadas. Un tercio de la superficie se remodeló para ubicar las oficinas y las áreas de formación, mientras que los otros dos tercios del local permanecieron como taller y almacén.

Todos los elementos del proyecto (distribución de las oficinas, mobiliario, iluminación, instalaciones) se diseñaron según una clara ordenación lineal que permite futuras ampliaciones. Las áreas de reunión y formación se colocaron cerca de la entrada, junto a las pocas ventanas existentes.

La interdependencia entre el taller y las oficinas se vio, asimismo, reforzada por la elección de los mismos materiales constructivos y la adopción de una estética compartida.

Uno de los problemas más graves que tuvieron que resolver los arquitectos fue el grado de iluminación de las oficinas, muy diferente al de un almacén o un taller. Como abrir más ventanas en los paneles prefabricados del edificio era imposible, se optó por introducir la luz natural a través de tragaluces en la cubierta, debajo de los cuales una plancha continua de fibra de vidrio ondulada difunde la luz en toda el área de oficinas.

Herbert Lewis Kruse Blunck Architecture ha progettato la trasformazione di un magazzino di 5.400 m², situato in un parco industriale, in un centro di lavorazione e distribuzione di componenti saldati. Un terzo della superficie è stata ristrutturata al fine di ubicare gli uffici e le aree di formazione, mentre gli altri due terzi del locale sono rimasti come officina e magazzino.

Tutti gli elementi del progetto (distribuzione degli uffici, arredi, illuminazione, impianti) sono stati progettati secondo una chiara disposizione lineare che possa permettere futuri ampliamenti. Le aree di riunione e formazione sono state collocate vicino all'entrata, accanto alle poche finestre esistenti.

L'interdipendenza tra l'officina e gli uffici è stata rafforzata dalla scelta degli stessi materiali costruttivi e l'adozione di un'estetica comune.

Uno dei problemi più gravi che gli architetti hanno dovuto risolvere è stato il grado di illuminazione degli uffici, molto diversa da quella di un magazzino o un'officina. Siccome non era possibile aprire ulteriormente le finestre nei pannelli prefabbricati, si è scelto di introdurre la luce naturale attraverso dei lucernari sul tetto, al di sotto dei quali è stato situato un pannello ondulato di fibra di vetro che diffonde la luce in tutta l'area degli uffici.

Architects: Herbert Lewis Kruse Blunck Architecture

Location: Ankeny, Iowa, United States

Photographs: Farshid Assassi

The architects left the exposed structure and ceiling intact throughout the entire building in order to formally express the industrial nature of the design.

Los arquitectos mantuvieron la estructura vista en todo el edificio y el cerramiento exterior sin revestir, con el propósito de expresar formalmente el carácter industrial de la intervención.

Gli architetti hanno conservato la struttura a vista in tutto l'edificio e la copertura esteriore senza rivestimento per esprimere formalmente il carattere industriale dell'intervento.

German Design Center
Centro Alemán del Diseño / Centro Tedesco del Design

Norman Foster
& Partners

Located in the heart of the most built-up part of Germany, Essen is a city characterized by industry, mining and building. Heavy industry has lost ground to new technologies, and many of the large factories are falling into disuse. In order to conserve the industrial heritage, these buildings were recovered to be devoted to new, varied uses. This was the challenged faced by the Norman Foster and Partners architectural firm when transforming a mining complex into the new headquarters of the German Design Center.

The old factory had been designed in 1927 by the architects Fritz Schupp and Martin Kremmer, but it was closed in 1986 when coal production ceased to be profitable.

The plan provided for the organization of both temporary and permanent exhibitions, to which almost all the interior space was devoted. One of the main objectives was to highlight the contrast between the powerful industrial aesthetic and small-scale architecture where the finishes, details and materials acquire a great deal of importance.

Essen, situada en el corazón de la Alemania más urbanizada, es una ciudad que se caracteriza por la industria, la minería y la edificación. La industria pesada ha perdido terreno frente a las nuevas tecnologías y muchas de sus grandes fábricas han entrado en decadencia. Para conservar el patrimonio industrial, se recuperaron estos edificios con la intención de destinarles usos nuevos y variados. Este fue el reto al que se enfrentó el despacho de arquitectura Norman Foster & Partners al transformar un complejo minero en la nueva sede del Centro Alemán del Diseño.

La antigua fábrica había sido diseñada en 1927 por los arquitectos Fritz Schupp y Martin Kremmer, pero fue clausurada en 1986, cuando la producción de carbón dejó de ser rentable.

El programa prevé la organización de exposiciones temporales y permanentes, a las que destina prácticamente la totalidad del espacio interior. Uno de los objetivos principales consistió en potenciar el contraste entre la poderosa estética de la industria y una arquitectura de pequeña escala donde los acabados, detalles y materiales adquieren gran importancia.

Essen, situata nel cuore della Germania più urbanizzata, è una città che si distingue per l'industria, il settore minerario e l'edilizia. L'industria pesante ha perso terreno con la diffusione delle nuove tecnologie e molte delle sue grandi fabbriche sono in declino. Al fine di conservare il patrimonio industriale, sono stati recuperati questi edifici per destinarli a nuovi usi. La sfida dello studio di architettura Norman Foster & Partners era di trasformare un complesso minerario nella nuova sede del Centro Tedesco del Design.

L'antica fabbrica fu progettata nel 1927 dagli architetti Fritz Schupp e Martin Kremmer e venne chiusa nel 1986 con la crisi dell'industria del carbone.

Il programma prevede l'allestimento di mostre temporanee e permanenti, alle quali è destinata la quasi totalità dello spazio interno. Uno degli obiettivi principali consisteva nel potenziare il contrasto tra la potente estetica dell'industria e un'architettura su piccola scala dove le rifiniture, i dettagli e i materiali acquistano molta importanza.

Architects: Norman Foster & Partners

Location: Essen, Germany

Photographs: Nigel Young

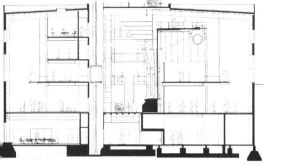

During its construction, the façade was remodeled, and elements that did not fit with the compositional language of its original design were eliminated. The chimney had to be demolished due to problems with its stability.

On the inside, the team of architects decided to highlight the building's industrial use, brutally exposing the original structure with almost no additional element or treatment.

Durante la construcción, la fachada fue rehabilitada y se eliminaron elementos que no pertenecían al lenguaje compositivo de su diseño original. La chimenea tuvo que ser demolida por problemas de estabilidad.

En el interior, el equipo de arquitectos decidió potenciar su pasado industrial descubriendo brutalmente la estructura original sin apenas elemento alguno o tratamiento adicional.

Durante la costruzione, è stata restaurata la facciata e sono stati eliminati elementi che non appartenevano al linguaggio compositivo del progetto originale. La ciminiera è stata demolita per problemi di stabilità.

All'interno, il team di architetti ha deciso di potenziare il suo passato industriale mettendo drasticamente a nudo tutta la struttura originale con pochi elementi o trattamenti supplementari.

Nuremberg
Núremberg / Norimberga

Wirth

These offices are located in an old industrial zone on the outskirts of Nuremberg. The plan, designed by the Wirth team, occupies a large warehouse with virtually no internal partitions.

The client wanted a single space in which to place all the tables, since the company's spirit is to avoid any type of hierarchy within the headquarters, encouraging teamwork and communication among the different working teams.

In accordance with these precepts, the architects placed no walls. They limited themselves to restoring the original space with a great deal of sensitivity and common sense. In order to retain the skylights, which are typical of the manufacturing idiom and useful for providing natural daylight all day long, the installations were hidden inside several tubes crisscrossing the space in both directions without dampening the overall perception of the space. The lighting is made of stainless steel which calls to mind the building's industrial past.

Estas oficinas están ubicadas en una antigua zona industrial de las afueras de Núremberg. El proyecto, ideado por el grupo Wirth, ocupa una gran nave que apenas tiene particiones verticales.

El cliente deseaba un único espacio donde colocar todas las mesas, ya que el espíritu de la empresa es rehuir cualquier tipo de jerarquía dentro de la sede, facilitar el trabajo en equipo y potenciar la comunicación entre los distintos equipos de trabajadores.

Siguiendo tales preceptos, los arquitectos no levantaron ningún tabique. Se limitaron a restaurar y habilitar el espacio original con gran sensibilidad y sentido común. Para mantener los lucernarios, típicos del lenguaje fabril y tan útiles para proporcionar luz natural durante todo el día, se colocaron las instalaciones en unos pocos tubos que cruzan la estancia en las dos direcciones principales sin enturbiar la percepción global del espacio. Las luminarias son de acero inoxidable y recuerdan el pasado industrial de la edificación.

Questi uffici sono situati in una vecchia zona industriale della periferia di Norimberga. Il progetto, ideato dal gruppo Wirth, occupa un gran capannone che quasi non ha muri divisori.

Il cliente desiderava un unico spazio dove collocare tutti i tavoli, visto che lo spirito dell'impresa è evitare qualsiasi tipo di gerarchia dentro la sede, facilitare il lavoro di gruppo e potenziare la comunicazione tra i diversi team di dipendenti.

Seguendo tali precetti, gli architetti non hanno progettato nessun tramozzo, ma si sono limitati a restaurare e ristrutturare lo spazio originale con notevole sensibilità e senso comune. Per conservare i lucernari, tipici del linguaggio industriale e tanto utili per sfruttare al massimo la luce naturale tutto il giorno, gli impianti sono stati collocati in pochi tubi che attraversano il locale nelle due direzioni principali senza intorbidare la percezione globale dello spazio. Le lampade sono di acciaio inossidabile e ricordano il passato industriale dell'edificio.

Architects: Wirth

Location: Nuremberg, Germany

Photographs: Karin Hessman/Artur

The photograph above shows the initial state in which the building was found.

La foto superior muestra cuál era el estado inicial en que se encontraba la edificación.

La foto in alto mostra lo stato dell'edificio prima della ristrutturazione.

Michaelides & Bednash

Buschow Henley

Through a series of minimal, restrictive interventions made on the third floor of a true art deco factory in the center of London, the architects Buschow Henley have designed a space that is full of surprises, intrigue, charm and provocative interior movement.

The client, Michaelides & Bednash, is an innovative firm specializing in communication strategies whose requirements for the new project were that it be original, challenging, provocative and suited to the space. These premises constituted the point of departure for a free-ranging discussion on functional simplicity and visual purity.

The structure suggests a series of intertwined "psychological" zones that define potential working areas. One of these mechanisms, within the hierarchical system of the intervention, consists of the design of a table at which each person works individually, but that is equipped with all the equipment needed in order for all the people on the team to meet around it.

Mediante una serie de mínimas y restrictivas intervenciones practicadas en la tercera planta de una auténtica fábrica *art déco* del centro de Londres, los arquitectos Buschow Henley han proyectado un espacio lleno de sorpresas, intriga, encanto y sugerente movimiento interior.

El cliente, Michaelides & Bednash, es una compañía innovadora de estrategias de la comunicación cuyas órdenes para la nueva propuesta eran que fuera original, desafiante, sugerente y acorde al lugar. Estas premisas constituyeron el punto de partida de una discusión liberada a favor de la sencillez funcional y la pureza visual.

La estructura plantea una serie de zonas «psicológicas» entrelazadas que definen áreas potenciales de trabajo. Uno de estos mecanismos, dentro del sistema jerarquizado de la intervención, consiste en el diseño de una mesa en la que cada persona trabaja de forma individual, pero que está equipada con todos los servicios que se requieren para reunir a su alrededor al personal del equipo.

Mediante una serie di interventi minimi e limitati effettuati al terzo piano di autentica fabbrica Art Déco nel centro di Londra, gli architetti Buschow Henley hanno progettato uno spazio pieno di sorprese, suspense, incanto e che evoca il movimento interno.

Il desiderio del cliente, Michaelides & Bednash, un'innovatrice azienda di strategie della comunicazione, era che la proposta fosse originale, audace, evocativa e consona al luogo. Queste premesse sono state il punto di partenza di una discussione libera a favore della semplicità funzionale e della purezza visuale.

La struttura offre una serie di zone «psicologiche» incrociate che definiscono aree potenziali di lavoro. Uno di questi meccanismi, dentro il sistema gerarchico dell'intervento, consiste nel progetto di un tavolo su cui ciascuna persona lavora individualmente, ma che è dotato di tutti i servizi necessari per riunire i membri del team.

Architects: Buschow Henley

Location: London, United Kingdom

Photographs: Nick Kane/Arcaid

The product resulting from manipulating space and psychology is a universally attractive installation, equally appropriate as a living area, a working zone or a public forum.

El producto resultante de manipular espacio y psicología es una instalación de atractivo universal, igualmente apto para vivienda, oficina o foro público.

Il prodotto che risulta dalla manipolazione dello spazio e della psicologia è una struttura che possiede un fascino universale, adatta ad essere adibita in ugual misura ad abitazione, ufficio o spazio pubblico.

Shepherd's Bush Studios

John McAslan
& Partners

The remodeling of this warehouse with a concrete structure covers a total of 3.000 m² laid out in a three-level structure.

The inside of the construction was organized around a new vertical opening that is three stories high and opens the warehouse's central axis onto a large horizontal window that allows for the vertical connection of the spaces, thus organizing the other spaces at either end of the warehouse. All movement revolves around it and the interactions that take place when the building is operating take place around this central connecting nucleus. On the roof, a skylight crowns this nucleus and provides lighting from above that reaches down to the lowest floor.

La reforma de este almacén de estructura de hormigón abarca un total de 3.000 m² distribuidos en un armazón de tres niveles.

El interior de la construcción se organizó en torno a una nueva abertura vertical que abarca tres pisos de altura y que abre en el eje central de la nave una gran ventana horizontal que permite la conexión vertical de los espacios, organizando a ambos extremos de la nave el resto de dependencias. Alrededor de este núcleo central de comunicaciones se resuelve toda la circulación y se establecen las interacciones propias del edificio en pleno funcionamiento. En cubierta, un lucernario corona este núcleo y aporta la luz cenital que cae rasante hasta la última planta.

La ristrutturazione di questo magazzino formato da una struttura di cemento comprende un totale di 3.000 m² distribuiti su 3 livelli.

L'interno della costruzione è stato organizzato attorno a una nuova apertura verticale che comprende 3 piani e apre nell'asse centrale dell'edificio una grande finestra orizzontale che consente la connessione verticale degli spazi, organizzando ad entrambi gli estremi dell'edificio il resto dei locali. Intorno a questo nucleo centrale di comunicazioni si svolge tutta la circolazione e si creano tutte le interazioni proprie dell'edificio in pieno funzionamento. Sul tetto, un lucernario corona questo nucleo e apporta la luce che scende radente fino all'ultimo piano.

Architects: John McAslan & Partners

Location: London, United Kingdom

Photographs: Richard Bryant/Arcaid

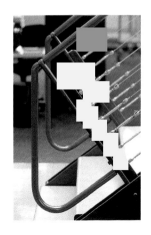

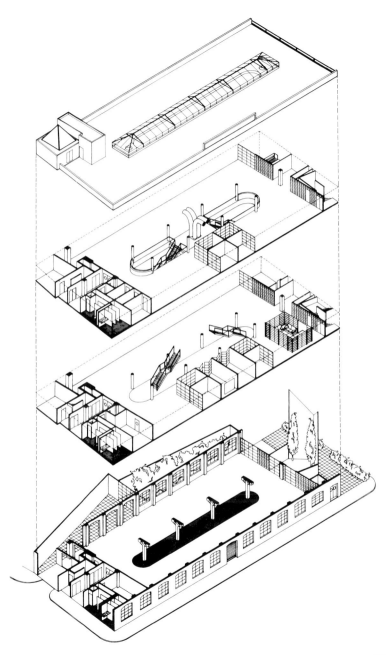

London Merchant Securities

John McAslan
& Partners

In an intervention of 17,500 m², this design combines the renovation of an important industrial building from the 1920s with the construction of a new office building that will house two activities: administration and a design studio.

Part of the original older building had to be demolished in order to allow for the construction of the new building that borders Rosebery Avenue and presents a refined, well-proportioned, detailed glass façade.

At all times the intention and desire to adapt the old structure to the new operational needs was taken into account, and this involved the adaptation of the old building in a daring contrast with the modernized services and utilities. The movement and service areas are concentrated in a new glass construction that has been placed at the point of intersection between both buildings (the pre-existing one and the newly designed one). Once the entire project is completed, the building complex will showcase the obvious, intentional contrast between modernity and history, which is reflected above all in the materials used.

En una intervención que abarca 17.500 m², el proyecto combina la rehabilitación de un importante edificio industrial de los años veinte con la construcción de un nuevo edificio de oficinas que acogerá dos actividades: administración y estudio de diseño.

Parte del edificio antiguo original tuvo que ser demolido para permitir la construcción del edificio de nueva planta que linda con la Rosebery Avenue y que se presenta con una fachada de cristal refinada, bien proporcionada y detallada.

En todo momento se tuvo la intención y la buena voluntad de adaptar la antigua estructura a las nuevas necesidades que aportaba el programa de funciones, lo cual implicó la readaptación de la misma en un atrevido contraste de puesta al día de los servicios e instalaciones de nueva implantación. La circulación y las áreas de servicio se concentran en una construcción nueva de cristal que se ha ubicado en el punto de intersección de ambos bloques (el preexistente y el de nueva planta). El complejo de edificios supone, una vez terminada toda la obra, el contraste evidente e intencionado entre lo nuevo y lo antiguo, entre modernidad e historia, y se refleja, sobre todo, en la elección de los materiales.

In un intervento che riguarda 17.500 m², il progetto combina la ristrutturazione di un importante edificio industriale degli anni Venti con la costruzione di un nuovo edificio di uffici che ospiterà due attività: amministrazione e studio di design.

Parte del vecchio edificio è stato demolito per consentire la costruzione del nuovo edificio che è adiacente alla Rosebery Avenue e vanta una facciata di vetro raffinata, ben proporzionata e dettagliata.

In ogni momento, hanno prevalso l'intenzione e la buona volontà di adattare la vecchia struttura alle nuove necessità richieste dal programma di attività, il quale ha implicato il riadattamento della stessa in un audace contrasto di servizi rinnovati e nuovi impianti. La circolazione e le aree di servizio si concentrano in una costruzione nuova di vetro che è stata collocata nel punto di intersezione di entrambi gli edifici (il preesistente e quello nuovo). Il complesso di edifici implica, una volta terminati tutti i lavori, il contrasto evidente e voluto tra il nuovo il vecchio, tra la modernità e la storia e si riflette soprattutto nella scelta dei materiali.

Architects: John McAslan & Partners

Location: London, United Kingdom

Photographs: Peter Cook/View

Side view   Sección   Sezione

The transition between the new and old building is reflected in the intentionally distinct treatment applied to the finishes.

La transición entre el edificio nuevo y el viejo se refleja en el tratamiento desigual e intencionado que se ha aplicado a los acabados.

La transizione tra l'edificio nuovo e il vecchio si riflette nel trattamento disuguale e voluto applicato alle rifiniture.

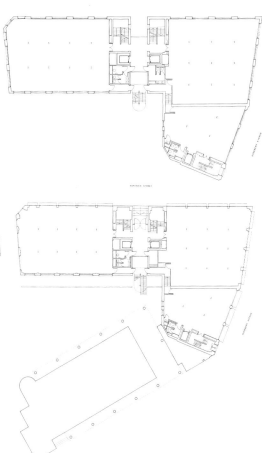

Advertising Agency
Agencia de publicidad / Agenzia di pubblicità

John McAslan
& Partners

This intervention on St. Peter's Street consisted of the re-conversion of a 800 m² Victorian warehouse into the studios for an advertising agency.

One of the main objectives of the intervention was to maintain the warehouse's original structure. The project proposed a double-high access façade that leads to the building's interior patio. The entrance space presents an exceptional elegant staircase that is a mediating element between the old façade and the back façade, which opens onto the patio. The configuration of this latter wall onto the patio consisted of a double window that echoes the double interior space and that is actually a double door on the lower level, along with a wall made of translucent concrete pieces that skillfully echoes the warehouse's interior layout. A large metallic beam organizes the façade's horizontal composition and serves as a frame for the translucent glass-brick wall, which is a reference to the architect Pierre Charreau's Maison de Verre.

La intervención en St. Peter's Street consistió en la reconversión de un almacén victoriano, de 800 m², en los estudios de una agencia de publicidad.

Uno de los objetivos principales de la intervención fue mantener la estructura original del almacén. El proyecto plantea una fachada de acceso a doble altura haciendo eco de la fachada que se resuelve en el patio interior del edificio. El espacio de entrada presenta una excepcional y elegante escalera que es el elemento mediador entre la antigua fachada y la posterior, que se abre al patio. La configuración de este último alzado al patio consiste en una doble ventana que reproduce el doble espacio interior y que es una doble puerta en planta baja, junto con una pared de piezas de hormigón translúcido que hábilmente reproduce la distribución interior de la nave. Una gran viga metálica estructura la composición horizontal de la fachada y sirve de marco a la pared translúcida de pavés, que es una referencia a la Maison de Verre del arquitecto Pierre Charreau.

Il progetto in St. Peter's Street prevedeva la ristrutturazione di un magazzino vittoriano di 800 m² per ubicare la sede di un'agenzia di pubblicità.

Uno degli obiettivi principali dell'intervento era conservare la struttura originale dell'edificio. Il progetto comprende una facciata di accesso a doppia altezza che è l'eco della facciata che dà sul patio interno dell'edificio. Lo spazio dell'entrata presenta un'eccezionale ed elegante scala, che è l'elemento mediatore tra la vecchia facciata e quella nuova, che si affaccia sul patio. La configurazione di quest'ultimo fronte rivolto al patio consiste di una doppia finestra che mostra il doppio spazio interno e di una doppia porta al piano terra, accanto a una parete di vetrocemento che abilmente lascia intravedere la distribuzione interna dell'edificio. Una grande trave metallica struttura la composizione orizzontale della facciata e serve da cornice alla parete semitrasparente che ricorda la Maison de Verre dell'architetto Pierre Charreau.

Architects: John McAslan & Partners

Location: London, United Kingdom

Photographs: Peter Cook/View

Composition of the façade
opening onto the interior patio.

Composición de la fachada
abierta al patio interior.

Composizione della facciata che
guarda sul patio interno.

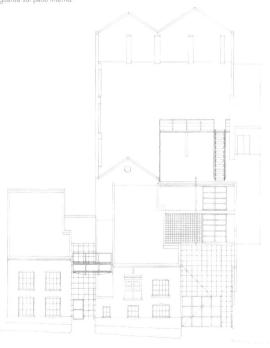

The only walls in the building are those
that make up the premises and the new
interior access façades.

Las únicas paredes del edificio son las
que conforman el recinto y las nuevas
fachadas de acceso a su interior.

Le uniche pareti dell'edificio sono quelle
che formano il perimetro e le nuove
facciate di accesso al suo interno.

Derwent Valley Holding

John McAslan
& Partners

The building that was restored to house the offices of Derwent Valley was completed in 1990. During the conversion, the point of departure was a 600 m² industrial warehouse that in conventional terms had no architectural qualities: an elementary roof dating from the year 1950 was found in terrible condition with its original but not noteworthy structure.

The renovation plan converted the building into a provocative working space through the application of simple parameters: special attention to the use of natural daylight, repairs to the warehouse's original finishes, and the insertion of a mezzanine along the entire inside space on only one side.

This new floor is supported by circular concrete pillars which are quite beautiful due to their careful and original joining with the upper floor. Attention to the use and combination of materials distinguishes any design: the exposed brick walls were simply painted and the oak floor was cleaned and varnished.

El edificio restaurado para habilitar las oficinas de la Derwent Valley fue completado en 1990. Durante la conversión, el punto de partida era una nave industrial de 600 m² que, en términos convencionales, no disponía de ningún interés arquitectónico: un elemental cobertizo en estado lamentable, datado en el año 1950, con una estructura original aunque poco destacable.

El proyecto de intervención convirtió el edificio en un sugerente lugar de trabajo mediante la aplicación de sencillos parámetros: especial atención al empleo de la luz natural, reparación de los acabados originales de la nave e inserción de una entreplanta a todo lo largo del espacio interior y únicamente en uno de sus lados.

Esta nueva planta está soportada por unos pilares circulares de hormigón de gran belleza debido a su cuidada y original entrega con la tarima del piso superior. La atención en el uso y la combinación de los materiales distinguen cualquier actuación del proyecto: las paredes de obra de ladrillo visto fueron simplemente pintadas y el suelo de madera de roble, limpiado y barnizado.

L'edificio, restaurato per ospitare gli uffici della Derwent Valley, fu completato nel 1990. Durante la ristrutturazione, il punto di partenza era una costruzione industriale di 600 m² che, in termini convenzionali, non era di nessun interesse architettonico: una semplice tettoia in pessimo stato risalente al 1950, con una struttura originale di scarsa importanza.

Il progetto ha trasformato l'edificio in un suggestivo luogo di lavoro tramite l'applicazione di parametri semplici: un'attenzione particolare per l'impiego della luce naturale, la riparazione delle rifiniture originali della costruzione e l'aggiunta di un soppalco per tutta la lunghezza dello spazio interno e solamente su un lato.

Questo nuovo piano è supportato da dei pilastri circolari di cemento di grande bellezza grazie all'accurato e originale addentellato del livello superiore. La cura nell'utilizzo e nella combinazione dei materiali distingue tutti gli elementi del progetto: le pareti di mattoni a vista sono state semplicemente dipinte e il pavimento di legno di rovere, pulito e verniciato.

Architects: John McAslan & Partners

Location: London, United Kingdom

Photographs: Peter Cook/View

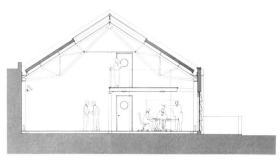

Side view   Sección transversal   Sezione trasversale

The asymmetry introduced by
the mezzanine enriches the
space with a balcony and a
ceiling with a different height.

La asimetría que introduce
la entreplanta enriquece el
espacio con un balcón y
un techo a otra altura.

L'asimmetria apportata dal
soppalco arricchisce lo
spazio con un ballatoio e
un soffitto a diversa altezza.

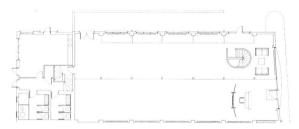

Top view   Planta de distribución   Pianta di distribuzione

553

Thames & Hudson Offices
Oficinas Thames & Hudson / Uffici di Thames & Hudson

John McAslan
& Partners

The English publishing house, Thames & Hudson charged the architectural team of John McAslan & Partners with the restoration of an old warehouse from 1930 located in London's West End. The building houses the new publishing house's headquarters in 2,000 m², in which equal attention is paid to the functional layout and to the design of the furniture which must accommodate approximately 120 persons.

The plan's scope of application was resolved rationally around an atrium located in the central axis of the building, which houses inside a library with a collection of approximately 12,000 volumes used for reference by the publishing house's production staff. The open floor plan is maintained on each of the building's levels, and visual communication between floors is made patently clear through three vertical connections that are open to the stairs, which are likewise located in the central axis. Various isolated nuclei, which are also organized around the central nucleus, contain the utilities and other maintenance elements. The offices and study areas are located lengthwise along the entire space in an orderly manner, and are open to the central atrium that visually connects the entire building.

La editorial anglosajona Thames & Hudson encargó al equipo de arquitectura John McAslan & Partners la restauración de un antiguo almacén de 1930 ubicado en el West End de Londres. El edificio alberga la nueva sede de la empresa editorial en 2.000 m², en los que se presta igual atención a la distribución del programa de funciones que al diseño del mobiliario, destinado a acomodar a unas 120 personas.

El ámbito de aplicación del programa se resuelve de manera racional en torno a un atrio situado en el eje central de la pieza, que incorpora en su interior una biblioteca con unos 20.000 ejemplares donde se puede consultar la producción propia de la editorial. La planta libre se mantiene en cada uno de los niveles del edificio y la comunicación visual entre ellos se hace patente mediante los núcleos verticales abiertos de las escaleras, igualmente ubicadas en el eje central de distribución. Varios núcleos aislados, igualmente dispuestos en el eje central, contienen los servicios y otros elementos de mantenimiento. Las oficinas y zonas de estudio se ubican longitudinalmente a todo lo largo de cada pieza de forma ordenada y abiertas al atrio central de comunicación que visualmente conecta con todo el edificio.

La casa editrice anglosassone Thames & Hudson ha affidato allo studio di architettura John McAslan & Partners il restauro di un vecchio magazzino del 1930 situato nel West End di Londra. L'edificio ospita la nuova sede della casa editrice in una superficie di 2.000 m², in cui è stata prestata la stessa cura nella distribuzione del programma di funzioni e nel design degli arredi, destinati ad accogliere circa 120 persone.

L'ambito di applicazione del programma si articola in maniera razionale attorno a un atrio situato sull'asse centrale del locale, che comprende al suo interno una biblioteca con circa 20.000 esemplari, dove è possibile consultare tutta la produzione della casa editrice. Tutti i piani dell'edificio sono a pianta aperta e la comunicazione visuale tra loro si rende evidente tramite i nuclei verticali aperti delle scale, anch'esse ubicate nell'asse centrale di distribuzione. Vari nuclei isolati sono inoltre situati sull'asse centrale e contengono i servizi e gli altri articoli di manutenzione. Gli uffici e le zone di studio sono posizionati longitudinalmente in tutta la lunghezza di ciascun locale in forma ordinata e aperta rispetto all'atrio centrale di comunicazione che visivamente collega tutto l'edificio.

Architects: John McAslan & Partners

Location: London, United Kingdom

Photographs: Peter Cook/View

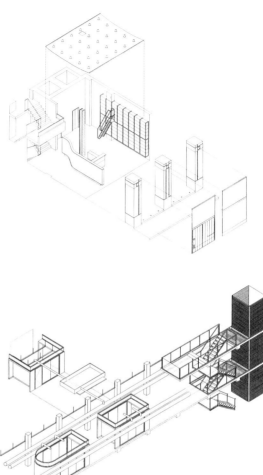

In this project, the placement of the air conditioning installation system represents a main organizing element that underlines the linear, rational floor plans.

La disposición del sistema de instalaciones del aire acondicionado representa en este proyecto un elemento estructurador principal que subraya la disposición lineal y racional de las plantas.

La disposizione dell'impianto di aerazione in questo progetto rappresenta un elemento principale della struttura, che sottolinea la disposizione lineare e razionale dei piani.

All the elements in the project are organized lengthwise, following the linear placement imposed by the building's structural pillars.

Todos los elementos del proyecto se organizan longitudinalmente según la disposición lineal impuesta por la estructura de pilares del edificio.

Tutti gli elementi del progetto sono organizzati longitudinalmente secondo una disposizione lineare imposta dalla struttura dei pilastri dell'edificio.

559

Williams Murray Banks

Pierre d'Avoine Architects

Williams Murray Banks (WMB) is a recently-formed graphic design and packaging company with headquarters in Heal's Building on London's West End. The design by Pierre d'Avoine Architects consists of remodeling two of its spaces: the main office (a large room 30 meters long by 6.5 meters wide and 2.7 meters high) and a small meeting room.

WMB wanted the main office to be an adaptable space that would normally be open on all sides, but that would also be capable of providing three independent offices when needed.

Almost all the new elements are located around a central axis covered by a wooden hanging ceiling. The tables, shelving, closets and benches set a rhythm along the length of the axis, which work as if they were a graphic scale. The existing structure (ceilings and perimeter walls) have been painted in a pale whitish tone; the concrete floor has been varnished in graphite.

Williams Murray Banks (WMB) es una empresa reciente de diseño gráfico y embalaje con sede en el Heal's Building del West End londinense. El proyecto de Pierre d'Avoine Architects consiste en la remodelación de dos de sus espacios: la oficina principal (una gran sala de 30 metros de longitud por 6,5 metros de anchura y 2,7 metros de altura) y una pequeña sala de reuniones.

WMB quería que la oficina principal fuese un espacio adaptable, normalmente abierto en todas las direcciones, pero también capaz de proporcionar tres oficinas independientes cuando fuera necesario.

Prácticamente todos los nuevos elementos se sitúan en un eje central cubierto por un falso techo de madera. Las mesas, las estanterías, los armarios y los bancos marcan un ritmo a lo largo del eje que funciona como si se tratase de una escala gráfica. La estructura existente (techos y muros perimetrales) se ha pintado en un tono pálido próximo al blanco; el suelo de hormigón se ha laqueado al grafito.

Williams Murray Banks (WMB) è uno studio di disegno grafico e imballaggi di fondazione recente con sede nell'Heal's Building del West End londinese. Il progetto dello studio Pierre d'Avoine Architects consiste nella ristrutturazione dei suoi due spazi: l'ufficio principale (una grande sala lunga 30 metri, larga 6,5 e alta 2,7 metri) e una piccola sala riunioni.

WMB voleva che l'ufficio principale fosse uno spazio flessibile, normalmente aperto in tutte le direzioni, ma che allo stesso tempo potesse essere diviso in tre uffici indipendenti, in caso di necessità.

Praticamente, tutti i nuovi elementi sono situati su un asse centrale coperto da un controsoffitto di legno. I tavoli, gli scaffali, gli armadi e le panchine seguono un ritmo lungo l'asse che funziona come se si trattasse di una scala grafica. La struttura esistente (il soffitto e le pareti perimetrali) è stata dipinta con una tonalità pallida simile al bianco; il pavimento di cemento è stato laccato con grafite.

Architects: Pierre d'Avoine Architects

Location: London, United Kingdom

Photographs: David Grandgorge

The architect's strategy was to emphasize the relationship between the extraordinary length of the room and its low ceilings. The walls and similar-sized doors have been replaced by sliding panels that serve both functions at the same time.

La estrategia de los arquitectos fue enfatizar la relación entre la extraordinaria longitud de la sala y su poca altura. Los muros y las puertas de tamaño similar han sido sustituidos por paneles correderos que hacen de ambas cosas a la vez.

La strategia degli architetti è stata enfatizzare la relazione tra la straordinaria longitudine e l'altezza ridotta della sala. I muri e le porte di dimensioni simili sono stati sostituiti con pannelli scorrevoli che svolgono entrambe le funzioni.

Metropolis Studios Ltd.

Powell-Tuck,
Connor & Orefelt

The company Metropolis Studios Ltd. obtained the needed municipal permits in order to redesign part of the building where the old electrical power plant in Chiswick, London had been located as a recording studio.

The initial requirements were total respect for the building's old structural elements, which dated from the 19th century, and rigorous sound proofing, which was obligatory due to its proximity to a residential area. They opted to create a spacious interior container that would house all the functions within the walls of the old building without actually touching them.

The design of the structures is defined along a central atrium, defining the premises as a system of asymmetrical volumes connected via multi-directional ramps and stairways. The service and bar area can be accessed from the platform in the reception and office area; a suspended ramp leads to the second floor on which the recording studios are located. On a higher level, a slightly tilted façade isolates the smaller area of technical studios.

La compañía Metropolis Studios Ltd. obtuvo los permisos municipales necesarios para proyectar en parte del edificio de la antigua central eléctrica de Chiswick, en Londres, un centro de grabaciones.

Los requisitos iniciales eran el absoluto respeto por las viejas estructuras del edificio, del siglo XIX, y un riguroso control acústico, obligado por la proximidad de un conjunto de viviendas. Se optó por la creación de un amplio contenedor interior que acogiera todas las funciones dentro de las paredes del antiguo edificio, sin llegar nunca a tocarlas.

El diseño de estructuras se articuló en torno al atrio central, definiendo el local como un sistema de prismas asimétricos comunicados mediante rampas y escaleras multidireccionales. Desde la plataforma de la zona de recepción y oficinas se accede a la superficie de servicios y al bar; una rampa suspendida conduce al segundo piso, en el que se encuentra el resto de las salas de grabación. En el nivel más elevado, una fachada ligeramente inclinada aísla el área de estudios técnicos menores.

La società Metropolis Studios Ltd. ottenne i permessi municipali necessari per progettare uno studio di registrazione in una parte dell'edificio della vecchia centrale elettrica di Chiswick, a Londra.

I requisiti iniziali erano il rispetto assoluto delle vecchie strutture dell'edificio del XIX secolo e un rigoroso controllo acustico, a causa della sua prossimità ad abitazioni. Si optò per la creazione di un grande contenitore interno che potesse accogliere tutte le strutture, entro le pareti del vecchio edificio senza arrivare mai a toccarle.

Il progetto delle strutture si articola attorno all'atrio centrale, definendo il locale come un sistema di prismi asimmetrici collegati da rampe e scale multidirezionali. Dalla piattaforma della zona di ricevimento e degli uffici si accede all'area dei servizi e al bar; una rampa sospesa conduce al secondo piano, nel quale è situato il resto delle sale di registrazione. Nel livello più alto, una facciata leggermente inclinata isola l'area degli studi tecnici minori.

Architects: Powell-Tuck, Connor & Orefelt

Location: London, United Kingdom

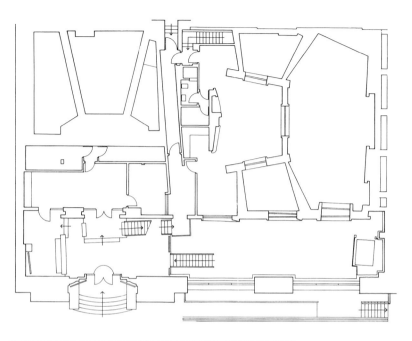

Layout of the top floor of the
building with the smaller
technical studios and the
mixing rooms.

Planta del último nivel del
edificio con los estudios técnicos
de menores proporciones y las
salas de mezclas.

Pianta dell'ultimo livello
dell'edificio con gli studi tecnici
più piccoli e le sale di missaggio.

Studio in Glasgow
Estudio en Glasgow / Studio a Glasgow

Anderson Christie
Architects

The space in which Anderson and Christie decided to located their offices had been an old bakery. Although its perimeter was highly irregular in shape, the space had interesting features, such as large steel bread ovens, exposed brick walls and metallic structural elements. The treated walls were painted in intense colors in order to exaggerate the contrast with the unrestored surfaces and create chromatic focal points. The brick and stone were conserved in certain areas.

In a parallel fashion, given the flimsy state of the existing ceilings, new floors were built. Above all of them a concrete surface was placed in situ, concrete being another material whose use on the floor and whose type of finish help call to mind the industrial construction idiom.

The project's sophistication lies in the details that make up the main elements organizing the interior space: the stairways, banisters, partitions, artificial lighting, doors and the choice of furniture.

El local en el que Anderson y Christie decidieron situar su despacho había sido una antigua panadería. Aunque su perímetro era muy irregular, el local tenía características interesantes, pues contaba con grandes hornos de acero para el pan, muros de ladrillo visto y estructura metálica. Las paredes tratadas se pintaron con colores muy intensos para exagerar el contraste con las superficies no restauradas y crear focos cromáticos. En determinadas zonas se ha conservado el ladrillo y la piedra.

Paralelamente, se construyeron nuevos forjados debido al precario estado de los existentes. Sobre todos ellos se colocó un pavimento de hormigón in situ, otro de los materiales cuyo vertido en el suelo y tipo de acabado ayudan a recordar el lenguaje constructivo industrial.

La sofisticación del proyecto se centró en los detalles que configuran los principales elementos de estructuración del espacio interior: las escaleras, las barandillas, las particiones, la iluminación artificial, las puertas o la selección del mobiliario.

Il locale in cui Anderson e Christie ha deciso di ubicare il suo studio era un vecchio panificio. Sebbene il perimetro fosse molto irregolare, il locale aveva caratteristiche interessanti: disponeva di grandi forni di acciaio per il pane, muri di mattoni a vista e una struttura metallica. Le pareti trattate sono state dipinte con colori molto intensi per creare un forte contrasto con le superfici non restaurate e creare fuochi cromatici. In determinate zone sono stati conservati i mattoni e la pietra.

Parallelamente, sono state costruite nuove solette, a causa dello stato precario di quelle esistenti. Sopra di esse è stato collocato un pavimento di cemento, un altro dei materiali che per struttura e tipo di finitura ricordano il linguaggio costruttivo industriale.

La sofisticazione del progetto è stata incentrata nei dettagli che rappresentano i principali elementi della strutturazione dello spazio interno: le scale, le ringhiere, le partizioni, l'illuminazione artificiale, le porte o la scelta dell'arredamento.

Architects: Anderson Christie Architects

Location: Glasgow, United Kingdom

Photographs: Kevin McCourt

The studio is located on a main street in Glasgow's West End. The entrance to the space is the ground floor of a Victorian-style housing building, while the back part, containing the ovens from the old bakery, contains the working area.

El estudio se encuentra en una calle importante del West End de Glasgow. La entrada del local es la planta baja de un edificio de viviendas de estilo victoriano, mientras que la parte trasera, que corresponde a los hornos de la vieja panadería, contiene la zona de trabajo.

Lo studio si trova in una via principale del West End di Glasgow. L'entrata del locale è al piano terra di un edificio di abitazioni in stile vittoriano, mentre sul retro in cui erano situati i forni del vecchio panificio, c'è la zona di lavoro.

Ground floor   Planta baja   Piano terra

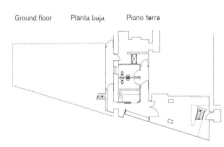

First floor   Planta primera   Primo piano

Second floor   Planta segunda   Secondo piano

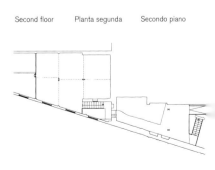

Labotron. Offices and workshops

Labotron. Oficinas y talleres / Labotron. Uffici e atelier

Pep Zazurca i Codolà

The purpose of the project was to make maximum use of natural daylight, which barely manages to enter from the street through skylights that cut across the roof of the large rear space of the premises.

Following this criteria, it was decided to eliminate intermediate partitions and thus foster fluidity, both physical and visual, throughout the entire space.

It is accessed via a hallway, where the reception counter is located, behind a entrance door made entirely of glass. The large space that the corridor opens onto contains the administrative area and the offices. Another hallway houses the workshop and receives natural daylight though its opening to the street, although it is visually protected by a acid-treated matte window. Finally, both hallways, which run parallel to the central walls, reach the central space, making a series of cubicles which contain the utilities and storage areas.

La finalidad del proyecto ha sido aprovechar al máximo la luz natural, que apenas llega desde la calle a través de las claraboyas que recortan la cubierta del gran espacio trasero del local.

Siguiendo este criterio, se decidió prescindir de las particiones intermedias y potenciar así la fluidez, tanto física como visual, en todo el espacio.

Se accede a través de un pasillo, donde se ubica el mostrador de recepción, tras una puerta de entrada totalmente acristalada. El gran espacio al que se abre el corredor contiene la zona de administración y los despachos. Otro pasillo alberga el taller y recibe la luz natural a través de su abertura a la calle, visualmente protegida con un cristal mate tratado al ácido. Finalmente, ambos pasillos, paralelos a las paredes medianeras, llegan al espacio central formando una serie de cubículos que contienen los servicios y los almacenes.

La finalità del progetto è stata sfruttare al massimo la poca luce naturale che arrivava dalla strada attraverso i lucernari del tetto del grande spazio sul retro del locale.

Seguendo questo criterio, si è deciso di eliminare le partizioni intermedie e di potenziare la fluidità, sia fisica che visuale, in tutto lo spazio.

La porta d'entrata totalmente di vetro conduce al corridoio, dove si trova il banco della reception. Alla fine del corridoio si arriva a un grande spazio che comprende la zona di amministrazione e gli uffici. Il laboratorio si trova in un altro corridoio che riceve luce naturale attraverso un'apertura che guarda sulla strada, protetta da un vetro opaco. Infine, entrambi i corridoi, paralleli alle pareti mezzane, conducono allo spazio centrale formato da una serie di box che contengono i servizi e i magazzini.

Architect: Pep Zazurca i Codolà

Location: Barcelona, Spain

Photographs: Eugeni Pons

The vertical dividers are light laminated wood panels, and they join the ceiling with a piece of glass that maintains visual continuity and maximizes the amount of daylight that enters.

Las separaciones verticales son paneles de madera laminada clara y la entrega con el cielo raso corre a cargo de una pieza de cristal que mantiene la continuidad visual y maximiza las entradas de luz.

Le partizioni verticali sono formate da pannelli di legno chiaro laminato con vetro nella parte superiore fino al soffitto, per mantenere la continuità visuale e massimizzare la diffusione della luce.

Crosswise view   Sección longitudinal   Sezione longitudinale

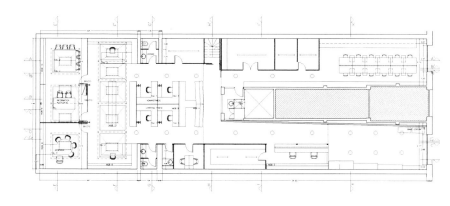

Floor plan   Planta de distribución   Pianta della distribuzione

Double You

Marc Viader i Oliva

Double You is an advertising and webpage design company. This team of creative professionals has installed its new headquarters in a 236 m² space within an industrial building in a residential area in the Barcelona neighborhood of Gracia.

The design, led by architect Marc Viader, is organized around three axes that define the entirety of the space. The three directives are three double rows of tables between which the cables feeding all the work stations run. The crosswise placement of these axes frees up for other uses the side façades with windows. In this way, we find that the main façade, facing a church, has 17 continuous meters of table on which a high working counter has been placed. And the façade facing the building's patio, on the access side of the space, marks the sequence of opposing volumes made by the opaque utility closet and the transparent cube containing the meeting room.

The tables are modular so that they can be placed according to the needs of each team for meetings at any given time. All the office furniture was designed with the same dynamic capacity and versatility with which the overall use of the space was envisioned.

Double You es una empresa de publicidad y diseño de páginas web. Este equipo de creativos ha instalado su nueva sede en un local de 236 m² que pertenece a un edificio industrial del tejido residencial del barrio de Gracia, en Barcelona.

El proyecto, ideado por el arquitecto Marc Viader, se organiza según tres ejes que articulan la totalidad del espacio. Las tres directrices son tres filas dobles de mesas entre las que circula el cableado que alimenta cada terminal de trabajo. La disposición transversal de estos ejes permite liberar las fachadas laterales de ventanas destinadas a otros usos. Así, encontramos que la fachada principal, frente a la iglesia, dispone de 17 metros continuos de mesa a todo lo largo que plantean un mostrador alto de trabajo. O bien la fachada que da al patio del edificio, en el eje de acceso al local, que pauta la secuencia de volúmenes opuestos que suponen la cabina opaca de servicios y el cubo transparente de la sala de reuniones.

La forma modular de las mesas permite disponerlas según la necesidad que cada equipo tenga de agruparse en un momento determinado. Todo el mobiliario de oficina se diseñó con la misma capacidad dinámica y versatilidad con que se ha concebido el uso global del espacio.

Double You è un'agenzia di pubblicità e progettazione di pagine Web. Questa equipe di creativi ha scelto di stabilire la propria sede in un locale di 236 m² che appartiene a un edificio industriale del tessuto residenziale del quartiere di Gràcia, a Barcellona.

Il progetto, ideato dall'architetto Marc Viader, si organizza secondo tre assi che articolano la totalità dello spazio. Le tre direttrici sono tre file doppie di tavoli tra cui circolano i cavi che alimentano i terminali. La disposizione trasversale di queste assi lasciano libere le facciate laterali delle finestre destinate ad altri usi. In questo modo, vediamo che lungo la facciata principale, di fronte alla chiesa, scorre un tavolo di 17 metri che funge da piano alto di lavoro. La facciata che è rivolta verso il patio dell'edificio, sull'asse di accesso del locale, crea la sequenza di volumi opposti che comprendono la cabina opaca dei servizi e il cubo trasparente della sala riunioni.

La forma modulare dei tavoli consente di disporli secondo le necessità di ciascun team in un determinato momento. Tutto l'arredamento degli uffici è stato progettato con la stessa capacità dinamica e versatilità con cui è stato concepito l'uso globale dello spazio.

Architect: Marc Viader i Oliva

Location: Barcelona, Spain

Photographs: Jordi Miralles

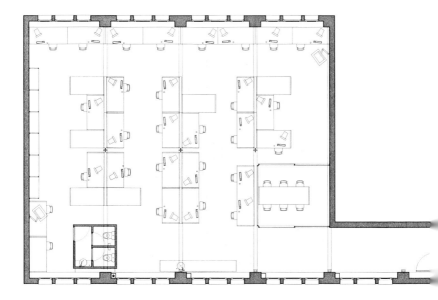

The stone wall and stained glass and rose windows of the church located across the street form part of the office's interior landscape.

El muro de piedra y los vitrales y rosetones de la iglesia situada al otro lado de la calle forman parte del paisaje interior del despacho.

Il muro di pietra, le vetrate colorate e i rosoni della chiesa situata sull'altro lato della strada formano parte del paesaggio interno dell'ufficio.

Hispano 20

José Ángel
Rodrigo García

The main objective of Hispano 20 was the creation of a specific corporate image for the offices designated for younger clients that could be adapted to any type of space. The designer developed a series of formal and aesthetic elements to create space.

Glass walls sinuously flow through the space and create transparent compartments, exposing the bank employees' activities to the public eye.

The most noteworthy element in its layout is the mezzanine, with a balcony that looks out onto the reception area and accesses to the front part of the offices. Two different levels can be distinguished on the ground floor: one near the façade where the cashiers are located, and another under the mezzanine, where the workplaces, the meeting room and a double-high area containing the journal library and money changing machines are located.

The lighting is centered around a profusion of dichromatic lamps embedded in the stuccoed hanging ceilings. Fluorescent lighting lies behind a large luminous lattice, and lights projecting onto the walls were hung on electric rails in the ceiling in the exhibition hall.

The furniture shows post-modern and avant-garde details in a daring mix of contrasts, in accordance with the image the company wish to convey to their new clients.

El objetivo principal de Hispano 20 era la creación de una imagen corporativa específica para las oficinas destinadas a los clientes más jóvenes y que pudiera ser adaptada a cualquier tipo de locales. El autor desarrolló una serie de elementos formales y estéticos creadores de espacios.

Unos muros de cristal recorren sinuosamente el local y crean compartimentos transparentes, mostrando la actividad de los trabajadores del banco a los ojos del público.

En su distribución, destacamos la entreplanta, que alberga una sala de exposiciones, con una balconada que da a la zona de recepción y accesos a la parte delantera de las oficinas. En la planta baja se distinguen dos niveles: uno próximo a la fachada, donde se sitúan las cajas, y otro bajo la entreplanta, donde se ubican los puestos de trabajo, la sala de reuniones y un área de doble nivel con hemeroteca y máquinas de cambio de moneda.

La iluminación se centra en una profusión de lámparas dicroicas empotradas en falsos techos de escayola. Detrás de la gran celosía luminosa se optó por la fluorescencia, y en la sala de exposiciones se situaron proyectores de pared sobre raíl electrificado en el techo.

El mobiliario tiene detalles posmodernos y vanguardistas en una mezcla atrevida de contrastes acorde con la imagen que desean transmitir a sus nuevos clientes.

L'obiettivo principale di Hispano 20 era la creazione di un'immagine aziendale specifica per gli uffici destinati ai clienti più giovani e che potesse essere adattata a qualsiasi tipo di locale. L'autore ha sviluppato una serie di elementi formali ed estetici creatori di spazi.

Pareti di vetro si snodano in modo sinuoso per il locale e creano compartimenti trasparenti, che consentono ai clienti di vedere l'attività dei dipendenti della banca.

Nella sua distribuzione, è degno di nota il piano rialzato che ospita una sala espositiva con una ringhiera che si affaccia sulla zona della reception e degli accessi alla parte anteriore degli uffici. Al piano terra si distinguono due livelli: uno vicino alla facciata, dove sono situate le casse e uno sotto il piano rialzato, dove si trovano i posti di lavoro, la sala di riunioni e un'area a doppio livello con un'emeroteca e macchine per il cambio di moneta.

L'illuminazione si basa su un'abbondanza di lampade dicroiche incassate nei controsoffitti. Dietro la grande gelosia luminosa si è optato per le luci al neon e nella sala espositiva sono stati collocati di proiettori da parete su una guida elettrificata sul soffitto.

L'arredamento ha dei dettagli postmoderni e avanguardisti in una combinazione audace di contrasti, in accordo con l'immagine che si desidera trasmettere ai nuovi clienti.

Architect: José Ángel Rodrigo García

Location: Barcelona, Spain

588

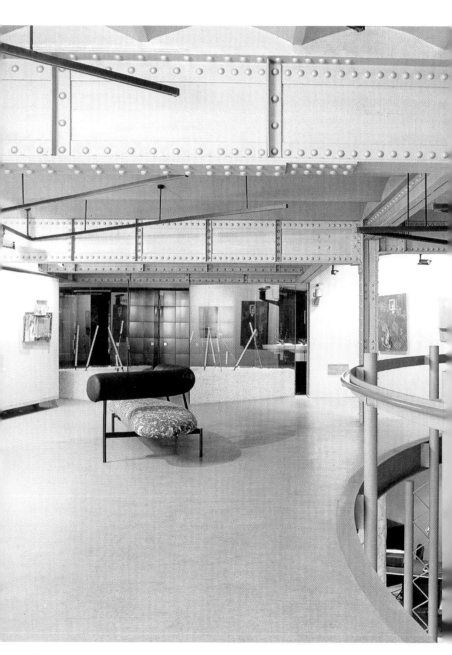

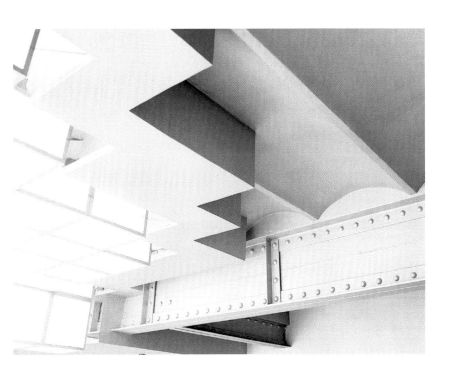

Montardit SA

Josep Juvé &
Núria Jolis

This well-known firm selling high quality food products entrusted the design of their main headquarters, offices and warehouse in the Barcelona Ensanche neighborhood to Josep Juvé & Núria Jolis's studio.

The space was a ground floor divided by a central nucleus that created two almost identical parts, with a façade facing the street. Thus, a single space was created that along its length integrates all the utilitarian needs of the agenda established by the promoters.

A tour through the indoor space begins with the access through the glass façade to the reception area, which has wooden floors and exposed brick walls. A crosswise wall, also covered in wood, divides the space in two: to the right is a waiting area and to the left a boardroom. The offices are accessed through a glass door on which the firm's letters (MT) are written. The furniture, which is functional and practical, is organized following the structure of the layout and creating different working areas. In the back, there are two separate spaces in the office area: a rest area and a new meeting room.

Esta reconocida firma comercial de productos alimenticios de alta calidad encargó al estudio de Josep Juvé & Núria Jolis el diseño de su sede principal, oficinas y almacén en un emplazamiento del Ensanche barcelonés.

El local era una planta baja dividida por un núcleo central que provocaba la formación de dos partes casi iguales, con fachada sobre la calle. Así se creó un espacio único que, a lo largo de su recorrido, integra todas las necesidades funcionales del programa establecido por los promotores.

El trayecto por el espacio interior se inicia con el acceso, a través de la fachada de vidrio, a la recepción, pavimentada en madera y con paredes de obra vista. Un paramento transversal, revestido también con madera, divide la planta en dos: a la derecha, una zona de espera y, a la izquierda, una sala de juntas. A las oficinas se accede mediante una puerta de cristal, con las letras emblemáticas de la firma. El mobiliario, funcional y práctico, se organiza siguiendo la estructura de la planta y creando las distintas zonas de trabajo. Al fondo, hay dos estancias separadas del sector de despachos: un área de descanso y una nueva sala de reuniones.

Questa conosciuta marca di alimentari di prima qualità ha affidato allo studio Josep Juvé & Núria Jolis la progettazione della sede principale, degli uffici e del magazzino in un locale dell'Ensanche barcellonese.

Il locale si trova al piano terra e consisteva in due parti quasi uguali divise da un nucleo centrale, con la facciata che dà sulla strada. Quindi, è stato creato uno spazio unico, soddisfando tutte le necessità funzionali del programma stabilito dagli imprenditori.

Il percorso dello spazio interno inizia con l'accesso, attraverso una porta di vetro, che conduce alla reception, con pavimento di legno e pareti di mattoni a vista. Un tramezzo trasversale, rivestito di legno, divide il piano in due: a destra una zona d'aspetto e a sinistra una sala riunioni direttive. Si accede agli uffici tramite una porta di vetro con il logo della ditta. L'arredamento, funzionale e pratico, si organizza in base alla struttura del piano e crea le distinte zone di lavoro. In fondo, ci sono due stanze separate dall'area degli uffici: un'area per i momenti di sosta e una nuova sala di riunioni.

Architects: Josep Juvé & Núria Jolis

Location: Barcelona, Spain

Photographs: Eugeni Pons

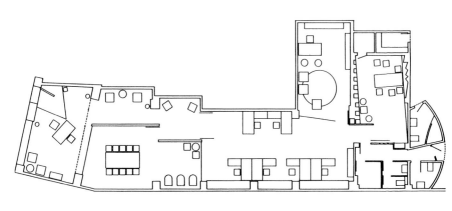

The spaces, which are opened or separated through glass walls, acts as a showcase of the professional activity while it also provides advertising for the company.

Las dependencias, abiertas o separadas mediante paramentos vidriados, actúan como escaparate de la actividad profesional y son el reclamo publicitario de la firma comercial.

I locali, aperti o separati con tramezzi di vetro, fungono da vetrina dell'attività professionale e sono la réclame della marca.

GCA

GCA
Arquitectes Associats

The studio of the GCA architectural team is immersed in the homogeneous urban fabric of Barcelona, occupying old textile warehouses located on the ground floor of a 1946 building.

The space had classically-inspired offices near the access, with cornices, moldings and compartmentalized spaces. The interior consisted of an open floor space held up by metallic struts and upright riveted legs.

The architects chose a dual strategy: first, they retained the image of the existing office, restoring the moldings and adding installations to place the reception, administrative, management and construction monitoring areas. Second, they created a clearly modern space devoted to design in the old warehouse. The design was based on a dialectic. It was envisioned as a large white box, lit from above by two large skylights.

Light is a key element. White walls, maple flooring and glass dividers have shaped a neutral, homogeneous and minimalist space.

El estudio del equipo de arquitectos GCA se encuentra inmerso en el homogéneo tejido urbano de Barcelona ocupando unos antiguos almacenes textiles situados en la planta baja de un edificio de 1946.

El local disponía de unos despachos de inspiración clásica junto al acceso, con cornisas, molduras y espacios compartimentados. El interior consistía en una planta libre soportada por perfiles metálicos de cerchas y pies derechos roblonados.

Los arquitectos optaron por una estrategia doble: por un lado, mantener la imagen de los despachos existentes, restaurando carpinterías y dotándolos de instalaciones, para ubicar en ellos las áreas de recepción, administración, dirección y control de obras. Por otro, crear un espacio claramente moderno dedicado al diseño en el antiguo almacén. El proyecto se basa en un diálogo de contrarios. Se concibió como una gran caja blanca, iluminada cenitalmente por dos grandes claraboyas.

La luz es el elemento primordial. Paredes blancas, pavimentos de arce y mamparas de cristal han ido configurando un espacio neutro, homogéneo y minimalista.

Lo studio di architetti GCA occupa i vecchi magazzini tessili situati al piano terra di un edificio che risale al 1946 ed è immerso nell'omogeneo tessuto urbano di Barcellona.

Il locale disponeva di alcuni uffici di ispirazione classica vicino all'entrata, con modanature e spazi separati. L'interno era a pianta libera supportata da capriate e piedritti fissati con ribattini.

Gli architetti hanno optato per una doppia strategia: in primo luogo, conservare l'aspetto degli uffici esistenti, restaurando i serramenti e dotandoli di impianti in modo da poter ubicare le aree di ricevimento, amministrazione, direzione e controllo dei lavori. In secondo luogo, creare uno spazio chiaramente moderno dedicato alla progettazione nel vecchio magazzino. Il progetto si basa su idee opposte. È stato concepito come una grande cassa bianca, illuminata da due grandi lucernari.

La luce è l'elemento principale. Pareti bianche, pavimenti di acero e paraventi di vetro creano uno spazio neutro, omogeneo e minimalista.

Architects: GCA Arquitectes Associats

Location: Barcelona, Spain

Photographs: Jordi Miralles

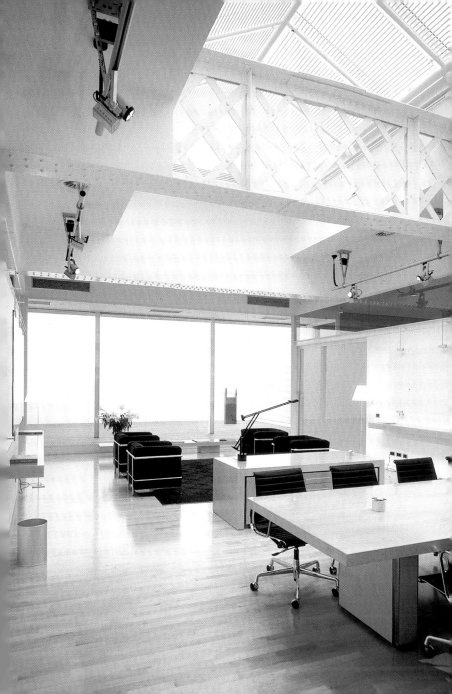

The offices house more than 200 employees. Thus, the meeting spaces were key elements in the design. The entrance vestibule especially was conceived as a multi-purpose zone in which even ping-pong could be played.

Las oficinas albergan a más de 200 trabajadores. Por eso, los espacios de reunión tienen una gran importancia en el proyecto. En particular, el vestíbulo de entrada está concebido como una zona multiuso en la que incluso se puede jugar a *ping-pong*.

Gli uffici ospitano più di 200 dipendenti. Per questo, gli spazi per le riunioni hanno una grande importanza nel progetto. In particolare, l'atrio d'ingresso è stato concepito come una zona multiuso, nella quale si può perfino giocare a ping-pong.

Casadesús Studio
Estudio Casadesús / Studio Casadesús

Antoni Casadesús

Antoni Casadesús remodeled a space that had previously been occupied by a textile company in order to convert it into his design and interior decoration studio and to accommodate his living space as well.

The size of the space (150 m²), its high ceilings, the back patio (facing south-west) and above all its excellent location, just a few meters from Paseo de Gracia in the center of Barcelona, made it a privileged location.

A central area, with a small garden and the kitchen, separates the more private area of the house (bedroom, bathroom and attic) from a large double-high room open to the rear garden. The placement of pieces allows the different functions to be independent and different degrees of privacy to be distinguished, while a visual connection among all parts of the house is maintained.

Despite the home's considerable depth, a high degree of natural illumination has been achieved in all the spaces.

Antoni Casadesús remodeló un local antiguamente ocupado por una empresa textil para convertirlo en su estudio de diseño e interiorismo y albergar asimismo su propia vivienda.

Las dimensiones del local (aproximadamente 150 m²), su gran altura, el patio trasero (de orientación sudeste) y, sobre todo, su excelente ubicación, a pocos metros del paseo de Gracia (en el centro de Barcelona) lo convierten en un espacio privilegiado.

Una franja central, con un pequeño jardín y la cocina, separa la zona más privada de la casa (dormitorio, baño y altillo) de una gran sala con doble altura abierta al jardín trasero. Esta disposición de piezas permite independizar las distintas funciones y distinguir diferentes grados de privacidad, a la vez que mantiene una conexión visual entre todos los puntos de la casa.

A pesar de la considerable profundidad de la vivienda, se ha conseguido un alto nivel de iluminación natural en todos los espacios.

Antoni Casadesús ha ristrutturato un locale che una volta era occupato da un'azienda tessile per trasformarlo nel suo studio di design e arredamento d'interni e nella sua abitazione.

Le dimensioni del locale (approssimativamente 150 m²), la notevole altezza, il patio sul retro (orientato a sud-est) e soprattutto la sua ottima posizione, a pochi metri dal Passeig de Gràcia (nel centro di Barcellona) ne fanno un luogo privilegiato.

Una sezione centrale, con un piccolo giardino e la cucina, separa la zona più privata della casa (camera da letto, bagno e soppalco) da una grande sala a doppia altezza aperta al giardino sul retro. Questa disposizione di locali permette di rendere indipendenti le varie funzioni e di distinguere i diversi gradi di intimità e allo stesso tempo mantiene una connessione visuale tra tutti i punti della casa.

Nonostante la notevole profondità del locale, è stato raggiunto un alto livello di illuminazione naturale in tutti gli spazi.

Architect: Antoni Casadesús

Location: Barcelona, Spain

Photographs: Eugeni Pons

The flooring throughout the entire home is white marble, except in the attic, where it is teak.

The work chairs are by Charles Eames; the table by Isern y Bernal.

Polished, shiny surface predominate in the bathroom. The faucets are by Philippe Starck.

El pavimento de toda la casa es de mármol blanco, salvo en el altillo, donde es de madera de teca.

Las sillas de trabajo son una creación de Charles Eames; la mesa, de Isern y Bernal.

En el baño dominan las superficies pulidas y brillantes. Los grifos son de Philippe Starck.

Il pavimento è di marmo bianco in tutta la casa, tranne quello del soppalco che è di legno di acero.

Le sedie per l'ufficio sono state disegnate da Charles Eames, mentre il tavolo è di Isern e Bernal.

Nel bagno dominano le superfici lucidate e brillanti. La rubinetteria è di Philippe Starck.

B&B Studio Home
B&B Estudio vivienda / Studio e abitazione B & B

Sergi Bastidas

On the island of Majorca we can find an old blacksmith's workshop which has been renovated by the architect Sergi Bastidas to be used for his studio and home. In order to retain the large utilitarian space provided by the workshop, he carefully chose the type of partitions needed for the new layout. The solutions adopted, with little visual impact as was intended, have consisted of the simultaneous use of the transparency of the windows, built-in separating panels and sliding walls, which manage to create parking, reception, meeting, working and utility spaces.

From an architectural standpoint, the industrial nature of the space was to be respected; thus simple lines, exposed structures, and rough materials such as polished cement for the floors have been chosen; many of the pre-existing mechanical elements were kept as well.

The area on the first floor reserved for the living space, meeting room and two offices has planned as a more private space, with isolated functional spaces: bedroom, bathroom and dressing room.

En la isla de Mallorca se encuentra una antigua herrería que ha sido reformada por el arquitecto Sergi Bastidas para ubicar su estudio y su vivienda. Con el fin de mantener el amplio espacio utilitario que brindaba la nave, ha trabajado con mucho cuidado el tipo de particiones necesarias para la nueva distribución. Las soluciones adoptadas, de poco impacto visual como se pretendía, han consistido en el empleo de la transparencia en las vidrieras, paneles separadores de obra y paredes correderas al mismo tiempo, que consiguen crear zonas de aparcamiento, recepción, reunión, trabajo y servicios.

Desde el punto de vista arquitectónico, se ha querido respetar el carácter industrial, por lo que se ha optado por la sencillez de líneas, estructuras vistas, materiales brutos como el uso de cemento pulido para los suelos, además de mantenerse muchos de los elementos mecánicos preexistentes.

El área del primer piso reservada al uso de vivienda, sala de reuniones y dos despachos ha sido pensada como una zona más íntima y privada, con espacios funcionales separados entre sí: dormitorio, baño y vestidor.

Nell'isola di Maiorca c'è una vecchia fucina che l'architetto Sergi Bastidas ha restaurato per ubicare il suo studio e la sua abitazione. Con l'obiettivo di conservare l'ampio spazio che offriva il locale, ha studiato bene il tipo di ripartizioni necessarie per la nuova distribuzione. Le soluzioni adottate, volutamente di ridotto impatto visivo, consistono nell'impiego della trasparenza delle vetrate, pannelli divisori solidi e pareti scorrevoli allo stesso tempo, che creano zone di parcheggio, ricevimento, riunione, lavoro e servizi.

Dal punto di vista architettonico, si è voluto rispettare il carattere industriale, quindi si è optato per la semplicità delle linee, strutture a vista, materiali grezzi, come l'uso di cemento lisciato per i pavimenti, oltre a conservare molti degli elementi meccanici preesistenti.

L'area del primo piano riservata ad uso abitativo, sala riunioni e due uffici, è stata pensata come una zona più intima e privata, con spazi funzionali separati tra loro: camera da letto, bagno e spogliatoio.

Architect: Sergi Bastidas
Location: Molinar, Palma de Mallorca, Spain
Photographs: Pere Planells

The stairway is a vertical connecting element that visually forms part of the floor due to the material chosen for its construction.

La escalera es un elemento de comunicación vertical que visualmente forma parte del suelo debido al material elegido para su construcción.

La scala è un elemento di comunicazione verticale che visivamente fa parte del pavimento, grazie al materiale scelto per la sua costruzione.

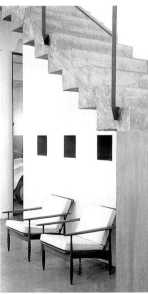

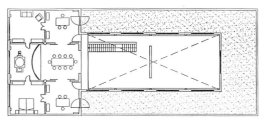

Upper floor. Two offices and a meeting room have been placed alongside the living space.
Planta alta. Se han dispuesto dos despachos y una sala de reuniones junto a la vivienda.
Piano superiore. I due uffici e la sala riunioni sono stati disposti accanto all'abitazione.

Ground floor   Planta baja   Piano terra

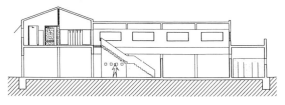

Crosswise view   Sección longitudinal   Sezione longitudinale

615

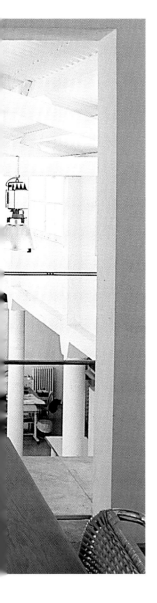

Studio in Madrid
Estudio en Madrid / Studio a Madrid

Enrique Bardají

Enrique Bardají, a Madrid architect, designed his own studio in a building that he had also designed. With this, Bardají has become both client and designer at the same time, which is reflected in the precision with which he carried out the definition of each element. The result is a spacious, luminous interior where the functions of studio are easily accommodated, making use of intentional industrial references that also characterize the rest of the building.

The other basic element in the design is luminosity. A central skylight, with a canvas that diffuses the light, illuminates the central space. On three of the perimeter walls, a series of windows running from floor to ceiling are protected by Venetian blinds that control the light entering all day long.

El estudio de Enrique Bardají fue diseñado por él mismo en un edificio proyectado a su vez también por este arquitecto madrileño. Con esta propuesta, Bardají se ha convertido en cliente y diseñador a un mismo tiempo, lo cual queda reflejado en la precisión con que ha llevado a cabo la definición de cada elemento. El resultado es un amplio y luminoso espacio interior donde se desarrolla sin complicaciones el programa funcional del estudio, con unas intencionadas connotaciones industriales que también marcan el resto del edificio.

El otro elemento básico del proyecto es la luminosidad. Un tragaluz central, con una lona que matiza la luz, ilumina el espacio central. En tres de los muros perimetrales, una serie de ventanas de suelo a techo se protegen con persianas de lama venecianas que controlan el recorrido del sol a lo largo del día.

Lo studio di Enrique Bardají è stato progettato da lui stesso in un edificio anch'esso opera di questo architetto madrileno. Con questa proposta, Bardají si è trasformato in cliente e architetto allo stesso tempo e questo si riflette nella precisione con cui ha completato ciascun elemento. Il risultato è un ampio e luminoso spazio interno dove si svolge senza complicazioni il programma funzionale dello studio, con volute connotazioni industriali che caratterizzano il resto dell'edificio.

L'altro elemento di base del progetto è la luminosità. Un lucernario centrale, con una tela che armonizza la luce, illumina lo spazio centrale. Su tre dei muri perimetrali, c'è una serie di finestre a tutta altezza protette da veneziane che elaborano la luce solare durante tutto il giorno.

Architect: Enrique Bardají

Location: Madrid, Spain

Photographs: Lionel Malka

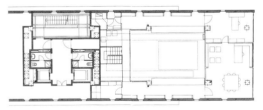

Attic floor
Enrique Bardají's office and archives are located in the attic.

Planta altillo
En el altillo se hallan los archivos y el despacho de Enrique Bardají.

Pianta del soppalco
Nel soppalco si trovano gli archivi e l'ufficio di Enrique Bardají.

Ground floor
A library, meeting room, machinery room, and kitchen-dining room are located around the central space.

Planta baja
Alrededor del espacio central se ubica una biblioteca, una sala de reuniones, una sala de maquinaria y una cocina comedor.

Piano terra
Attorno allo spazio centrale sono ubicate una biblioteca, una sala riunioni, una sala di macchinari e una cucina e sala da pranzo.

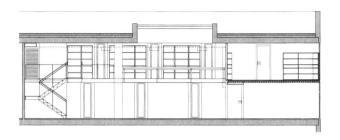

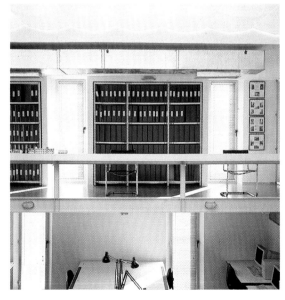

The attic floor is made of two DM panels filled with material that provides sound proofing and a linoleum finish. The panels are supported on a structure of metallic beams.

El forjado del altillo está formado por dos tableros de DM con un relleno de material de aislamiento acústico y un acabado de linóleo. Los tableros se sustentan sobre una estructura de viguetas metálicas.

La soletta del soppalco è formata da due pannelli di legno compresso tra cui è inserito del materiale di isolamento acustico e una rifinitura in linoleum. I pannelli sono appoggiati su una struttura di longherine metalliche.

Empty SA

Víctor López Cotelo

The project consisted of adapting a 700 m² commercial space for the offices of the company Empty SA. The architect of this project which was finished in 1998, Víctor López, along with his associates, decided from the start to adopt a strategy of minimal intervention. The changes involved stripping the space of interior design elements in a different style that are frequently used in construction, thus promoting the natural daylight that entered in order to compensate for the lack of outside views.

After the demolition of all the existing parts, the structural skeleton of the space was exposed, into which the new systems of installations that equip the offices were integrated. The greatest degree of flexibility and versatility in the spaces, which are especially open and airy, are required conditions for the effective functioning of the office.

El proyecto consistió en la adaptación de un local comercial de 700 m² para oficinas de la empresa Empty SA. El arquitecto de esta obra finalizada en 1998, Víctor López, junto a sus colaboradores, decidió plantear desde un principio una estrategia de justa intervención. La actuación llevada a cabo consistió en despojar el local de elementos de interiorismo de otro orden y que frecuentemente se emplean para vestir las intervenciones, así como en potenciar la luz natural para compensar la falta de vistas hacia el exterior.

Tras la demolición de toda la obra preexistente reapareció el esqueleto, la estructura vista del local en la que se integraron los nuevos sistemas de instalaciones que equipan las oficinas. La máxima flexibilidad y versatilidad en los espacios, especialmente diáfanos, son condiciones indispensables para un eficaz funcionamiento de la oficina.

Il progetto è la ristrutturazione di un locale commerciale di 700 m² per gli uffici dell'impresa Empty SA. L'architetto di questo progetto completato nel 1998, Victor López, assieme ai suoi collaboratori, ha deciso di applicare fin dall'inizio una giusta strategia di intervento. Sono stati eliminati gli elementi di arredamento di altra natura e che frequentemente si impiegano come ornamento ed è stata potenziata la luce naturale per compensare la mancanza di viste sull'esterno.

Dopo la demolizione di tutti gli elementi esistenti è riapparso lo scheletro, la struttura del locale a cui sono stati integrati i nuovi impianti per gli uffici. La massima flessibilità e versatilità degli spazi, particolarmente aperti, sono le condizioni indispensabili per un efficace funzionamento dell'ufficio.

Architect: Víctor López Cotelo

Location: Madrid, Spain

Photographs: Luis Asín

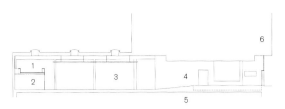

Lengthwise view

Sección longitudinal

Sezione longitudinale

6

1
2
3
4
5

Lengthwise view
1. Administrative area
2. Meeting room
3. Room
4. Ramp
5. Garages
6. Existing building

Sección longitudinal
1. Administración
2. Sala de reuniones
3. Sala
4. Rampa
5. Garajes
6. Edificio existente

Sezione longitudinale
1. Amministrazione
2. Sala riunioni
3. Sala
4. Rampa
5. Garage
6. Edificio esistente

Crosswise view

Sección transversal

Sezione trasversale

1
2
4
5
3

Crosswise view
1. Administrative area
2. Office
3. Garages
4. Management
5. Storage area

Sección transversal
1. Administración
2. Despacho
3. Garajes
4. Dirección
5. Almacén

Sezione trasversale
1. Amministrazione
2. Ufficio
3. Garage
4. Direzione
5. Magazzino

Floor plan   Planta   Pianta

Floor plan
1. Storage area
2. Utilities
3. Management
4. Room
5. Patio
6. Bathroom
7. Office
8. Meeting room
9. Closet
10. Photocopies
11. Kitchen
12. Garbage chute

Planta
1. Almacén
2. Instalaciones
3. Dirección
4. Sala
5. Patio
6. Aseo
7. Despacho
8. Sala de reuniones
9. Ropero
10. Fotocopias
11. Cocina
12. Vertedero

Pianta
1. Magazzino
2. Impianti
3. Direzione
4. Sala
5. Patio
6. Servizi
7. Ufficio
8. Sala riunioni
9. Guardaroba
10. Fotocopie
11. Cucina
12. Area rifiuti

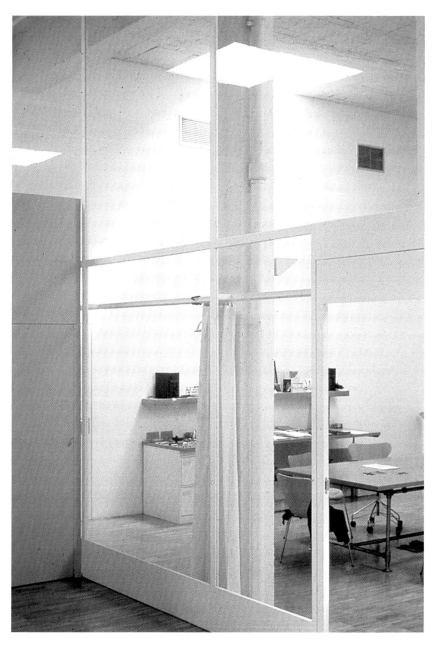

Salamanca Neighborhood
Barrio de Salamanca / Quartiere di Salamanca

Manuel Serrano,
Marta Rodríguez Ariño

An industrial warehouse in the Salamanca neighborhood of Madrid was adapted as an architectural studio for the architects who designed the intervention. After the demolition of all the existing walls, the warehouse was left open and airy. Skylights were built into the roof, and the window openings were extended to the floor; the roof was also removed in the new indoor garden area.

The working area, meeting room, layout printing area, storage area, kitchen, and bathroom were placed on the ground floor. The offices were placed on the mezzanine. The meeting room was placed next to the indoor garden and is used simultaneously as an informal meeting place. In the layout printing area, a freight elevator provides access to the office mezzanine. In the back a storage area, a bathroom covered in gresite, and a small kitchen are located.

On the roof, the skylights were made with transparent cellular polycarbonate panels over an iron structure, and on the bottom they are finished with reinforced glass on a metallic structure.

Una nave industrial en el barrio de Salamanca de Madrid se adecuó como estudio de arquitectura de los arquitectos autores de la intervención. Tras la demolición de toda la tabiquería existente, la nave quedó diáfana. Se abrieron lucernarios en cubierta y se agrandaron los huecos de las ventanas hasta el suelo; además, se procedió a la demolición de la cubierta en la zona del nuevo jardín interior.

En la planta baja se sitúan la zona de trabajo, la sala de reuniones, el área de impresión de planos, el almacén, la cocina y el aseo. En la entreplanta se ubican los despachos. La sala de juntas se ubica junto al jardín interior y éste se utiliza a su vez como lugar para las reuniones informales. En la zona de impresión de planos, un montacargas da acceso a la entreplanta de los despachos. Al fondo se sitúa un almacén, un aseo revestido de gresite y una pequeña cocina.

En la cubierta, los lucernarios se hacen con placas de policarbonato celular incoloro sobre bastidor de hierro y en su parte inferior se rematan con vidrio armado sobre perfilería metálica.

Un edificio industriale nel quartiere di Salamanca di Madrid ristrutturato per ospitare lo studio di architettura degli architetti che lo hanno progettato. Sono stati eliminati tutti i tramezzi esistenti. Sono stati aperti lucernari sul tetto e ampliate le finestre fino al pavimento; inoltre è stato demolito il tetto nella zona del nuovo giardino interno.

Al piano terra si trovano la zona di lavoro, la sala riunioni, l'area di stampa dei piani, il magazzino, la cucina e i servizi. Gli uffici sono ubicati nel piano rialzato. La sala del consiglio direttivo è situata accanto al giardino interno e viene utilizzata anche per le riunioni informali. Nella zona di stampa dei piani, un montacarichi dà accesso al piano rialzato degli uffici. In fondo ci sono un magazzino, un bagno rivestito in mosaico e una piccola cucina.

Sul tetto, la parte superiore dei lucernari è fatta con lastre di policarbonato cellulare incolore su un telaio di ferro e la parte inferiore è di vetro retinato e profili metallici.

Architects: Manuel Serrano, Marta Rodríguez Ariño

Location: Madrid, Spain

Photographs: José Latova

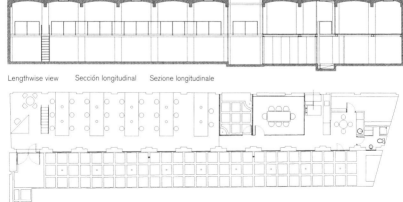

Lengthwise view   Sección longitudinal   Sezione longitudinale

Ground floor   Planta baja   Piano terra

632

There is a walkway in the working area that contains the library made of a projecting tramex metallic structure which is accessed through a metallic spiral staircase.

En la zona de trabajo existe una pasarela que soporta la biblioteca fabricada con estructura metálica en voladizo y tramex a la que se accede por una escalera de caracol también metálica.

Nella zona di lavoro c'è una passerella che supporta la biblioteca fabbricata con una struttura metallica sporgente e rete metallica, a cui si accede tramite una scala a chiocciola metallica.

The floor of the mezzanine is made of metallic sheeting, sound proofing, boarding, and industrial parquet finishing.

El forjado de la entreplanta está hecho con una chapa metálica, absorbente acústico, tablero y acabado en parqué industrial.

La soletta del piano rialzato è formata da una lastra metallica, materiale di isolamento acustico, una tavola e finitura con parquet industriale.

Ciclorama

Manuel Serrano,
Marta Rodríguez Ariño

The cyclorama is a continuous backdrop. Initially built on one floor, this approximately 300 m² warehouse from the 1930's has been totally transformed and now houses two platforms, one with natural daylight and another in the mezzanine, suspended by a light structure into which the smallest platforms and the utility rooms fit. With the greatest spatial and constructional economy, these latter spaces are reached by two stairways, one inserted into the entrance zone and another that keeps the crossed ties and beams of the roof. The space is accessed through a succession of metal, wood and glass doors. The reception area is totally opened to the large distribution hallway. Across from this, the bathroom nucleus, the kitchen, and the storage area are an open volume covered in sheeting that has been rusted and subsequently varnished.

The reinforced concrete struts from the original warehouse have been left intact as pieces of industrial archaeology that are naturally incorporated into the timeless eclecticism of the cyclorama space.

El ciclorama es un fondo continuo. Construida inicialmente en una planta, esta nave de los años treinta, de unos 300 m², ha sido trasformada por completo y ahora alberga tres platós, uno con luz natural y otro en la entreplanta, suspendida ésta de una ligerísima estructura en la que caben el plató más pequeño y los cuartos de instalaciones. Con la mayor economía espacial y constructiva, a estos últimos espacios se llega por medio de dos escaleras, una insertada en la zona de entrada y otra que salva los cruces de tirantes y vigas de la cubierta. El acceso se produce a través de una sucesión de puertas de metal, madera y vidrio. La recepción se abre completamente al gran pasillo de acogida y distribución. Frente a esta zona el núcleo de aseos, la cocina y el almacén son un volumen exento revestido de chapa con tratamiento de oxidación y barnizado posterior.

Se han respetado las cerchas de hormigón armado de la nave original que, como piezas de arqueología industrial, se incorporan de forma natural al eclecticismo intemporal de la envolvente de los cicloramas.

Il ciclorama è un fondale continuo. Inizialmente formato da un solo piano, questo capannone degli anni Trenta di circa 300 m² è stato completamente trasformato e ora ospita tre teatri di posa, uno con luce naturale e un altro nel piano rialzato, che è supportato da una struttura leggerissima su cui sono situati il teatro di posa più piccolo e le stanze degli impianti. Con una grande economia costruttiva e di spazio, si può accedere a questi due ultimi spazi tramite due scale, una inserita nella zona dell'entrata e l'altra situata tra le intersezioni di tiranti e le travi del tetto. L'entrata è composta da una successione di porte di metallo, legno e vetro. La reception è situata sul grande corridoio di ricevimento e distribuzione. Di fronte a questa zona il nucleo di servizi, la cucina e il magazzino sono un volume esteso rivestito di lamiera con trattamento di ossidazione e verniciatura.

Sono state conservate le capriate di cemento armato della costruzione originale che, come elementi di archeologia industriale, si integrano in maniera naturale all'eclettismo atemporale del ciclorama.

Architects: Manuel Serrano, Marta Rodríguez Ariño

Location: Madrid, Spain

Photographs: Julio Limia

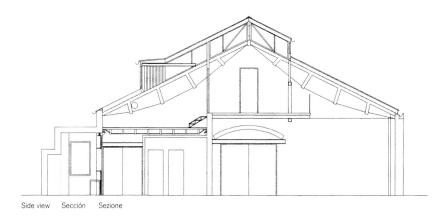

Side view   Sección   Sezione

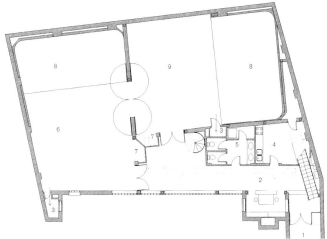

Lower level
1. Access
2. Reception area
3. Dark room
4. Kitchen
5. Bathroom
6. Platform 1, with
   natural daylight
7. Make-up room
8. Cyclorama
9. Platform 2

Planta baja
1. Acceso
2. Recepción
3. Cámara oscura
4. Cocina
5. Baño
6. Plató 1, con luz de día
7. Maquillaje
8. Ciclorama
9. Plató 2

Piano terra
1. Entrata
2. Reception
3. Camera oscura
4. Cucina
5. Bagno
6. Teatro di posa 1 con
   illuminazione naturale
7. Angolo per il trucco
8. Ciclorama
9. Teatro di posa 2

The room has been composed of
varnished metal sheets and
the skylight on the first platform is cellular
metacrylate, all of which is supported by
a light metallic structure.

La cubierta se ha compuesto con
planchas de metal lacado y el lucernario
del plató 1 es de metacrilato celular,
todo ello apoyado en un ligero
entramado de estructura metálica.

Il tetto è composto da lastre di metallo
laccato e il lucernario del teatro di posa 1
è in metacrilato cellulare, appoggiato su
una leggera struttura metallica.

Architectural Studio
Estudio de arquitectura / Studio di architettura

José Miguel
Usabiaga Bárcena

This construction, located in the city of San Sebastián, was originally a railway roundhouse, a place damaged and transfigured by successive interventions throughout time that masked its constructional identity and building type. For this reason, a formal and constructional unfolding was decided on with the aim of rescuing the historicity of the location.

The action was carried out along two main axes: first, the physical intervention on what already existed, which was approached with an almost archaeological approach. Then, only referring to what is new, the innovation is inscribed within the same stance, with special care taken in the transitions made with glass sheets, which are both transparent and translucent, a delicate material that allows the building's history to shine through.

The materials actively participate in the proposed battle against time, contrasting their genesis and integrating into the atmosphere in the industrial and railway ambiance of the old recovered building. The new walkway, which is defined by pure steel bars which are neither treated nor protected, will gradually acquire a patina of rust as they age, and it is supported on the old wood structure without holes being drilled into it; the banister, made of the same steel, and a handrail made with plumbing pipes run alongside it.

Esta construcción, ubicada en la ciudad de San Sebastián, fue en su origen un almacén ferroviario, un lugar herido y transfigurado por sucesivas intervenciones en el tiempo que enmascararon su identidad constructiva y tipológica. Por esta razón se planteó un despliegue formal y de intervención dispuesto a rescatar la historicidad de este emplazamiento.

La acción se desarrolló sobre dos ejes principales; por un lado, la intervención física sobre lo existente, que se abordó con una actitud casi arqueológica. Y por otro, en lo que se refiere estrictamente a lo nuevo, la intervención se inscribe dentro de la misma vocación, con especial cuidado en las transiciones hechas con láminas de vidrio, transparente y translúcido, material delicado y respetuoso con la historia.

Los materiales participan activamente en el combate de tiempos propuesto, contrastando su génesis e integrándose en la atmósfera, en el aura industrial y ferroviaria del viejo edificio recuperado. La nueva pasarela, definida por perfiles de acero puro, sin tratamiento ni protección, crece con su vejez tiznada de óxido y se apoya en la vieja estructura de madera sin agujerearla; con ella también va la barandilla, en el mismo acero, y un pasamanos fabricado con tubos de fontanería.

Questa costruzione, che si trova a San Sebastián, è stata un magazzino ferroviario, un luogo ferito e sfigurato da lavori che hanno mascherato la sua identità costruttiva e tipologica. Per questa ragione si è intrapreso un programma di lavori mirato a riscattare la storicità di questo edificio.

Le azioni hanno riguardato due assi principali: in primo luogo il recupero di elementi esistenti, che è stato fatto con una metodologia quasi archeologica. In secondo luogo, per quanto riguarda le parti nuove, i lavori sono stati eseguiti sulla base dello stesso principio, con un'attenzione speciale per le pareti divisorie di vetro, trasparente o semitrasparente, materiale delicato e rispettoso della storia.

I materiali partecipano attivamente nello scontro dei tempi, contrastando la sua genesi e integrandosi nell'atmosfera, nell'aura industriale e ferroviaria del vecchio edificio recuperato. La nuova passerella è dotata di profili di acciaio puro che, non essendo stati trattati o rivestiti, sono macchiati di ossido e si combinano perfettamente alla vecchia struttura; la ringhiera fatta con lo stesso acciaio è dotata di un corrimano fabbricato con i tubi che si usano per gli impianti idraulici.

Architect: José Miguel Usabiaga Bárcena

Location: San Sebastian, Spain

Photographs: José Manuel Bielsa

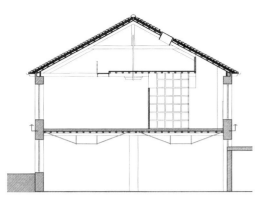

Cross section   Sección transversal   Sezione trasversale

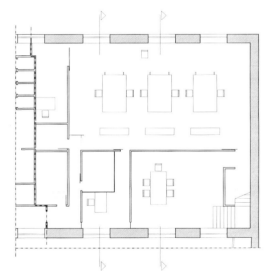

Floor plan   Planta de distribución   Pianta della distribuzione

The floor has been covered with industrial-strength wood in narrow and thicker planks, lined along its perimeter by a metal panel that stops it before it joins the old walls.

El suelo se ha revestido con madera industrial en tablilla estrecha y gruesa, recercado en todo su perímetro por un angular metálico que la detiene antes del choque con los viejos muros.

Il pavimento è stato rivestito con legno industriale in listelli stretti e grossi e bordato in tutto il perimetro da un profilo metallico per addolcire il contrasto con le vecchie pareti.

The new walls that divide the workshop and other spaces are made of plasterboard, with a light gray varnished finish.

Los nuevos tabiques que dividen el taller y otras estancias son de cartón yeso, con un acabado lacado gris claro.

I nuovi tramezzi che dividono il laboratorio e altre stanze sono di cartongesso, con una finitura di vernice grigio chiaro.

The building's volume is recovered with a partial emptying of the wooden floor of the upper level, which is no longer an attic and the calligraphy of the fixings that hold up the walkway and the struts that elevate the space can be appreciated.

El volumen del edificio se recupera con un vaciado parcial del suelo de madera del piso superior, donde ahora deja de ser desván y puede apreciarse la caligrafía de las fijaciones que sostienen la pasarela y las cerchas que encumbran el espacio.

I volume dell'edificio si recupera con uno scavo parziale del pavimento di legno del piano superiore, che ora non è più un semplice solaio e si possono apprezzare i supporti della passerella e le capriate che elevano lo spazio.

Central Headquarters of IU-EB
Sede central IU-EB / Sede centrale dell'IU-EB

José Miguel
Usabiaga Bárcena

The project is the renovation of an old industrial space located in an interior patio right in the middle of Bilbao, in order to place there the central headquarters of the Basque Country's political organization Izquierda Unida.

On the ground floor, the access gallery crosses an apartment building before reaching the factory. At the end of the gallery, lead by the red idiom of the ceiling painting, a glass box makes the transition with the main building. The factory becomes a regenerated volume, once again through the red exhibited in its skirting board and filtered up to the upper floors through the cellular polycarbonate and wooden enclosure, superimposed in order to improve the building's air conditioning and heating systems. On the first floor, which is used for administrative offices, the sequence of private spaces along the open, fluid hallway contrasts with the new geometric shapes and volumes: another glass box and cylinder for the more important meetings.

El proyecto es la rehabilitación de un viejo espacio industrial situado en el patio interior en pleno centro de Bilbao, para ubicar en él la sede central de la organización política Izquierda Unida del País Vasco.

La galería de acceso atraviesa en la planta baja un edificio de viviendas para llegar a la fábrica. Al final de la galería, conducidos por la lengua roja que supone la pintura del techo, una caja de vidrio se encarga de la transición con el edificio principal. La fábrica se convierte en un prisma regenerado, de nuevo a través del rojo exhibido en su zócalo, y tamizado en los pisos superiores tras el cerramiento de policarbonato celular y madera, superpuesto para mejorar las condiciones de climatización del edificio. En la planta primera, de uso administrativo, la secuencia de recintos privados a lo largo de un pasillo abierto y fluido contrasta con los nuevos volúmenes y formas geométricas: otra caja de vidrio y un cilindro para las reuniones más importantes.

Il progetto è la ristrutturazione di un vecchio spazio industriale situato in un patio interno in pieno centro di Bilbao per l'ubicazione della sede centrale dell'organizzazione politica Izquierda Unida del Paese Basco.

La galleria di accesso attraversa il piano terra di un edificio di abitazioni fino alla fabbrica. Alla fine della galleria, accompagnati dalla lingua rossa rappresentata dalla pittura del tetto, si raggiunge una cassa di vetro che segna il passaggio con l'edificio principale. La fabbrica si trasforma in un prisma rigenerato, ancora una volta attraverso il rosso dello zoccolo e filtrato ai piani superiori dietro il tramezzo in policarbonato cellulare e legno, sovrapposto per migliorare le condizioni di climatizzazione dell'edificio. Al primo piano, adibito ad uso amministrativo, la sequenza di locali privati lungo un corridoio aperto e fluido contrasta con i nuovi volumi e le forme geometriche: un'altra cassa di vetro e un cilindro per le riunioni più importanti.

Architect: José Miguel Usabiaga Bárcena

Location: Bilbao, Spain

Photographs: José Manuel Bielsa

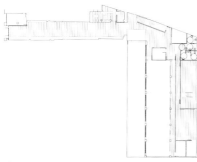

Ground floor   Planta baja   Piano terra

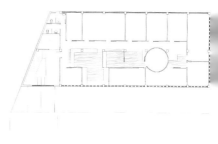

First floor   Planta primera   Primo piano

The lighting reinforces the industrial atmosphere through a system of halogen lights suspended on stripped, exposed cables.

La iluminación refuerza la atmósfera industrial mediante un sistema de luces halógenas suspendidas sobre cable desnudo y visto.

L'illuminazione rafforza l'atmosfera industriale tramite un sistema di luci alogene sospese su un cavo senza alcun rivestimento.

econd floor   Planta segunda   Secondo piano

Lengthwise view   Sección longitudinal   Sezione longitudinale

The main meeting room is a double-high space whose upper part connects with the library and the archives.

La sala de actos principal es un espacio a doble altura cuya parte superior comunica con la biblioteca y el archivo.

La sala conferenze principale è uno spazio a doppia altezza, la cui parte superiore comunica con la biblioteca e l'archivio.

Studio Naço Offices
Oficinas Studio Naço / Uffici Studio Naço

Studio Naço

The same architects who make up the firm Naço renovated and converted this old lumber warehouse into their central headquarters, their place of work.

With the garage dismantled, the patio located on the northern side of the ground floor became the setting for the entrance. This patio will set a distance from which to view the new façade while crossing the patio until arriving at the entrance nook.

Once the façade was stripped of its old, worn-out wooden covering, the spectacular wooden structure that had always held up the old warehouse re-emerged in shapes that might symbolically represent the trees whose wood was kept there. With the intention of rescuing this structure and exhibiting and describing it, it was decided to make the façade radically transparent, such that a glass membrane that used to be sustained by a metallic structure now envelops the façade and is activated through an electronic system that opens and closes the windows.

Los mismos arquitectos que constituyen la firma Naço se encargaron de rehabilitar y convertir este antiguo y viejo almacén de maderos en su sede central, su lugar de trabajo.

Desmantelado el garaje, el patio situado al norte de la planta baja se convierte en el escenario que indica la entrada. Este patio marcará una distancia de la cual se servirá la nueva fachada para ser observada mientras se atraviesa el patio hasta llegar al hueco de la entrada.

Una vez despojada la fachada de su antiguo cerramiento de maderas viejas y gastadas, resurgió la espectacular estructura de madera que siempre había sostenido al viejo almacén, y formas que, simbólicamente, podían representar los árboles cuya madera allí se guardaba. Con la intención de rescatar dicha estructura y de mostrarla y explicitarla, se ha decidido transparentar radicalmente la nueva fachada, de manera que una piel de cristal que antes estaba soportada por una subestructura metálica envuelve ahora dicha fachada y queda accionada mediante un sistema electrónico que abre y cierra las ventanas.

Gli stessi architetti che formano parte della ditta Naço si sono occupati di ristrutturare e trasformare questo vecchio magazzino di legname nella loro sede centrale e luogo di lavoro.

Dopo aver demolito il garage, il patio situato a nord del piano terra si è trasformato nello scenario che contraddistingue l'entrata. Questo patio segna la distanza per osservare la facciata mentre lo si attraversa fino ad arrivare all'entrata.

Dopo aver spogliato il fronte del vecchio rivestimento di legno consumato, è apparsa la spettacolare struttura di legno che sosteneva il vecchio magazzino, con forme che simbolicamente possono ricordare gli alberi, il cui legno era conservato al suo interno. Con lo scopo di riscattare questa vecchia struttura e di metterla in mostra, si è deciso di rendere radicalmente trasparente la nuova facciata, che prima era sostenuta da una sottostruttura metallica, avvolge ora questa facciata ed è azionata tramite un sistema elettronico di apertura e chiusura delle finestre.

Architect: Studio Naço

Location: Paris, France

Photographs: Mario Pignata-Monti

In the end, the old warehouse is divided in order to display the different working areas of the Naço offices. From the building, one has an overall view of the space, both horizontally and vertically, despite its being divided into three totally open floors, 120 m² each.

The only closed space is in the shape of a cube. It has been christened the boîte and there is one on each floor. It is used as a container for different services for each floor: bathrooms and closets on the ground floor, photocopier and archives on the second floor, and fax and storage area on the third floor. Partitions, doors and hanging ceilings were excluded as elements of the project.

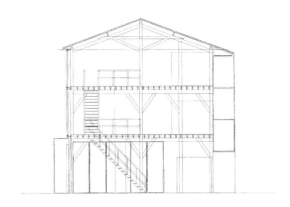

El viejo almacén, queda finalmente seccionado con la intención de exhibir las diferentes áreas de trabajo de las oficinas Naço. Del edificio se tiene una percepción global del espacio, tanto horizontal como verticalmente, a pesar de encontrarse dividido en tres plantas absolutamente diáfanas de unos120 m² cada una.

Una única estancia cerrada en forma de cubo, bautizada como la *boîte* y ubicada en cada piso, se utiliza como contenedor de diferentes servicios para cada planta: aseos y guardarropa en planta baja, fotocopiadora y archivo en la segunda, y fax y almacén en la tercera. Particiones, puertas y falsos techos quedaron excluidos en el planteamiento del proyecto.

Il vecchio magazzino è stato sezionato per mostrare le diverse aree di lavoro degli uffici Naço. L'edificio offre una sensazione globale dello spazio, sia orizzontale che verticale, anche se è diviso in tre piani assolutamente liberi di 120 m² ciascuno.

L'unica stanza chiusa a forma di cubo, battezzata la *boîte* e situata in tutti i livelli, si utilizza come contenitore dei diversi servizi di ogni piano: servizi e guardaroba al piano terra, fotocopiatrice e archivio al secondo e fax e magazzino al terzo. Nel progetto sono stati esclusi partizioni, porte e controsoffitti.

Silos in Amsterdam
Silos en Amsterdam / Silo ad Amsterdam

Die architectengroep

The building where the offices of Die Architectengroep are located used to be a glass flour silo which supplied all the bakeries in Amsterdam.

A fundamental premise of the project was the distinction between a northern and a southern zone in the building. The drafting rooms are located in the southern zone, while the spaces housing more independent functions were placed in the northern zone, including meeting rooms, administrative offices, the offices of the architect partners, accounting, and a service stairway.

This division was carried out through a glass enclosure mounted on thick wooden frames.

The construction of a skylight in the roof and numerous niches in the walls make it possible for natural daylight to reach all the corners in the building.

El edificio que actualmente ocupan las oficinas de Die architectengroep era antiguamente un silo que abastecía de harina a todas las panaderías de Amsterdam.

Una premisa fundamental del proyecto fue la distinción en el edificio de una zona norte y una zona sur. En ésta ultima se encuentran las salas de dibujo, mientras que en la primera se ubican los espacios con funciones más independientes: salas de reunión, administración, despachos de los socios arquitectos, contabilidad y la escalera de servicio.

Esta división se lleva a cabo mediante un cerramiento de vidrio montado en robustas carpinterías de madera.

La construcción de un tragaluz en la cubierta y numerosos huecos practicados en los forjados hace posible que la luz natural no distinga rincones en todo el edificio.

L'edificio, che attualmente ospita gli uffici di Die architectengroep, una volta era un silo in cui si conservava la farina per tutti i panifici di Amsterdam.

Una premessa fondamentale del progetto era la distinzione nell'edificio tra una zona nord e una zona sud. In quest'ultima si trovano le sale progetti, mentre nella prima si trovano spazi con funzioni più indipendenti: sale riunioni, amministrazione, studi dei soci architetti, contabilità e scala di servizio.

Questa divisione è stata attuata mediante un tramezzo di vetro montato su una robusta struttura di legno.

La costruzione di un lucernario sul tetto e numerosi fori praticati nelle solette fanno sì che la luce naturale raggiunga tutti gli angoli dell'edificio.

Architects: Die architectengroep

Location: Amsterdam, Netherlands

Photographs: Christian Richters

The building's structure of concrete porticos converts the large open space that makes up the drafting area into a highly versatile place from which the more private, compartmentalized zones making up the offices can be accessed behind sliding glass doors.

La estructura de pórticos de hormigón del edificio convierte el gran espacio diáfano que constituye la zona de dibujo en un lugar muy versátil desde donde se accede a las zonas más privadas y compartimentadas que conforman los despachos tras unas correderas de cristal.

La struttura di portici di cemento dell'edificio trasforma il grande spazio aperto della zona progetti in un luogo molto versatile da cui si accede alle zone più private e suddivise in compartimenti che formano gli uffici dietro porte di vetro scorrevoli.

Architecture Office
Oficina de arquitectura / Studio di architettura

Jacob Zeilon & Partners

In 1999, the architects Z&P placed their own architectural studio in a building from the 1960s. The building had been a banking headquarters and later an advertising agency, so that their initial commitment was to recover a large, open working space. Previously, the large vault that covered the bank had been torn down, and in its place a mezzanine was created in an open space which contained the areas devoted to client service, utilities, supply area and two meeting rooms. Likewise, a zone was reserved for a spacious cafeteria and rest areas.

The ground floor is a working zone, and from either end one can see a visual connection with the upper level. The walls have been covered with forceful, strong and quite functional materials, whose discreet design balances a neutral complex with little visual impact.

En un inmueble de los sesenta los arquitectos Z&P ubicaron en 1999 su propio estudio de arquitectura. El edificio había correspondido a una sede bancaria y posteriormente a una agencia de publicidad, de manera que su compromiso inicial fue recuperar un amplio y diáfano espacio de trabajo. Previamente se derruyó la gran bóveda que cubría el banco y en su lugar se creó una entreplanta, en forma de volumen exento, que contiene las áreas destinadas a la atención al cliente, servicios, zona de suministros y dos salas de reuniones. Igualmente, se destinó una zona a cafetería y áreas de descanso muy espaciosas.

La planta baja es la zona de trabajo y desde cualquiera de sus extremos se puede apreciar una conexión visual con la planta superior. Los paramentos han sido revestidos con materiales contundentes y robustos, bastante funcionales, cuyo discreto diseño equilibra un conjunto neutro, de poco impacto visual.

In un immobile degli anni Sessanta gli architetti Z&P ubicarono nel 1999 il loro studio di architettura. L'edificio era stato sede di una banca e in seguito di un'agenzia di pubblicità, quindi il primo passo è stato recuperare uno spazio di lavoro ampio e libero. La volta che sovrastava la banca è stata demolita e al suo posto è stato creato un piano rialzato, con un volume esteso, che contiene le aree di attenzione al cliente, servizi, zone di fornitura e due sale riunioni. Sono stati creati anche un bar e aree per i momenti di sosta molto spaziose.

Il piano terra è la zona di lavoro e da qualsiasi punto si può vedere il piano superiore. Le pareti sono state rivestite con materiali particolari e resistenti, il cui disegno discreto si conforma con un insieme neutro, di ridotto impatto visivo.

Architects: Jacob Zeilon & Partners

Location: Stockholm, Sweden

Photographs: Tomas Fälth

"An important factor in the success of alternative spaces, such
as galleries holding shops inside, consists of projecting the image of
an artistic production."

Sharon Zukin, "Loft living: culture and capital in urban change"

(Baltimore, Md., The Johns Hopkins University Press, 1982)

«Un factor importante para el éxito del espacio alternativo, tal como ocurre
en las galerías que también incorporan tiendas en su interior, consiste en
proyectar la imagen de una producción artística.»

Sharon Zukin, *Loft living: culture and capital in urban change*

(Baltimore, Md., The Johns Hopkins University Press, 1982)

«Un fattore importante per il successo dello spazio alternativo, così come
avviene nelle gallerie che incorporano negozi al proprio interno, è di
proiettare l'immagine di una produzione artistica.»

Sharon Zukin, *Loft living: culture and capital in urban change*

(Baltimore, Md., The Johns Hopkins University Press, 1982)

shopping
in a loft

comprar
en un loft

comprare
in un loft

R 20th Century

Mike Solis + Nick Dine.
Dinersan Inc.

This trading company, which works with furniture and history-making design objects, has just opened a new space in the Tribeca neighborhood on the island of Manhattan.

The space comprises approximately 355 m² on various levels, following the design by Mike Solid and Nick Dine. The retail space, located on the main floor, is distinguished by its exposed brick walls, which highlight the impressive uniform gray flooring (treated with epoxy resin) and a high white ceiling. A metal and glass staircase leads to the lower level on which the exhibition gallery is located. Alongside this is access to an exceptional library on design, as well as a meeting room and a space for art.

Esta empresa comercial, que trabaja con mobiliario y objetos de diseño que han hecho historia, acaba de estrenar recientemente un nuevo local en el barrio de Tribeca, en la isla de Manhattan.

El local comprende alrededor de 355 m² distribuidos en varios niveles según el diseño de Mike Solis y Nick Dine. El espacio de venta al público, ubicado en la planta principal, se distingue por sus muros de ladrillo visto, que destacan en el impresionante pavimento gris continuo (tratado con resina epoxy) y de un alto techo de color blanco. Una escalera de metal y cristal conduce al nivel inferior, en el que se encuentra la galería de exposiciones. Junto a ésta se tiene acceso a una excepcional biblioteca dedicada al diseño, así como a una sala de reuniones y un espacio destinado al arte.

Questa azienda, che opera nel settore dell'arredamento e degli oggetti di design che hanno fatto storia, recentemente ha inaugurato un nuovo locale nel quartiere di Tribeca nell'isola di Manhattan.

Il locale occupa una superficie di 355 m² circa, distribuiti in vari livelli secondo il progetto di Mike Solis e Nick Dine. Lo spazio dedicato alla vendita al pubblico, ubicato al piano nobile, si distingue per i suoi muri di mattoni a vista, che risaltano con l'impressionante pavimento grigio uniforme (trattato con resina epossidica) e per il soffitto alto di color bianco. Una scala di metallo e vetro conduce al livello inferiore, nel quale sono situati una galleria espositiva, un'eccezionale biblioteca dedicata al design, una sala riunioni e uno spazio dedicato all'arte.

Interior Designers: Mike Solis + Nick Dine. Dinersan Inc.

Location: Manhattan, New York, United States

Photographs: Jordi Miralles

Independent counters exhibit small
collections of ceramic or exquisite
glass objects.

Mostradores independientes exhiben
pequeñas colecciones de cerámica
o trabajos exquisitos de cristal.

Espositori indipendenti mostrano
piccole collezioni di oggetti di ceramica
e raffinate creazioni di cristallo.

Original designs by Arne Jacobsen,
Edward Wormley and Eero Saarinen
provide the counterpoint to the equally
remarkable although less well known
works by Cees Braakman, Kho Liang Le
and Tapio Wirkkala.

Diseños originales de Arne Jacobsen,
Edward Wormley y Eero Saarinen son
el contrapunto de los igualmente
destacados, aunque menos conocidos,
de Cees Braakman, Kho Liang Le y
Tapio Wirkkala.

Design originali di Arne Jacobsen,
Edward Wormley e Eero Saarinen fanno
da contrappeso agli altrettanto rinomati,
anche se meno conosciuti, Cees
Braakman, Kho Liang Le e Tapio
Wirkkala.

Spazionavigli

RBA. Roberto Brambilla
& Associates

Spazionavigli by Cyrus Company established it presence in the North American market with its new showroom open to the public in December 1999 on Mercer Streets, a major shopping artery in New York City.

The new space's atmosphere remains on the margin of the other showrooms in Manhattan. Elegance, simplicity and resplendence constitute the mark of their aesthetic. The purity of lines and shapes covered with gentle pastel colors and whitish touches emphasize the company's ideals in furniture and interior design.

Spazionavigli by Cirus Company estableció su presencia en el mercado norteamericano con su nuevo *showroom*, abierto al público en el mes de diciembre de 1999 en la comercial Mercer Street de la ciudad de Nueva York.

La atmósfera del nuevo local neoyorquino permanece al margen de los demás *showrooms* de Manhattan. Elegancia, simplicidad y resplandor constituyen el sello de su estética. La pureza de líneas y formas vestidas con suaves colores pastel y aspectos blanquecinos enfatizan el ideal de la firma en cuanto a mobiliario y diseño de interiores.

Spazionavigli di Cirus Company si è imposto nel mercato americano con il suo nuovo *showroom*, aperto al pubblico in dicembre 1999 nella via dei negozi Mercer Street di New York.

L'atmosfera del nuovo locale newyorkese rimane al margine degli altri showroom di Manhattan. Eleganza, semplicità e fasto caratterizzano la sua estetica. La purezza delle linee e delle forme vestite con soavi colori a pastello e sembianze biancastre enfatizzano l'ideale della marca per quanto riguarda l'arredamento e design di interni.

Architects: RBA. Roberto Brambilla & Associates

Location: Manhattan, New York, United States

Photographs: Jordi Miralles

Cyrus Company manufacturers iron and wood beds, large and small armchairs, tables, seats, lamps, and lighting elements.

Cyrus Company produce camas de hierro o madera, sillones grandes y pequeños, mesas, sillas, lámparas y elementos para la iluminación.

Cirus Company produce letti di ferro o legno, poltrone grandi e piccole, tavoli, sedie, lampade e articoli per l'illuminazione.

Shin Choi in New York
Shin Choi en Nueva York / Shin Choi a New York

Wormser + Associates

Located in Manhattan's Soho district, this simple yet elegant shopping space reflects the style and serenity conveyed by the clothing creations by the designer Shin Choi. The retail shop occupies approximately 235 m² of loft-type space in a historical building dating from 1890, with high ceilings, wooden floors and skylights that architecturally enrich the space.

The main feature of the shop is the movable changing room with outer walls made of mirrors which spectacularly floats under the natural light that floods in through the skylights. Inside it, birch plywood panels complete this independent and necessary unit that adds versatility and flexibility to the display space and internal layout of the store. The birch wood furniture and minimalist inspiration end up defining this retail space.

Situado en el distrito del Soho de Manhattan, este sencillo aunque elegante local comercial refleja el estilo y la serenidad que desprenden las creaciones de ropa de la diseñadora Shin Choi. La tienda de venta al público ocupa alrededor de 235 m² de espacio tipo loft de un edificio histórico, datado en 1890, con techos altos, pavimentos de madera y tragaluces que enriquecen arquitectónicamente el lugar.

El objeto protagonista del local es el probador móvil, con paredes exteriores de espejo, que flota espectacularmente bajo la iluminación natural que penetra abundantemente por los lucernarios. En su interior, paneles contrachapados de madera de abedul completan esta unidad independiente y necesaria que añade versatilidad y flexibilidad al espacio de exposición y distribución interna de la tienda. El mobiliario de madera de abedul e inspiración minimalista define finalmente el espacio de venta.

Situato nel distretto di Soho di Manhattan, questo semplice ma elegante negozio riflette lo stile e la serenità che infondono le creazioni della stilista Shin Choi. Il negozio occupa circa 235 m² di spazio stile loft di un edificio storico, datato 1890, con soffitti alti, pavimenti di legno e lucernari che arricchiscono il locale dal punto di vista architettonico.

L'elemento protagonista è il camerino mobile, con pareti esteriori di specchio, che galleggia spettacolarmente sotto l'illuminazione naturale che penetra abbondantemente dai lucernari. Al suo interno, pannelli di compensato di legno di betulla completano questa unità indipendente e necessaria che aggiunge versatilità e flessibilità allo spazio espositivo e alla distribuzione interna del negozio. L'arredamento di legno di betulla e di ispirazione minimalista caratterizza lo spazio di vendita.

Architects: Wormser + Associates

Location: Manhattan, New York, United States

Photographs: Jordi Miralles

694

Rice paper panels create
provocative structures that highlight
the clothing.

The furniture is made along simple
lines and birch wood, in line with the spirit
of the clothing designed by Shin Choi.

Los paneles de papel de arroz crean unas
estructuras sugerentes que destacan las
piezas de ropa.

El mobiliario es de líneas sencillas y hecho
de madera de abedul, en línea con el
espíritu del diseño de moda de Shin Choi.

Pannelli di carta di riso creano delle
strutture suggestive che mettono in
risalto i capi di abbigliamento.

L'arredamento ha linee semplici ed è
fatto di legno di betulla, in linea con lo
spirito delle creazioni di Shin Choi.

Géneros de punto

Bailo + Rull
ADP. Arquitectes Associa

The old Esteve knitwear factory is located in Igualada, a town near Barcelona. The warehouse where the design is located is defined by a 6 x 6 meter structure made up of concrete pillars and arched master beams, covered topographically by spherical domes with square bases and interrupted by the orthogonal street crossing of the chamfer where the factory is located.

The factory has various accesses from the outside, and on this occasion, the idea was to delimit a small space around one of these accesses—the old main entrance, located on the chamfer—in order to create a retail outlet.

Given that the structure defining the building is partially hidden by a hanging ceiling, the intervention took place under an opening made around one of the joints in this structure.

La antigua fábrica de géneros de punto Esteve está situada en Igualada, una población cercana a Barcelona. La nave industrial donde se sitúa el proyecto viene definida por una trama estructural de 6 x 6 metros, formada por pilares de hormigón y jácenas en arco, cubierta topográficamente por cúpulas esféricas de base cuadrada e interrumpida por el cruce ortogonal de calles que dan lugar al chaflán de la fábrica.

La fábrica dispone de varios accesos desde el exterior y, en esta ocasión, se trata de delimitar un pequeño espacio alrededor de uno de estos accesos —la antigua entrada principal, situada en el chaflán— para generar el establecimiento de venta al público.

Puesto que la trama que define la fábrica está parcialmente oculta por un falso techo, la intervención se plantea bajo una abertura practicada alrededor de uno de los nudos estructurales de la misma.

La vecchia fabbrica di articoli di maglieria Esteve è situata a Igualada, una cittadina vicino a Barcellona. L'edificio industriale dove è ubicato il progetto è caratterizzato da una trama strutturale di 6 x 6 metri, formata da pilastri di cemento e travi maestre ad arco, tetto topograficamente a cupole sferiche a base quadrata e interrotta dall'incrocio ortogonale di strade che fanno angolo con la fabbrica.

La fabbrica dispone di varie entrate e in questo caso si è trattato di delimitare un piccolo spazio attorno a uno di questi accessi (la vecchia entrata principale situata in una parete del negozio di vendita al dettaglio.

Visto che la trama che caratterizza la fabbrica è parzialmente coperta da un controsoffitto, l'intervento è stato effettuato sotto un'apertura praticata attorno a uno dei nodi strutturali della stessa.

Architects: Bailo + Rull ADP. Arquitectes Associats

Location: Igualada, Barcelona, Spain

Photographs: Jordi Bernadó

The structure that delimits the shop
is made of polycarbonate, whose the
transparency allows one to discern the
size of the factory and the activities
taking place inside it.

La estructura que delimita la tienda es
de policarbonato, que permite entrever
desde su transparencia la extensión de
la fábrica y las actividades que en ella
se desarrollan.

La struttura che delimita il negozio è
di policarbonato, la cui trasparenza
consente di intravedere il resto della
fabbrica e le attività che vi si svolgono.

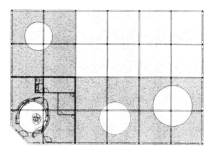

Overall design proposal   Propuesta de actuación global   Progetto globale proposto

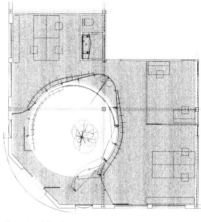

Floor plan of the shop

Planta de distribución de la tienda

Pianta di distribuzione del negozio

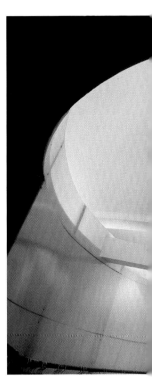

Round Store

Pep Zazurca i Codolà

Round Store is a clothing shop located on the ground floor of a historically catalogued building in Barcelona which had been in poor shape, with cracked walls and reinforcements applied in recent years. The ceiling was made of bricks and wooden and iron beams. The space is 20 meters deep by 4.5 meters wide, with a height of 4.5 meters.

The design included particleboard shelving running along the entire length and height of the wall. An extremely lightweight walkway allows access to the upper level, with stairways at either end that facilitate the flow of movement and offer the possibility of moving in both directions.

The shelving is slightly tilted to accommodate the unevenness of the wall and provide different depths for displaying the clothes. At the end lie the changing rooms with flat façades but diverse degrees of depth. Rail lighting installed in the shelving provides different types of lighting that reinforce the perspective.

The space's back wall showcases a mirror that visually prolongs the perspective.

Round Store es una tienda de ropa ubicada en los bajos de un edificio catalogado de Barcelona que se encontraba en muy mal estado, con muros agrietados y refuerzos aplicados en los últimos años. El techo era de casetones de tochana y vigas de madera y hierro. Las dimensiones de la planta son 20 metros de profundidad por 4,5 metros de anchura, con una altura de 4,5 metros.

El proyecto propone una estantería de aglomerado de madera que recorre todo lo largo y alto del muro. Una pasarela muy ligera permite el acceso a la parte alta de ésta, con escaleras a sus dos extremos que facilitan la fluidez de la circulación y ofrecen la posibilidad de un doble recorrido.

La estantería tiene una cierta inclinación que permite absorber los accidentes de la pared y que provee de diferentes profundidades para ordenar la ropa. Al final se sitúan los probadores, lo que consigue una fachada plana que, sin embargo, presenta profundidades muy diversas. Un carril de luz instalado en la estantería ofrece diferentes formas de iluminación que refuerzan la perspectiva.

En la pared del fondo del local destaca un espejo que prolonga visualmente la perspectiva.

Round Store è un negozio di abbigliamento che si trova al piano terra di un edificio protetto dai beni culturali di Barcellona, che era in cattive condizioni, con crepe nei muri e rinforzi applicati negli ultimi anni. Il soffitto era a cassettoni di mattoni e travi di legno e ferro. Il locale è lungo 20 metri, largo 4,5 metri e alto 4,5 metri.

Il progetto presenta una scaffalatura di agglomerato di legno che si estende per tutta la lunghezza e l'altezza del muro. Una passerella molto leggera permette l'accesso alla parte superiore della stessa, con scale alle due estremità che consentono una circolazione fluida e la possibilità di un doppio percorso.

La scaffalatura ha una certa inclinazione per assorbire le irregolarità della parete e fornisce diverse profondità in cui disporre i capi di abbigliamento. I camerini sono situati in fondo lasciano libero il resto del locale che, tuttavia, presenta profondità molto diverse. Una guida di luci collocata nella scaffalatura offre diverse forme di illuminazione che rafforzano la prospettiva.

Nella parete in fondo del locale spicca uno specchio che estende la prospettiva.

Architect: Pep Zazurca i Codolà

Location: Barcelona, Spain

Photographs: Eugeni Pons

The glass floor on the walkway acts as the shop's display window.

El suelo acristalado de la pasarela se convierte en el escaparate de la tienda.

Il pavimento di vetro della passerella si trasforma nella vetrina del negozio.

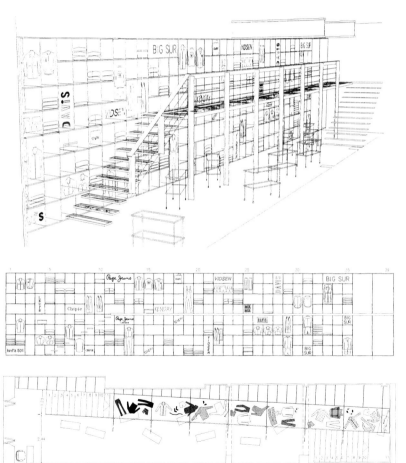

Joan Lao Furniture

Joan Lao

The sales outlet for the interior design firm Joan Lao is located in what used to be a large car dealership. The space's U-shaped layout strategically provides the display area, the management area and the firm's creative studio.

The first room, devoted to general display, is a space that acts as a single volume through a wooden vault covering the entire area. At the end of this room one reaches the shop. The counter joins with the space's embedded structure through a functional swath of wooden pieces that house part of the air conditioning system. Behind the shop, the second display area is a more ambiguous room than the first, in which a more specific product is displayed in a less flexible space, but where the architectural features take center stage.

El punto de venta de la firma de interiorismo Joan Lao está ubicado en un antiguo taller de venta de coches de gran superficie. La distribución del local en forma de U dispone estratégicamente la zona de exposición, el área de gestión y ventas junto con el estudio de creación de la firma.

La primera sala, destinada a la exposición general, es un espacio resuelto como un volumen continuo mediante una bóveda de madera que cubre toda el área. Finalizado el recorrido de esta primera sala se llega al punto de ventas. El mostrador se une a la estructura del local encastrado en uno de los pilares y sujeto ópticamente por una trama funcional de lamas de madera que sirve de retorno del aire acondicionado. Tras la zona de ventas, la segunda área de exposición es una sala más ambigua que la primera, en la que se expone un producto más concreto en un espacio menos flexible, pero donde los elementos arquitectónicos toman protagonismo.

Il punto vendita della marca di arredamenti Joan Lao è ubicato in un vecchio salone di vendita di automobili di grandi dimensioni. La distribuzione a forma di U del locale consente una disposizione strategica della zona espositiva, dell'area di gestione e vendita assieme allo studio di creazione.

La prima sala, destinata all'esposizione generale, è uno spazio caratterizzato da un unico volume mediante una volta di legno che sovrasta tutta l'area. Dopo aver percorso questa prima sala si arriva ai punti vendita. Il banco è unito alla struttura del locale, incassato in uno dei pilastri e fissato a una struttura di lame di legno attraverso cui avviene il riciclaggio dell'aria condizionata. Dopo la zona di vendita, la seconda area espositiva è una sala più ambigua della prima, in cui si espone un prodotto più concreto in uno spazio meno flessibile, ma dove gli elementi architettonici acquistano maggiore importanza.

Interior Designer: Joan Lao

Location: Barcelona, Spain

Photographs: Joan Mundó

The flooring on the patio, smoothed marble gravel, penetrates the interior space and physically introduces the presence of the outdoors inside.

El pavimento del patio, grava de mármol redondeada, penetra en el interior del local introduciendo físicamente la presencia del exterior en la sala.

Il pavimento del patio, ghiaia di marmo arrotondata, penetra all'interno del locale, introducendo fisicamente la presenza dell'esterno nella sala.

The glass walls in the retail area reach the meeting room on the upper floor; both are separated by a crosswise element covered in stone panels.

El paramento acristalado de la zona de ventas sube hasta el de la sala de juntas del piso superior; ambos están separados por un elemento transversal aplacado con piedra.

La parete di vetro della zona di vendita si innalza fino a quella della sala riunioni direttive del piano superiore; le due pareti sono separate da un elemento trasversale rivestito di pietra.

The original ceiling vaults set the rhythm for the placement of the light beams.

Los revoltones originales del forjado marcan el ritmo de distribución de los haces de luz.

Le volte originali del soffitto conferiscono un effetto speciale ai fasci di luce.

Esprit

Citterio & Dwan

The Esprit shop in Antwerp is an example of high technology applied to interior design.

The establishment's total space is 1,800 m², laid out on different levels and connected by a series of metallic staircases. The retail area is located on the ground floor, while the offices are located on the building's upper level. For the interior design of this part the same materials have been applied as in the rest of the space: floors covered in parquet, white walls and metallic structures that showcase functional and avant-garde furniture. The difference between the office area and the retail space lies in the finishes: carpet and white walls in the offices to provide greater brightness, while in the retail zone the color black predominates. The top-down lighting provides warmth to an atmosphere dominated by metallic structural elements.

El local de Esprit en Amberes es un ejemplo de la tecnología *high-tech* aplicada al interiorismo.

El espacio total del establecimiento alcanza los 1.800 m², distribuidos en distintos niveles y comunicados por un entramado de escaleras metálicas. En la parte baja del local está situada la zona de venta, mientras que en la parte superior del edificio se encuentran las oficinas. Para el diseño del interior de esta parte se han empleado los mismos materiales que en el resto: suelos pavimentados con parqué, paredes blancas y estructuras de perfilería metálica que dan forma a un mobiliario funcional y vanguardista. La diferencia entre la zona de oficinas y la de venta está en los acabados: moqueta y paredes blancas en las oficinas para dar mayor luminosidad, mientras que en la zona de ventas predomina el color negro. La iluminación cenital aporta calidez a un ambiente presidido por estructuras metálicas.

Il locale di Esprit ad Anversa è un esempio di architettura High Tech.

Lo spazio totale del locale è di 1.800 m², distribuiti in diversi livelli e collegati da un intreccio di scale metalliche. Al piano terra si trova la zona di vendita, mentre nella parte superiore dell'edificio ci sono gli uffici. Per questa parte sono stati utilizzati gli stessi materiali usati nel resto del locale: parquet, pareti bianche e strutture metalliche che formano un arredamento funzionale e all'avanguardia. La differenza tra la zona degli uffici e di vendita sta nelle finiture: moquette e pareti bianche negli uffici per donare più luminosità, mentre nelle aree di vendita prevale il nero. L'illuminazione dall'alto rende più caldo un ambiente dominato da strutture metalliche.

Architects: Citterio & Dwan

Location: Antwerp, Belgium

Preu bo

Joan Lao

The design by Joan Lao for Preu Bo consisted of creating a totally open space that would capture the timelessness and warmth of the original space, in which the leading brands of international fashion that characterize this company can be displayed.

The site had two 160 m² floors and a basement with a storage area and offices. The project connected this storage area via the display windows through a stairway and a freight elevator, such that the movement of sales merchandise was always visible. This idea generated a double space approximately seven meters high that became a highly interesting volume.

The space is deep, but it widens at the back where it is presided over by three structural columns covered in wood that define the fitting rooms, the waiting area and the general display. An elliptical mirror and three vertical lamps from Joan Lao's furniture collection dominate the wall at the end of the space.

El diseño de Joan Lao para Preu bo consistió en crear un espacio totalmente diáfano que plasmara la atemporalidad y la calidez del espacio original, en el que exponer las primeras firmas de la moda internacional que caracterizan a esta empresa. El local contaba con dos plantas de 160 m², y en el sótano se dispusieron el almacén y las oficinas. El proyecto comunicó este almacén desde el escaparate a través de una escalera y un montacargas, de manera que se viera el movimiento del material de venta. Esta idea genero un doble espacio de unos siete metros de altura que resultó muy interesante volumétricamente.

El local es profundo, pero se amplía al fondo, presidido por tres columnas estructurales revestidas de madera que definen la zona de probadores, el área de espera y la exposición general. Un espejo probador elíptico y tres lámparas verticales de la colección de mobiliario de Joan Lao presiden la pared final del local.

Il progetto di Joan Lao per Preu bo mirava a creare uno spazio totalmente libero che plasmasse l'atemporalità e il calore dello spazio originale, in cui esporre le principali marche della moda internazionale che caratterizzano questa azienda. Il locale era composto da due piani di 160 m² e nel sotterraneo sono stati collocati il magazzino e gli uffici. Sono stati costruiti una scala e un montacarichi per collegare il magazzino e il negozio, in modo che si vedesse il movimento di materiale di vendita. Questa idea ha generato un doppio spazio di sette metri circa di altezza, che è molto interessante dal punto di vista volumetrico.

Il locale è profondo, dominato da tre colonne strutturali rivestite di legno che delimitano la zona dei camerini, l'area d'aspetto e lo spazio espositivo generale. Uno specchio ellittico e tre lampade verticali della collezione di arredamento di Joan Lao spiccano sul muro in fondo al locale.

Interior Designer: Joan Lao

Location: Barcelona, Spain

Photographs: Eugeni Pons y Joan Mundó

The back of the shop is reserved for a waiting area that is reminiscent of the glamour of sophisticated clothing boutiques.

En el fondo del local se reserva una zona de estar que recupera el *glamour* de las sofisticadas boutiques de moda.

In fondo al locale, c'è un salottino che possiede il *glamour* delle sofisticate boutique di moda.

The flowers and plants form part of the design crowning the shop's mirrors.

La ornamentación vegetal forma parte del diseño en la coronación de los espejos del local.

Gli ornamenti vegetali abbelliscono gli specchi del locale.

La Farinera del Clot

Josie Abascal

La Farinera (flour mill) is a brick and iron manufacturing complex with ceramic decorations and a sloped Arab-style tile roof designed by the architect Josep Pericàs around the year 1898, within the 19th century Catalan modernist (art deco) aesthetic.

With a total of 2,634 m², the building, is organized around a new elevator shaft and stairwell located on the southeastern façade. This nucleus, drawn along a northwestern orientation, is inserted into the lot and allows access from the ground floor to the other floors in the building, where we can find a museum, and Internet café, a bar-cafeteria, an exhibition hall, spaces for different organizations, meeting spaces, workshops, offices, a theater/conference hall, and a space devoted to new information and communication technologies (Internet, multimedia, music, television, and radio space), which is located in the basement.

La Farinera (harinera) es un conjunto fabril de mahón y hierro con decoraciones cerámicas y cubierta de teja árabe a dos aguas proyectado por el arquitecto Josep Pericàs en torno al año 1898, dentro de la estética modernista de la Cataluña del siglo XIX.

Con un total de 2.634 m², el edificio,se organiza mediante un nuevo núcleo de comunicación vertical situado en la fachada sudeste. Este núcleo, trazado según la directriz norte-sur, se inserta en el terreno y permite el acceso desde la planta baja hasta el resto de plantas del edificio, donde encontramos un museo, un café internet, un bar cafetería, una sala de exposiciones, salas de entidades, espacios de reunión, talleres, oficinas, un teatro sala de actos y un espacio dedicado a las nuevas tecnologías de la comunicación y la información (internet, multimedia, música, espacio de televisión y radio), ubicado en la planta sótano.

La Farinera (mulino) è un complesso industriale costruito con mattoni e ferro con decorazioni di ceramica e tetto di coppi a due falde, progettato da Josep Pericàs nel 1898, secondo l'estetica modernista della Catalogna del XIX secolo.

L'edificio, con un totale di 2.634 m², è organizzato mediante un nuovo nucleo di comunicazione verticale situato sul fronte sud-est. Questo nucleo, tracciato secondo la direttrice nord-sud, si integra nel terreno e consente l'accesso dal piano terra al resto dei piani dell'edificio, dove troviamo un museo, un caffè internet, un bar, una sala espositiva, sale per assemblee associative, spazi per riunioni, laboratori, uffici, un teatro/sala conferenze e uno spazio dedicato alle nuove tecnologie della comunicazione e dell'informazione (Internet, sistemi multimediali, musica, spazio per televisione e radio), che si trova nel sotterraneo.

Architect: Josie Abascal

Location: Sant Martí, Barcelona, Spain

Photographs: Zona 5. Boatella + Lloria

First floor   Planta primera   Primo piano

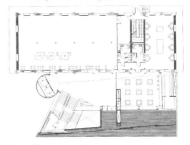

Ground floor   Planta baja   Piano terra

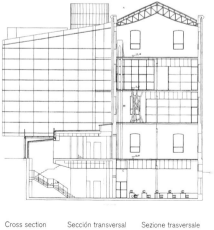

Cross section   Sección transversal   Sezione trasversale

On the inside, part of the original machinery and the flour transport system—pine wood conduits that fed the different machines and mills—have been conserved.

En el interior se ha conservado parte de la maquinaria original y el sistema de transporte de la harina, conductos de madera de pino que alimentaban las diferentes máquinas y molinos.

All'interno è stata conservata una parte dei macchinari originali e il sistema di trasporto della farina, dei condotti di legno di pino che alimentavano le diverse macchine e mulini.

ArtQuitect

Francesca Ricós Martí

In 1993, ArtQuitect's showroom near the El Born market in Barcelona was installed on the ground floor of a turn of the century building that was envisioned as a fruit warehouse and that later housed an art gallery.

The irregular layout divided 259 m² into three levels that consisted of a broken volume characterized by the rhythm of the wrought iron beams. The design by Francesca Ricós Martí proposed that the site's open spaces be enhanced through display cases placed around the perimeter, some of them suspended and others self-contained, all with industrial wheels in order to facilitate their being moved, and all made with perforated zinc sheeting and beech wood.

The upper floor was a small 72 m² room divided by a central arch made of exposed brick and reinforced by an iron beam. The board room and sales offices were placed in this area, with both halogen and fluorescent lighting. The warehouse is located in the basement.

El *showroom* de ArtQuitect, cercano al mercado de El Born de Barcelona, estaba situado en 1993 en la planta baja de un edificio de principios de siglo que se concibió como almacén de frutas y que después albergó una galería de arte.

La forma irregular de la planta repartió 259 m² en tres niveles que conformaban un volumen triturado y marcado por el ritmo de las vigas de hierro del forjado. El proyecto de Francesca Ricós propuso potenciar los espacios diáfanos del local mediante un programa de expositores dispuestos perimetralmente, algunos suspendidos y otros autoportantes, que incorporaban ruedas industriales para facilitar su desplazamiento, todos ellos realizados con plancha perforada zincada y madera de haya.

La planta superior era un pequeño habitáculo de 72 m² dividido por un arco central de ladrillo visto y reforzado por una viga de hierro. En esta zona se dispusieron la sala de juntas y los despachos comerciales, con una iluminación halógena y fluorescente. En el sótano se situó el almacén.

Lo showroom di ArtQuitect, vicino al mercato de El Born di Barcellona, era situato nel 1993 al piano terra di un edificio che risale all'inizio del secolo scorso e che era stato concepito come magazzino ortofrutticolo e successivamente aveva ospitato una galleria d'arte.

La forma irregolare del locale comprendeva 259 m² distribuiti in tre livelli che creavano un volume frammentato e contraddistinto dal ritmo di travi di ferro del soffitto. Il progetto di Francesca Ricós mirava a potenziare gli spazi aperti del locale mediante un programma di espositori disposti lungo il perimetro, alcuni sospesi e altri dotati di ruote industriali per facilitarne lo spostamento, tutti realizzati di lamiera perforata zincata e legno di faggio.

Il piano superiore era un piccolo locale di 72 m² diviso da un arco centrale di mattoni a vista e rinforzato da una trave di ferro. In questa area sono stati disposti la sala delle riunioni direttive e gli uffici commerciali, con un sistema di illuminazione alogena e al neon. Nel sotterraneo è stato situato il magazzino.

Interior Designer: Francesca Ricós Martí

Location: Barcelona, Spain

Photographs: Eugeni Pons

Breaking with the space's use of color, a neo-classically inspired fresco made using the technique of esgrafiado presides over the space's access area.

Rompiendo con el cromatismo ambiental, un fresco de inspiración neoclásica realizado con la técnica del esgrafiado preside la zona de acceso al local.

Rompendo il cromatismo ambientale, un affresco di ispirazione neoclassica realizzato con la tecnica del graffito sovrasta la zona d'entrata del locale.

In Mat. ArtQuitec

José Luis López Ibáñez

This 200 m² space is located on the ground floor of a building in the old quarter of Barcelona. The resulting perimeter space, with the irregularities of the layout, allows for a highly varied space where the polished concrete flooring helps to unify all the environments.

In the first environment, a black wall serves as a backdrop for exhibiting the ideas expressed in a text made with white vinyl characters. Later, a translucent plane extends in a linear fashion throughout the entire space, unifying and resolving—through its horizontal axis—the development of the exhibition. This plane is made of an extremely lightweight structure of galvanized steel frames supporting riveted polyester sheets. This two-millimeter thick membrane has the ideal degree of transparency in order to achieve ambiguous views, undefined shadows, iridescent reflections—an interesting stimulus for the imagination.

El local, de 200 m², está ubicado en la planta baja de un edificio de la Ciutat Vella barcelonesa. El espacio perimetral resultante, con las irregularidades de la planta, permite disponer de un espacio muy variado donde el pavimento de hormigón pulido ayuda a unificar todos los ambientes.

En un primer ambiente un paramento negro sirve de soporte para exponer las ideas en un texto de caracteres de vinilo blanco. A continuación, un plano translúcido se extiende linealmente por todo el local, unificando y resolviendo, en la horizontalidad, el desarrollo de la exposición. Este plano está formado por una estructura muy ligera de perfiles de acero galvanizado que soporta las láminas de poliéster remachadas. La membrana, de dos milímetros de espesor, posee un grado de transparencia idóneo para lograr visiones ambiguas, sombras indefinidas, reflejos iridiscentes; un interesante estímulo para la imaginación.

Il locale, di 200 m² si trova al piano terra di un edificio della Ciutat Vella barcellonese. Lo spazio perimetrale che ne risulta, con le irregolarità del piano, consente una distribuzione molto varia dove il pavimento di cemento lisciato aiuta ad unificare tutti gli ambienti.

In un primo ambiente, una parete nera funge da supporto per esporre le idee con lettere di vinile bianco. Dopo di che, un pannello translucido si estende in modo lineare per tutto il locale, unificando e organizzando in modo orizzontale lo spazio della mostra. Questo pannello è formato da una struttura molto leggera di profili di acciaio zincato che supportano lastre di poliestere fissate con ribattini. La pellicola, di due millimetri di spessore, possiede un grado di trasparenza che crea effetti visivi ambigui, ombre indefinite, riflessi iridescenti, un interessante stimolo per l'immaginazione.

Architect: José Luis López Ibáñez

Location: El Born, Barcelona, Spain

Photographs: Joan Mundó

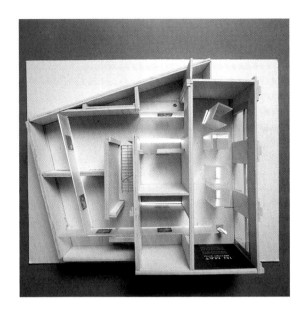

The prismatic volumes—with a
1.3 x 1.33 meter structure of varnished
steel and covered in polyester—
harmonize with the rest of the exhibition.

Los módulos prismáticos –con 1,30 x
1,33 metros, estructura de acero
barnizado y revestimiento de poliéster–
armonizan con el resto de la exposición.

I moduli prismatici – 1,30 x 1,33 metri,
struttura di acciaio verniciato e
rivestimento di poliestere – sono in
armonia con il resto dell'esposizione.

The graphic application of Fornasetti's enigmatic female faces help to visually define the poetic situations of the exhibition.

La aplicación gráfica de los enigmáticos rostros femeninos de Fornasetti ayudaron a definir visualmente las situaciones poéticas de la exposición.

L'applicazione grafica degli enigmatici volti di Fornasetti hanno aiutato a rappresentare dal punto di vista visivo le situazioni poetiche dell'esposizione.

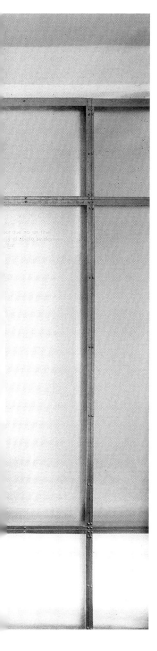

The light enlivens the entire exhibition. A line of screened neon lighting is located in the polyester panels, generating an effect of unreality.

La luz genera la vida de todo el montaje. Una línea de neón apantallada se sitúa en los planos de poliéster, lo que genera un efecto ascendente de irrealidad.

La luce dà vita a tutto l'allestimento. Una linea di neon schermati è situata nei pannelli di poliestere, generando un effetto ascendente di irrealtà.

Magna Pars

Luciano Maria Colombo

Located on Tortona de Milan street, Magna Pars is a multi-purpose space resulting from the complete re-conversion of a 3,450 m² building that used to be occupied by a cosmetic factory. It is the expression of all the stigmas of bourgeois Milanese architecture from the Ottocento.

The project involved a revolutionary use of materials, a functional reorganization, and a new definition of the main spaces in a building which is dedicated in part to offices and in part to conferences and similar events. Numerous environments devoted to diverse activities are located around the central area. There is a restaurant zone near the conference rooms, where a walkway channels access to the upper floor, neatly resolving the problem of connecting the two spaces.

The larger rooms, which are mainly used for conferences and exhibitions, are located on the lower level. The entire intervention took pains to respect the structure. The large openings letting in daylight have been retained, where the activities related to fashion, tourism and publicity are now carried out. In general, the majority of the environments have been envisioned with alternating transparent and opaque elements that allow for rich and interesting connections between the spaces.

Situado en la calle Tortona de Milán, Magna Pars es un espacio polifuncional resultado de la reconversión completa de un edificio de 3.450 m² ocupado antiguamente por una fábrica de cosméticos. Supone la expresión de todos los estigmas de la arquitectura burguesa milanesa del Ottocento.

El proyecto supone una revolución de los materiales, una reestructuración funcional y una nueva definición de los espacios principales en un edificio destinado en parte a oficinas y en parte a congresos y actos similares. En torno al área central se sitúan varios ambientes destinados a diversas actividades. Seguidamente se desarrolla una zona de restauración cercana a las salas de conferencias donde una pasarela organiza el acceso a la planta superior y resuelve con gran soltura las comunicaciones.

En la planta baja se hallan las salas de mayores dimensiones, destinadas principalmente a conferencias y exposiciones. Un gran respeto por la estructura ha presidido toda la intervención. Se han mantenido las grandes aberturas *daylight*, donde ahora se desarrollan las actividades relacionadas con la moda, el turismo y la publicidad. En general, la mayoría de los ambientes se han concebido con la alternancia de elementos transparentes y opacos que han permitido unas relaciones de comunicación entre los espacios muy ricas e interesantes.

Situato in via Tortona a Milano, Magna Pars è uno spazio polifunzionale ottenuto dalla riconversione completa di un edificio di 3.450 m² che precedentemente era stato una fabbrica di cosmetici. È l'espressione di tutti gli stigmi dell'architettura borghese milanese dell'Ottocento.

Il progetto comporta una rivoluzione dei materiali, una ristrutturazione funzionale e nuova configurazione degli spazi principali in un edificio destinato in parte a uffici e in parte a congressi e a eventi simili. Intorno all'area centrale sono situati vari ambienti adatti a diverse attività. Dopo di questa, segue un'area di ristorazione vicina alla sala di conferenze dove una passerella organizza l'accesso al piano superiore consentendo una grande facilità di comunicazione.

Al piano terra si trovano le sale di dimensioni maggiori, destinate principalmente a conferenze ed esposizioni. Il progetto è stato impostato sul rispetto della struttura esistente. Sono stati conservati i grandi spazi *daylight*, dove ora si svolgono attività che riguardano la moda, il turismo e la pubblicità. In generale, la maggioranza degli ambienti sono stati concepiti con l'alternanza di elementi trasparenti e opachi che hanno consentito eccellenti e interessanti relazioni di comunicazione tra gli spazi.

Architect: Luciano Maria Colombo

Location: Milan, Italy

Photographs: Matteo Piazza

Progetto Lodovico

Located in the city of Milan, Progetto Lodovico is a space for professionals and creators in the worlds of architecture, urban planning, design, and communication, who find there an up-to-date center of operations within a renowned cultural space.

The layout and functional design plans for the 3,000 m² of usable space currently available to be extended to the adjacent areas, thus redefining a final 8,500 m² macrostructure. The laboratory is divided into workshops capable of holding approximately 80 professionals from the different specialties. As a support service and specialization of the different disciplines, there are varied infrastructures: a conference room, two meeting rooms, a law office, an administrative area and a secretarial area, all coordinated by a single management body that is likewise promoted by its own department of public relations.

Situado en la ciudad de Milán, Progetto Lodovico es un espacio destinado a profesionales y creadores del mundo de la arquitectura, el urbanismo, el diseño y la comunicación, que pueden encontrar en él un centro de operaciones al tiempo que un referente cultural.

El proyecto de distribución y funcional prevé que los 3.000 m² de espacio operativo actual puedan extenderse a las áreas adyacentes hasta redefinir una macroestructura final de 8.500 m². El laboratorio está dividido en talleres de trabajo capaces de recibir alrededor de 80 profesionales de las diversas especialidades. Como servicio de soporte y especialización de las distintas disciplinas, ofrece variadas instalaciones de infraestructura: una sala de conferencias, dos salas de reuniones, un gabinete de leyes, una administración y una secretaría, según un todo coordinado por un órgano directivo unitario que está igualmente promocionado por su propio departamento de relaciones públicas.

Situato a Milano, Progetto Lodovico è uno spazio destinato a professionisti e a creatori del mondo dell'architettura, dell'urbanistica, del design e della comunicazione, i quali possono contare su un centro operativo e allo stesso tempo di un punto di riferimento culturale.

Il progetto di distribuzione e funzionale prevede che l'attuale spazio operativo di 3.000 m² possa estendersi alle aree adiacenti fino a generare una macrostruttura finale di 8.500 m². Il laboratorio è diviso in aree di lavoro con una capienza di circa 80 professionisti di diverse specialità. Come servizio di appoggio e specializzazione delle varie discipline, offre varie infrastrutture: una sala conferenze, due sale riunioni, un ufficio di consulenza legale, un'amministrazione e una segreteria, il tutto organizzato da un organo direttivo unitario, promosso da un proprio dipartimento di relazioni pubbliche.

Architect: Luciano Maria Colombo

Location: Milan, Italy

Photographs: Matteo Piazza

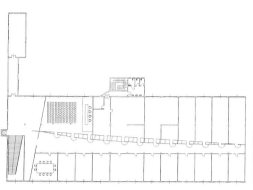

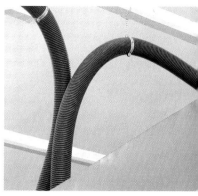

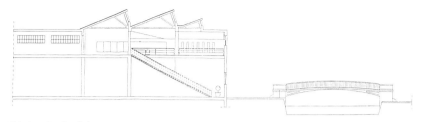

Side view   Sección   Sezione

Nani Marquina Showroom

Nani Marquina

The showroom of the company Nani Marquina is located in a large industrial building in the Barcelona neighborhood of Gracia, an urban enclave that is largely residential.

The reform of the site have sought an open space full of light where the firm's rugs could be displayed and their design and color could be brought out in as neutral a setting as possible. With this in mind, the luminosity of the color white was chosen for the floors and walls.

A transparent glass wall separates the office space from the showroom space, allowing a visual, continuous connection throughout the entire space, as well as allowing the rugs displayed to be viewed from different angles.

El *showroom* de la empresa Nani Marquina se encuentra ubicado en un gran edificio industrial que pertenece al barrio de Gracia de Barcelona, un enclave de tejido urbano mayoritariamente residencial.

La reforma del local ha buscado un espacio abierto lleno de luz donde poder ubicar las alfombras de la firma y resaltar así su diseño y color en un escenario lo más neutro posible. Con esta intención se eligió la luminosidad del color blanco para suelos y paredes.

Un paramento transparente de cristal separa el espacio de oficina del estrictamente dedicado a *showroom*, lo que permite mantener una conexión visual y continua de todo el espacio, así como el control de las alfombras expuestas desde diferentes ángulos.

Lo *showroom* dell'azienda Nani Marquina è ubicato in un grande edificio industriale che appartiene al quartiere di Gràcia di Barcellona, un enclave in un tessuto urbano prevalentemente residenziale.

La ristrutturazione del locale ha cercato uno spazio aperto pieno di luce in cui collocare i tappeti dell'azienda e far risaltare il loro disegno e i colori in un ambiente più neutro possibile. Con questo obiettivo, è stato scelto il colore bianco per pavimenti e pareti.

Una parete trasparente di vetro separa lo spazio dell'ufficio da quello dedicato allo *showroom* e consente di mantenere una connessione visuale ininterrotta di tutto lo spazio e allo stesso tempo il controllo dei tappeti esposti da angoli diversi.

Interior Designer: Nani Marquina

Location: Barcelona, Spain

Photographs: Jordi Miralles

Montaje 97
Montaje 97 / Allestimento 97

Estudi Metro

The objective of this montage consisted of creating a showroom loft for a photographer. The original space was the floor of an old factory.

The control of natural daylight has been maximally enhanced and is one of the reasons why it was decided to paint the house with light, neutral colors, and with mainly natural textiles. The overall lighting is incandescent, with certain more intense points of halogen lighting; auxiliary lights have also been placed in specific areas.

The furniture is the main feature of this loft, given the fact that it individualizes and clearly distinguishes each of the different spaces; in addition, all the pieces chosen are mutually harmonious through the simple lines of their design. Wood is the material chosen for the pieces: varnished and dyed DM for tables and cherry wood dyed is walnut in the china display cabinet and the dining room table and office.

El objetivo de este montaje consistió en crear un espacio *showroom loft* para un fotógrafo. El espacio original era la planta de una antigua fábrica.

El control de la luz natural se ha potenciado al máximo y es una de las razones por las que se decide vestir la casa con colores claros y neutros, y con tejidos naturales en su gran mayoría. La iluminación general es incandescente, con algunos puntos halógenos que logran mayor intensidad; además, en algunas zonas se han empleado lámparas auxiliares.

El mobiliario es protagonista en este loft, dado que personaliza y distingue sobremanera cada una de las diferentes estancias, al margen de que todas las piezas elegidas guarden una armonía común respecto a una tendencia clara en la simplicidad de líneas de su diseño. La madera es el material elegido para las piezas: DM barnizado y teñido para mesas y también madera de cerezo tintada en color nogal en el mueble vajillero y la mesa de comedor y despacho.

Lo scopo di questo progetto era creare uno spazio *showroom loft* per un fotografo. Lo spazio originale era una vecchia fabbrica.

Il controllo della luce naturale è stato potenziato al massimo ed è una delle ragioni per cui si è scelto di adornare la casa prevalentemente con colori chiari e neutri e tessuti naturali. L'illuminazione generale è a incandescenza, con alcuni punti di luce alogena che donano una maggiore intensità; in alcune zone sono state aggiunte anche delle lampade.

L'arredamento è il protagonista in questo loft, dato che personalizza e distingue oltremodo ciascuna delle stanze, sebbene tutti gli articoli scelti possiedano un'armonia comune riguardo a una chiara tendenza alla semplicità delle linee del suo design. Il legno è il materiale scelto per i pezzi: legno compresso verniciato e dipinto per i tavoli e anche legno di ciliegio dipinto con color legno di noce per il mobile per le stoviglie e i tavoli della sala da pranzo e dell'ufficio.

Interior Designer: Estudi Metro

Location: Barcelona, Spain

Photographs: Zona 5. Boadella + Lloria

Montaje 96
Montaje 96 / Allestimento 96

Francesc Rifé
& Associats

The Casa Decor'96 exhibition was located in an old industrial factory in the center of Barcelona which had been divided into independent modules that re-created models of living spaces designed according to different criteria.

The interior designer Francesc Rifé displayed an experimental home model. In a rectangular 56 m² space, 5.4 meters high with openings to the outside on both sides—which obligated the perimeter structures to be free in order to make the most of the natural daylight—he created two levels and converted the livable space in the most useful way possible.

The central featured element of the project was the bathroom, which articulated the different spaces. A stairway integrated into this module allows access to the attic, where the bedroom was located, including a reading area. The bathtub was installed inside the central space: the shower in the back and the toilet were delimited by a sliding door. The injected glass sink appears centered under the upper orifice.

The kitchen is viewed as a continuation of the central module, in which all the water and electrical utilities are located. The cooking area is located in a granite block that also acts as a table for eating.

The audio-visual relaxation area has armchairs that compensate for the free space created by the location of the stairway.

En una antigua fábrica industrial del centro de Barcelona se ubicó la exposición Casa Decor'96, dividida en módulos independientes que recreaban modelos de espacios habitables según distintos criterios.

El interiorista Francesc Rifé expuso un módulo de vivienda experimental. En una planta rectangular de 56 m² y una altura de 5,4 metros con aberturas exteriores a ambos lados de la nave —lo que condicionó la liberación de los perímetros estructurales para sacar mayor rendimiento de la luz natural—, creó dos niveles y convirtió el espacio útil en el más adecuado.

El proyecto plantea un elemento central protagonista: el baño, que articula las diferentes estancias. Una escalera integrada a este módulo permite acceder al altillo, donde se sitúa el dormitorio, que cuenta con un área de lectura. La bañera se ubica en el interior del bloque central; la ducha, al fondo, y el inodoro queda delimitado por una puerta corredera. El lavabo de cristal inyectado aparece centrado respecto al orificio superior.

La cocina se entiende como una continuidad del módulo central, en cuyo interior se ubican todos los servicios, tanto de agua como eléctricos. La zona de cocción se sitúa en un bloque de granito que también sirve de mesa para comer.

La zona de relax audiovisual dispone de unos sillones que compensan el espacio libre que deja la situación de la escalera.

La fiera Casa Decor'96 si svolse in una vecchia fabbrica nel centro di Barcellona e divisa in moduli indipendenti che ricreavano spazi abitativi secondo diversi criteri.

L'architetto d'interni Francesc Rifé espose un modulo di abitazione sperimentale. In un piano rettangolare di 56 m² e con un'altezza di 5,4 metri e apertura verso l'esterno su entrambi i lati dell'edificio — per questo sono stati liberati i perimetri strutturali per sfruttare al meglio la luce naturale — sono stati creati due livelli e lo spazio utile è stato trasformato in modo funzionale.

Il progetto presenta un elemento centrale protagonista: il bagno, in base al quale sono organizzate le diverse stanze. Una scala integrata a questo modulo consente di accedere al soppalco in cui si trova la camera da letto e un'area di lettura. La vasca da bagno è situata all'interno del blocco centrale; la doccia è in fondo, mentre la tazza è separata da una porta scorrevole. Il lavandino di vetro iniettato appare centrato rispetto ai suoi bordi.

La cucina è stata concepita come una continuazione del modulo centrale, al cui interno si trovano tutti gli impianti, sia idraulico che elettrico. L'area di cottura è situata in un blocco di granito che funge anche da tavolo per mangiare.

La zona audiovisiva di relax dispone di poltrone che compensano lo spazio libero lasciato dalla scala.

Interior Designer: Francesc Rifé & Associats

Location: Barcelona, Spain

Photographs: Zona 5. Jaume Boadella. Toni Lloria

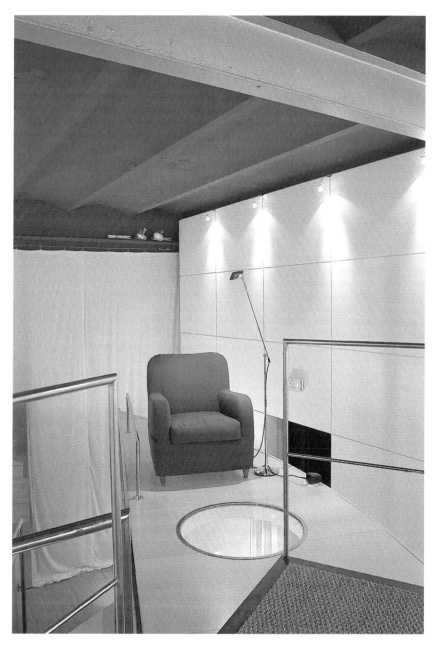

A circular glass window opens out in the floor and can be walked over; it visually connects the attic with the bathroom.

En el suelo se abre una ventana circular de cristal que se puede pisar y que conecta visualmente el altillo con el baño.

Sul pavimento è situata una finestra circolare, che si può attraversare, con vista sul bagno.

The extracting fan is suspended from the ceiling structure in order to cover the electric oven. A double-high glass case integrated into one of the lengthwise walls finishes off this culinary space.

La campana extractora está suspendida de la estructura superior para servir a la encimera eléctrica. Una vitrina a doble altura integrada en uno de los paramentos longitudinales remata este espacio culinario.

L'aspiratore è sospeso dalla struttura superiore sopra la cucina elettrica. Una cristalliera incassata nella parete longitudinale completa questo angolo cottura.

Floor plan   Planta   Pianta

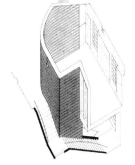

Two Showrooms in Italia
Dos showrooms en Italia / Due showroom in Italia

The Rossa house is an old brick building that houses part of the installations of the company Aplicacioni SRL, manufacturers of dividing panels for offices in Palo Alto.

Built at the beginning of the century and fitted out for years as a factory, it is a two-floor warehouse that was later connected to another lower body, thus enlarging its total surface area to more than 1,000 m².

The company's agenda called for the definition of three main areas: offices, a showroom, and a storage area. The architects decided to place the warehouse on the ground floor alongside the utilities area and the air conditioning and heating systems, leaving the upper level for the offices and the showroom.

In addition to the showroom, the plan for the second project, this time for a company manufacturing air conditioning and heating units, Olimpia Splendid SpA, also included the main entrance to the offices, the reception area and three rooms for visits. The total surface area is 190 m².

The irregular perimeter of the space is determined by the fan-shaped structure of the ceiling: the beams incorporate a series of circular lamps and spotlights. Beams, walls, frames, and skirting boards are all in the same bluish tone, while the hanging ceiling, which is slightly tilted, is white in order to make the play of lights and reflections stand out.

La casa Rossa es un antiguo edificio de ladrillo que alberga parte de las instalaciones de la empresa Aplicacioni SRL, fabricante de paneles divisorios para oficinas de Palo Alto.

Construida a principios de siglo y habilitada durante años como fábrica, se trata de una nave de dos plantas a la que posteriormente se adosó un segundo cuerpo, de menor altura, para ampliar su superficie total a más de 1.000 m².

El programa de la empresa preveía la definición de tres áreas principales: oficinas, sala de exposición y almacén. Los arquitectos decidieron ubicar el almacén en la planta baja, junto a las zonas de servicio y la maquinaria de climatización, dejando la planta superior para las oficinas y la sala de exposición.

El programa del segundo proyecto, para la empresa de aparatos de climatización Olimpia Splendid SpA, además del espacio de exposición, también incluye la entrada principal de las oficinas, la recepción y tres salas para visitas. La superficie total abarca una superficie de 190 m².

El perímetro irregular de la planta viene determinado por la estructura en forma de abanico que adopta el techo: las vigas incorporan series de lámparas circulares y focos. Vigas, paredes, carpintería y zócalos son de un mismo tono azulado, mientras que el falso techo, ligeramente inclinado, es blanco para resaltar el juego de luces y de reflexiones.

La casa Rossa è un antico edificio di mattoni che ospita parte dei locali dell'azienda Applicazioni SRL, fabbricante di pannelli divisori per uffici di Palo Alto.

Costruito all'inizio del secolo scorso e per anni sede di una fabbrica, è un capannone di due piani, al quale successivamente è stata affiancata una seconda costruzione più bassa al fine di ampliare la superficie totale a più di 1.000 m².

Il programma dell'azienda prevedeva la creazione di tre aree principali: uffici, sala espositiva e magazzino. Gli architetti hanno ubicato il magazzino al piano terra, assieme alle zone di servizio e all'impianto di climatizzazione, destinando il piano superiore agli uffici e all'area espositiva.

Il programma del secondo progetto, per la ditta di impianti di climatizzazione Olimpia Splendid Spa, oltre allo spazio espositivo comprende l'entrata principale degli uffici, la reception e tre sale per i visitatori. La superficie copre un totale di 190 m².

Il perimetro irregolare del piano è dovuto alla struttura a forma di ventaglio del tetto: le travi comprendono una serie di lampade circolari e riflettori. Travi, pareti, serramenti e zoccoli sono di una tonalità bluette, mentre il controsoffitto, leggermente inclinato, è bianco per far risaltare il gioco di luci e riflessi.

Architects: King-Miranda Associati

Location: Treviso, Italy

Photographs: Andrea Zanzi

780

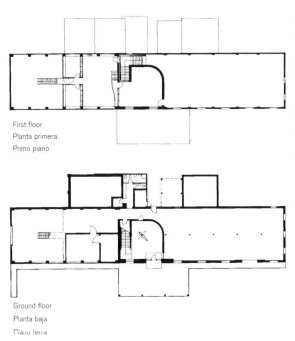

First floor
Planta primera
Primo piano

Ground floor
Planta baja
Piano terra

A canopy protects the access area
from the parking lot. The reception
area separates the building from the
new one. The stairway, walls, a pillar
covered in steel and brass, and even the
artificial lighting are envisioned as
artistic, sculptural elements.

Una marquesina protege el acceso
desde el aparcamiento. La recepción
separa el nuevo edificio del antiguo.
La escalera, los muros, un pilar revestido
de acero y latón e incluso la iluminación
artificial están concebidos como
elementos plásticos y escultóricos.

Una tettoia protegge l'accesso dal
parcheggio. La reception separa il
nuovo edificio dal vecchio. La scala,
i muri, un pilastro rivestito d'acciaio e
ottone, inclusa l'illuminazione artificiale,
sono stati concepiti come elementi
plastici e scultorei.

From the stairway landing the general offices, which are located in the adjacent body, can be accessed. The stairway continues to the second floor of the main volume. In it, the same curved wall from the reception area, with a rough bronze finish, closes off a room designed to be the management office. The rest of the floor is an open space where different product displays can be set up. Throughout the upper floor of the warehouse, a dark patterned carpet has been laid, specially designed by King and Miranda for this project.

Desde el descansillo de la escalera se accede a las oficinas generales, situadas en el cuerpo adosado. La escalera continúa hasta la segunda planta del cuerpo principal. En ella, el mismo muro curvado de la recepción, con un acabado rugoso de bronce, cierra una habitación destinada a oficina de dirección. El resto de la planta es un espacio libre donde se pueden montar los diferentes expositores de productos. En toda la planta superior de la nave se extiende una moqueta de dibujo oscuro, especialmente diseñada por King y Miranda para este trabajo.

Dal pianerottolo della scala si accede agli uffici generali, situati nell'edificio attiguo. La scala prosegue fino al secondo piano dell'edificio principale. All'interno di questo, il muro curvo della reception, con una finitura rugosa di bronzo, chiude una stanza destinata a ufficio della direzione. Il resto del piano è uno spazio aperto dove si possono collocare i diversi espositori dei prodotti. In tutto il piano superiore dell'edificio si estende una moquette con un disegno scuro, disegnata appositamente da King e Miranda per questo progetto.

Across from the entrance, a counter defines the reception area in one corner of the space. The rest of the space is available for the display units of projects according to the season or the new products being released.

Frente a la entrada, un mueble mostrador define la zona de recepción en una de las esquinas del espacio. En el resto de la planta se disponen libremente las unidades de exposición de productos en función de la época del año o de la incorporación de posibles novedades.

Di fronte all'entrata, un banco delimita la zona della reception in uno degli angoli dello spazio. Nel resto del piano, le unità espositive dei prodotti sono disposte liberamente a seconda dell'epoca dell'anno o della necessità di presentare possibili novità.

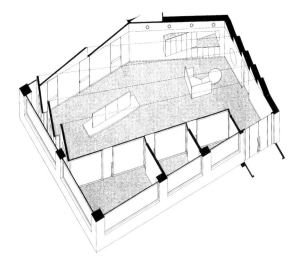

General axonometrical drawing of the company Olimpia Splendid's showroom.

Axonometría general del *showroom* de la empresa Olimpia Splendid.

Assonometria generale dello *showroom* dell'azienda Olimpia Splendid.

P.S. 1 Museum
Museo P.S.1 / Museo P.S.1

Frederick Fisher,
David Ross, Joseph
Coriaty

Frederick Fisher's career is closely linked to the world of art. For many years, P.S.1 Museum has been one of the hallmarks of the movement toward found spaces.

This building, an old school located in an industrial neighborhood near Queens, is 7,800 m², and its main value lies in the wide variety of spaces available, including the outdoor patios. An initial decision consisted of moving the entrance to the U-shaped back of this building, which was renovated by Fisher using concrete walls that enclose outdoor spaces where art work can displayed outside. The central building on the patio was converted into the entrance, such that the central stairway is featured.

La trayectoria de Frederick Fisher está íntimamente ligada al mundo del arte. El Museo P.S.1 ha sido durante muchos años una de las señas de identidad del movimiento *found space*.

Este edificio, una antigua escuela situada en una zona industrial próxima a Queens, tiene 7.800 m² y su principal valor estriba en la gran variedad de espacios disponibles, incluidos los patios exteriores. Una primera decisión consistió en trasladar la entrada a la parte trasera de este edificio en forma de U, renovado por Fisher con muros de hormigón que encierran espacios exteriores donde exponer obras al aire libre. La torre central del patio se convierte en la entrada al edificio, de manera que la escalera central cobra mayor protagonismo.

L'evoluzione di Frederick Fisher è strettamente legata al mondo dell'arte. Il Museo P.S.1 è stato per molti anni uno dei segni di riconoscimento del movimento *found space*.

Questo edificio, una vecchia scuola situata nella zona industriale vicino a Queens, ha una superficie di 7.800 m² e il suo principale valore consiste nella grande varietà di spazi disponibili, compresi patii esterni. La prima decisione è stato spostare l'entrata nella parte posteriore di questo edificio a forma di U, ristrutturato da Fisher con muri di cemento che chiudono spazi esterni in cui si possono collocare opere all'aperto. La torre centrale del patio si trasforma nell'entrata dell'edificio, per dare maggiore rilievo alla scala centrale.

Architects: Frederick Fisher, David Ross, Joseph Coriaty

Location: New York, United States

Photographs: Michael Moran

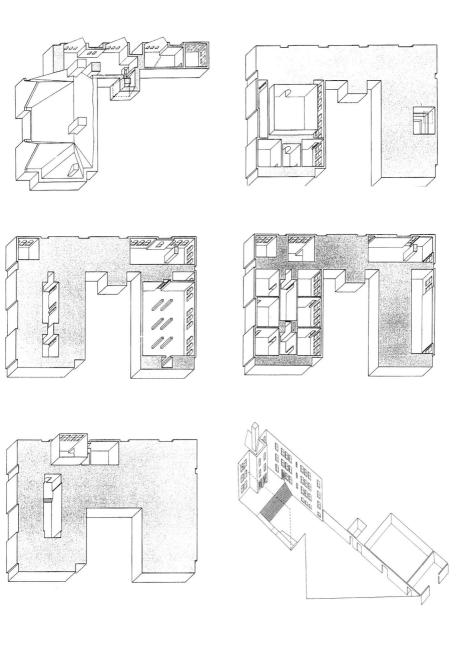

Dromokart

Florencia Costa
Architecture

Dromokart is located in a dismantled post-industrial area near the Naviglio Pavese canal in Milan. The old 6,000 m² building was used to manufacture wrought iron especially for boat propellers and has been transformed into a highly ingenious and high quality Go-Kart center.

The project by the architect Florencia Costa consisted of laying covered go-karting tracks that were equipped with a bar and a restaurant looking out over the tracks, as well as spaces for meetings and medical services. The circuit is used alternately for free time activities and training for professional drivers.

"The ecological conception of go-karting and the silence experienced through speed inspired me to create this dreamlike idea of space: the industrial environment contributed to imagining an almost seamless neutral container in which to accentuate its repetition and rigor. Unlike any other montage of this type, Dromokart is colorless; thus, it allows natural daylight to be the only feature of the space, just as occurs with other special effects," claims the architect.

Dromokart se encuentra en un área postindustrial desmantelada junto al canal Naviglio Pavese, en Milán. El antiguo edificio, de 6.000 m², estuvo dedicado a la fabricación de hierro forjado especial para hélices de barco y ha sido transformado en un *go kart* cubierto de gran ingenio y calidad.

El proyecto de la arquitecta Florencia Costa consiste en el planteamiento de unas pistas de *karting* cubiertas que están equipadas con un bar y un restaurante, cuyas vistas dan al circuito de *karts*, y unas estancias de reunión y de servicios médicos. El circuito planteado alterna su actividad de ocio con la prestación de sus pistas al entrenamiento de pilotos profesionales.

«La concepción ecológica del *karting* y el silencio que experimenta la velocidad me inspiraron esta onírica idea del espacio: el entorno industrial contribuyó a imaginar un contenedor neutro sin apenas costuras que acentuaran su repetición y rigor. A diferencia de cualquier otro montaje de este tipo, Dromokart no tiene color; por lo tanto, permite que sea la luz natural la única protagonista del espacio, como igualmente ocurre con los demás efectos especiales», afirma la arquitecta.

Dromokart si trova in una ex-area industriale smantellata assieme al canale Naviglio Pavese, a Milano. L'antico edificio, di 6.000 m², era adibito alla fabbricazione di ferro battuto speciale per eliche di imbarcazioni ed è stato trasformato in un circuito di go-kart coperto di grande ingegno e qualità.

Il progetto dell'architetto Florencia Costa comprende delle piste di kart coperte dotate di bar e ristoranti con vista sul circuito di kart e alcune sale riunioni e servizi medici. Nel circuito si svolgono attività ricreative e sessioni di allenamento di piloti professionisti.

«Il concetto ecologico del kartismo e il silenzio della velocità mi hanno suggerito questa idea onirica dello spazio: l'ambiente industriale ha contribuito a creare un contenitore neutro con poche interruzioni, che ne avrebbero altrimenti accentuato le ripetizioni e il rigore. A differenza di qualsiasi altro allestimento di questo tipo, Dromokart è incolore, quindi permette che la luce naturale sia l'unica protagonista dello spazio, come succede con il resto degli effetti speciali», afferma l'architetto.

Architects: Florencia Costa Architecture

Location: Milan, Italy

Photographs: Pino Guidolotti

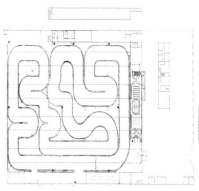

The central piece in the kitchen is covered in five-centimeter thick Carrara marble, while the extracting fan and the bar counters are made of beech wood.

The bar, with 14-meter high ceilings, contrasts with the lower, more intimate space of the restaurant, whose ceiling is 3.5 meters high.

El elemento central de la cocina está revestido de mármol de carrara de cinco centímetros de espesor, mientras que la campana y los mostradores del bar son de madera de abedul.

El bar, de 14 metros de altura, contrasta con el espacio más bajo e íntimo del restaurante, de 3,5 metros de alto.

L'elemento centrale della cucina è rivestito di marmo di Carrara di cinque centimetri di spessore, mentre l'aspiratore e i banchi del bar sono di legno di betulla.

Il bar, alto 14 metri, contrasta con l'ambiente più basso e intimo del ristorante, alto 3,5 metri.

Talls Tallats

Eugeni Boldú,
Orlando González

This site, located in the Barcelona neighborhood of Sants, was originally a copper pot manufacturing workshop. It currently houses two activities: a hair salon and a café, the combination of which within a single environment is an example of commercial mixing that lately make up a new conception of free time.

The floor plan is conditioned by the site's geometry, which is deeper than it is wide, with the café located in front along the façade and the hair salon occupying the more private area further from the street. The location of the access and the bathroom define a lengthwise axis that affects movement, grouping the main areas of the café and the hair salon on the same side.

Este local, ubicado en el barrio barcelonés de Sants, fue en sus orígenes un taller de fabricación de cazuelas y ollas de cobre. Actualmente alberga dos actividades, peluquería y cafetería, cuya combinación en un mismo ambiente es un ejemplo del mestizaje comercial que en los últimos tiempos conforma una nueva concepción del ocio.

La organización en planta viene condicionada por la geometría del local, más profundo que ancho, que sitúa la cafetería en el frente de fachada, mientras que la peluquería ocupa la zona más privada y alejada de la calle. Asimismo, la situación del acceso y el aseo define un eje longitudinal que resuelve las circulaciones agrupando a un mismo lado los ámbitos principales destinados a cafetería y peluquería.

Questo locale, ubicato nel quartiere barcellonese di Sants, una volta era un'officina di padelle e pentole di rame. Attualmente, è la sede di due attività commerciali, un parrucchiere e un caffè, la cui combinazione nello stesso ambiente è un ibrido commerciale che oggigiorno caratterizza il nuovo concetto di tempo libero.

L'organizzazione del piano è influenzata dalla geometria del locale, più lungo che largo. Il caffè è situato nella parte anteriore dell'edificio, mentre il parrucchiere occupa la zona più privata e lontana dalla strada. L'entrata e i servizi formano un asse longitudinale che organizza la circolazione raggruppando sullo stesso lato gli ambienti principali destinati al caffè e al parrucchiere.

Architects: Eugeni Boldú, Orlando González

Location: Barcelona, Spain

Photographs: Zona 5. Boadella + Lloria

The hair salon's amoeba-shaped counter and the bookshelves, either varnished or dyed, were ordered directly from the suppliers according to the everyday needs of the business.

El mostrador de la peluquería, en forma de ameba, así como los estantes para libros, lacas o tintes, se encargaron directamente a los industriales según las necesidades cotidianas del negocio.

Il banco del parrucchiere a forma di ameba e gli scaffali per libri, lacche o tinte, sono fatti su misura, secondo le necessità quotidiane dell'attività.

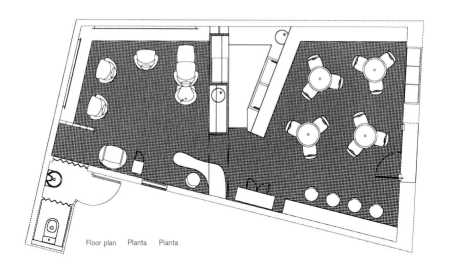

Floor plan   Planta   Pianta

Bar Zoom

Pau Disseny Associats

The intervention consisted of the rehabilitation and decoration of an underground space that had been a kitchen. The almost rectangular 19 x 9.5 meter space, which is three meters high, is crossed by a row of four columns with their corresponding one-meter high socles.

Due to the old building's general state of disrepair, large base socles were added in the structural foundations, and the floor was lowered as a result. The project enveloped the socles as if they were large boxes, covering them with wooden strips of rustic Galician pine; they thus resemble the concept of packaging.

For sound proofing, the need to have a double enclosure on the access led to the idea of a box-shaped vestibule oriented such that it would shamelessly invade the space as if it were an intruder. This box is full of orifices which act as eyes, mouths and ears that seem to be monitoring what is happening inside the space, satiating the visitor's curiosity as he or she looks inside before entering.

The bar was oriented to avoid interruptions in the existing architectural forms, such as socles and steps.

La intervención consistió en la habilitación y decoración de un local ubicado en un subterráneo que había sido una cocina. La planta, casi rectangular, de 19 x 9,5 metros y tres metros de altura, está atravesada por una fila de cuatro columnas con sus correspondientes zapatas de un metro de altura.

Debido a la degradación general del antiguo edificio, se añadieron unas grandes zapatas en el basamento de la estructura y, en consecuencia, se rebajó el nivel del suelo. El proyecto envolvió las zapatas como si fueran unas grandes cajas forrándolas con listones de madera de pino gallego rústico; así se aproximaba al concepto de embalaje.

La necesidad, por cuestiones de insonorización, de disponer un doble cerramiento de acceso sugirió la idea de un vestíbulo en forma de caja orientada de manera que invadiera descaradamente el espacio como si se tratara de un intruso. Esta caja se llena de orificios que son ojos, bocas u orejas que parecen estar pendientes de lo que ocurre en el interior del local, saciando la curiosidad del visitante que mira antes de entrar.

La barra del bar se orientó de forma que evitara las interrupciones arquitectónicas existentes, tales como zapatas y desniveles.

Il progetto comprendeva la ristrutturazione e l'arredamento di un locale ubicato in un sotterraneo che era stato una cucina. Il locale quasi rettangolare, 19 x 9,5 metri e tre metri di altezza, è attraversato da una fila di quattro colonne con i rispettivi rinforzi di un metro.

A causa del degrado generale del vecchio edificio, sono stati aggiunti dei rinforzi al basamento della struttura e di conseguenza è stato abbassato il livello del pavimento. I rinforzi sono stati creati a forma di grandi casse rivestite con legno di pino rustico della Galizia per ricordare il concetto di imballaggio.

La necessità, per ragioni di insonorizzazione, di disporre di una doppia copertura dell'entrata, ha suggerito l'idea di un ingresso a forma di cassa orientata in maniera che invadesse insolentemente lo spazio, come se si trattasse di un intruso. Questa cassa è piena di fessure che sono come occhi, bocche e orecchie che sembrano spiare nell'interno del locale e spingono i visitatori a guardare quello che succede dentro prima di entrare.

Il banco del bar è stato orientato in modo da evitare le interruzioni architettoniche esistenti, come i rinforzi o i dislivelli.

Interior Designers: Pau Disseny Associats

Location: Lloret de Mar, Spain

Photographs: Eugeni Pons

The bar has a lighting system consisting of 475 low-wattage bulbs and a sofa reminiscent of the shape of the lovely coast of Lloret.

El bar tiene una barra, una luminaria colgada en superficie de 475 bombillas de baja potencia y un sofá que dibuja el bonito litoral de Lloret.

Il bar comprende un banco, un sistema di illuminazione con 475 lampadine a bassa potenza e un divano che raffigura il bel litorale di Lloret.

Floor plan

Planta

Planta

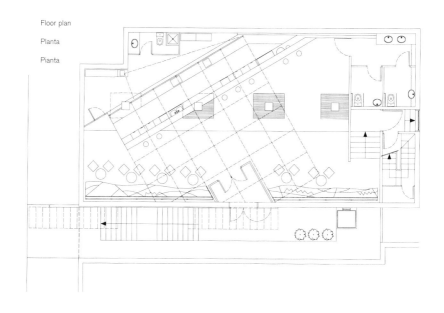

The lighting behind the sofa is made of glass with pergamine adhesive. The sofa upholstered in imitation leather re-creates the beaches of Lloret in a combination of swaths of color; it is the parameter that defines the space.

La luminaria tras el sofá es de vidrio con adhesivo en pergamino. El sofá tapizado con imitación de piel recrea las playas de Lloret en una combinación de retales de colores y es el parámetro que dimensiona el espacio.

Il punto luce dietro il divano è composto da vetro con pellicola opaca. Il divano rivestito di materiale similpelle riproduce le spiagge di Lloret con una combinazione di ritagli colorati ed è il parametro che modella lo spazio.

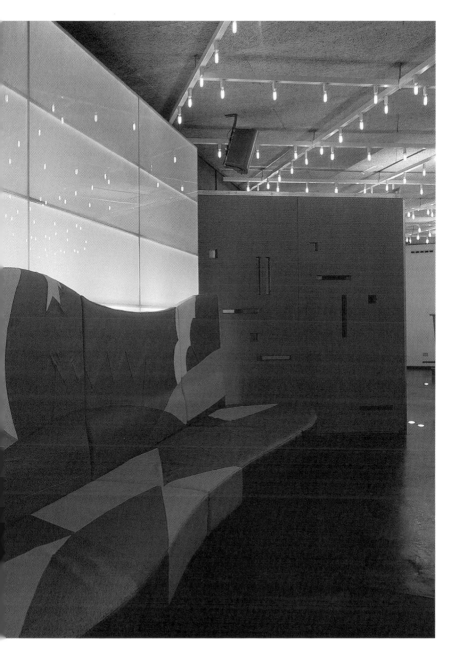

Club Cabool

Lorens Holm,
Ray Simon

This project involves the conversion of an industrial textile building dating from 1917 into a nightclub.

The main façade is covered in concrete, a material already used in the previous restoration and that is used to rediscover two deteriorated twin arches that were conserved.

The lower level is a deep space between two walls which is divided by five columns along its central axis. On the floor, the concrete covering is tilted toward the street. In the interior space, three elements have been inserted: a double-glazed façade with steel framing, a metallic wall inside that can be folded between the columns, and a monumental tilted mirror across from the entrance, the reflection of which covers the dead space behind it used for utilities.

There is a zone of transformable chairs across from the main space. In the back there is a small cabaret and the music platform. We can also find curtains that modulate the acoustic reverberations and a video stall. The bar runs along a wall across from the metallic wall; behind it, a stairway leads to the private space on the upper floor.

El proyecto es la conversión en club nocturno de un edificio textil industrial que data de 1917.

La fachada principal se revistió con hormigón, material empleado ya en una restauración anterior y que sirvió para redescubrir dos arcos gemelos bastante deteriorados que decidieron conservar.

La planta baja del local es un espacio profundo entre dos muros y dividido por cinco columnas en su eje central. En el suelo, la solera de hormigón se inclina hacia la calle. En el espacio interior se han insertado tres elementos: una doble fachada de cristal y perfilería de acero, una pared metálica en el interior que se dobla entre las columnas y un monumental espejo inclinado frente a la entrada, que recupera, por reflexión, el espacio muerto de los servicios situados a su espalda.

Frente al espacio principal se encuentra una zona de asientos transformable. Al fondo hay un pequeño cabaret y la plataforma de música. También encontramos cortinas que modulan la reverberación acústica y una cabina de vídeo. El bar corre a lo largo de un muro frente a la pared de metal; tras él, una escalera conduce al espacio privado del piso superior.

Il progetto è la conversione di una fabbrica tessile datata 1917 in un locale notturno.

La facciata principale è stata rivestita di cemento, un materiale già utilizzato nel restauro precedente per riscoprire due archi gemelli abbastanza deteriorati che si era voluto conservare.

Il piano terra del locale è uno spazio profondo tra due muri e diviso da cinque colonne situate sull'asse centrale. Il pavimento di cemento è inclinato verso la strada. Nello spazio interno sono stati aggiunti tre elementi: una doppia facciata di vetro e profili di acciaio, una parete metallica all'interno che si estende tra le colonne e un enorme specchio inclinato di fronte all'entrata, che recupera per riflesso lo spazio morto dei servizi situati alle sue spalle.

Di fronte allo spazio principale si trova una zona di posti a sedere trasformabile. In fondo c'è un piccolo teatro e una piccola pista da ballo. Ci sono anche delle tende che modulano la riverberazione acustica e un'unità video.

Il bar è disposto lungo il muro di fronte alla parete di metallo; dopo di questo, una scala conduce allo spazio privato del piano superiore.

Architects: Lorens Holm, Ray Simon

Location: Saint Louis, Missouri, United States

Photographs: Hedrich Blessing

Club Cabool has a website under the same name.
Inside, eight video cameras record live images of the
club, which are then broadcast on the Internet.

Club Cabool dispone de una web del mismo nombre.
En el interior ocho cámaras de vídeo registran
imágenes reales del club que se emiten por Internet.

Club Cabool dispone di un sito Web che porta lo stesso
nome. All'interno, otto telecamere registrano immagini
reali del locale che sono trasmesse su Internet.

The monitors, controlled by the disk
jockey, mix images of music and other
websites that serve as a real and virtual
counterpoint to the club.

Los monitores, controlados por el *disc-
jockey*, mezclan imágenes de música
y de otras webs que contraponen el
entorno real y virtual del club.

I monitor, controllati dal dj, trasmettono
video e immagini di altri siti Web,
mostrando l'ambiente reale e virtuale
del locale.

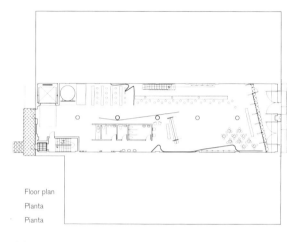

Floor plan
Planta
Pianta

Taxim Nightpark

Branson Coates

Taxim Nightpark in Istanbul emerged from the desire to transform an old factory building into a leisure multi-purpose space similar to those already existing in Europe, Japan, and the United States.

The team made up of the British architects Nigel Coates and Doug Branson were faced with a structure and volume characteristic of the industrial building idiom; a long, narrow initial sector that leads to a much larger space two- and three-stories high.

A complex network of stairways connects the different levels where the different utility areas are located. To the right of the entrance is the restaurant, envisioned as an elegant, indigenous bazaar where one can find the curtain and what is claimed to be the largest leather sofa in the world. The drinks area simulates an airport runway, with special effects-type lighting. Turkish Airlines has donated several pieces, such as the luggage containers, which are used here as stalls for screening videos.

El Taxim Nightpark de Estambul surge del deseo de transformar el edificio de una antigua fábrica en un multiespacio lúdico similar a los existentes en Europa, Japón y Estados Unidos.

El equipo formado por los arquitectos británicos Nigel Coates y Doug Branson se encontró con una estructura y una volumetría características del lenguaje constructivo fabril: un sector inicial, estrecho y alargado, que desemboca en un espacio mucho más amplio desarrollado en dos y tres alturas.

Un complejo entramado de escaleras conecta los diferentes niveles donde se disponen las distintas áreas de servicios. A la derecha de la entrada se ubica el restaurante, concebido como un elegante bazar autóctono donde se encuentran la cortina de cuentas y el sofá de piel más largos del mundo, según se dice. La zona de copas simula una pista de aeropuerto, con una iluminación muy efectista. Turkish Airlines ha cedido algunas piezas, como los contenedores de equipaje, empleados aquí como cabinas para la visualización de vídeos.

Il Taxim Nightpark di Istanbul sorge dal desiderio di trasformare l'edificio di una vecchia fabbrica in uno spazio polifunzionale per il tempo libero, simili a quelli esistenti in Europa, Giappone e Stati Uniti.

Il team, formato dagli architetti britannici Nigel Coates e Doug Branson, aveva a disposizione una struttura e una volumetria tipica del linguaggio costruttivo industriale: un settore iniziale, stretto e lungo, che si affaccia su uno spazio molto più ampio distribuito in due o tre livelli.

Un complesso intreccio di scale collega i diversi livelli, dove si trovano le diverse aree dei servizi. A destra dell'entrata c'è il ristorante, concepito come un elegante bazar autoctono, dove si trovano la tenda di perline e il divano di pelle più lunghi del mondo, secondo quello che si dice. L'area del bar imita la pista di un aeroporto, con un'illuminazione spettacolare. Turkish Airlines ha ceduto alcuni pezzi, come i vani per i bagagli che sono utilizzati come unità per la trasmissione di video.

Architects: Branson Coates

Location: Istanbul, Turkey

Photographs: Valerie Bennet

The Nightpark constitutes a masterly combination of indigenous and designer elements in at atmosphere dominated by a certain physical deterioration coming from the building itself.

La realización de este parque nocturno constituye una magistral combinación de procedimientos autóctonos y de diseño, inscritos en un ambiente dominado por un cierto deterioro material propio del edificio.

La realizzazione di questo parco notturno è una magistrale combinazione di elementi autoctoni e di design, situati in un ambiente dominato da un certo degrado materiale proprio dell'edificio.

823

Paci Restaurant
Paci Restaurant / Ristorante Paci

Roger Ferris +
Partners Llc.

The team of architects made up of Roger Ferris and his associate Robert Parisot believed that by highlighting the constructional qualities of the building and providing it with an appropriate function, such as a restaurant, it would become a focus of interest for the city. The first operation consisted of stripping the building of all materials and elements that were not original, discovering in the process the interesting wooden structure that supported the ceiling, which had to be reinforced and left exposed the brick on the perimeter walls. On the inside, the idea was that of a container built using birch wood panels which would simulate an old train car. The container has a bar, lavatories and rest rooms, and the dining room is located above it.

El equipo de arquitectos formado por Roger Ferris y su colaborador Robert Parisot consideró que resaltando las cualidades constructivas del edificio y adjudicándole una función adecuada, como un restaurante, se convertiría en un foco de interés para la ciudad. La primera operación consistió en despojar al edificio de todo material y elemento que no fuera original, lo que descubrió una interesante estructura de madera (que soporta la cubierta), que tuvo que ser reforzada y dejó a la vista el ladrillo de los muros perimetrales. En el interior se ideó un contenedor construido con paneles de madera de arce que simula ser un vagón robado a la memoria del viejo tren. El contenedor dispone de bar, servicios y habitaciones de descanso, y sobre él se sitúa la zona del comedor.

Il team di architetti formato da Roger Ferris e il suo collaboratore Robert Parisot ha voluto mettere in risalto le qualità costruttive dell'edificio e trasformarlo in ristorante, per fare di questo luogo un punto di interesse della città. L'edificio è stato spogliato di tutti i materiali e gli elementi non originali e questo ha consentito di scoprire un'interessante struttura di legno (la quale supporta il tetto), che è stata rinforzata. I mattoni dei muri perimetrali sono stati lasciati a vista. All'interno è stato costruito un contenitore fatto di pannelli di legno di acero che imita un vagone rubato alla memoria del vecchio treno. Il contenitore dispone di bar, servizi e sale di relax e sopra di esso si trova la zona ristorante.

Architects: Roger Ferris + Partners Llc.

Location: Southport, Connecticut, United States

Photographs: Michael Moran

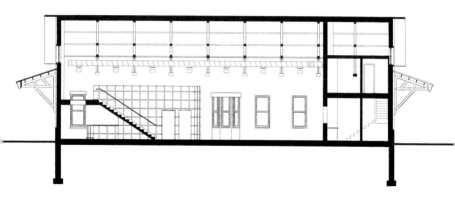

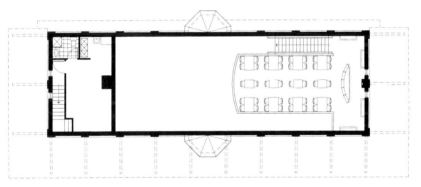

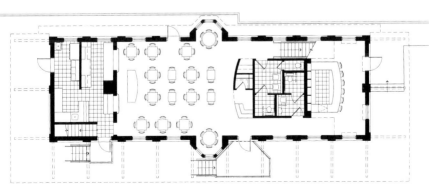

Porto Colom Restaurant
Restaurante Porto Colom / Ristorante Porto Colom

B&B
Estudio de arquitectura

Located in Porto Colom, Majorca, Spain, this old building enjoys splendid views that allow for the placement of an additional terrace used for less formal dining.

From an architectural standpoint, the building is an example of traditional island architecture which the project attempted to conserve: walls made of sea stones and structures using wooden beams reinforced with iron master beams. Likewise, the simple composition of the façade, as well as the internal layout of the old wine cellar, have been maintained, respecting the simple lines of the original design.

On the ground floor, the indoor floor plan includes a kitchen and a better dining area than that found on the terrace, where local gastronomic specialties can be savored. On the upper level, the bathrooms have been placed away from the dining room in a more private, reserved space.

Interior decoration is highly important when attempting to create a warm yet somewhat sophisticated atmosphere. Materials that bring warmth to the space, such as leather and wood, have been chosen. Along the same lines, diffused light has been chosen for general ambiance along with low lamps on the tables that make both daytime and nighttime meals more appealing.

Situada en Porto Colom, Mallorca, esta antigua construcción disfruta de espléndidas vistas que permiten ubicar una terraza complementaria que se destina a un servicio más informal.

Desde el punto de vista arquitectónico, el edificio es un ejemplo de las construcciones tradicionales de la isla, que el proyecto ha querido conservar: paredes de piedra de marés o estructuras de vigas de madera reforzadas por jácenas de hierro. De igual forma, la sencilla composición de la fachada, así como la distribución interior de la antigua bodega, se ha mantenido respetando la sencillez de líneas de su diseño original.

La distribución interior resuelve en la planta baja una sala comedor de más categoría que la terraza, donde se pueden saborear especialidades gastronómicas típicas del lugar, y la zona cocina. En planta piso se han situado los aseos, independientes de la sala comedor, en un lugar más íntimo y reservado.

La decoración interior es de gran importancia si se quiere crear una atmósfera acogedora y algo sofisticada a la vez. Se han elegido materiales que aportan calidez al conjunto, como el cuero y la madera. En la misma línea se dispone de una iluminación tamizada de ambiente general y una luz baja y fija sobre las mesas que ameniza las comidas tanto de día como de noche.

Situata a Porto Colom, a Maiorca, questa antica costruzione gode di splendide viste che consentono di ubicare una terrazza complementare destinata a un servizio di ristorazione più informale.

Dal punto di vista architettonico, l'edificio è un esempio delle costruzioni tradizionali dell'isola, che il progetto ha voluto conservare: pareti di pietra arenaria delle Baleari (marés) o strutture di travi di legno rafforzate da travi maestre di ferro. Allo stesso modo, la semplice composizione della facciata, così come la distribuzione interna della vecchia enoteca, è stata conservata rispettando la semplicità delle linee del progetto originale.

La distribuzione interna colloca al piano terra la sala da pranzo del ristorante di una categoria superiore a quello della terrazza, dove si possono gustare le specialità gastronomiche tipiche del posto, e la zona cucina. Al piano di sopra sono stati collocati i servizi, indipendenti dalla sala ristorante, in un luogo più intimo e riservato.

L'arredamento interno è molto importante se si vuole creare un'atmosfera accogliente e, allo stesso tempo, un po' sofisticata. Sono stati scelti materiali che rendono il locale più intimo, come la pelle e il legno. Seguendo lo stesso concetto, l'illuminazione generale dell'ambiente è diffusa e sui tavoli ci sono lampade basse e fisse, che rendono piacevoli i pasti sia di giorno che di notte.

Architects: B&B Estudio de arquitectura
Location: Majorca, Spain
Photographs: Pere Planells

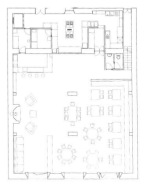

Floor plan

Planta de distribución

Pianta di distribuzione

The atmosphere created in this space allows for the display of large and small original paintings by painters and artists, who find this to be an ideal place for their works to be seen.

El ambiente creado en este espacio permite la exposición de grandes y pequeñas obras de pintores y artistas que encuentran en este lugar un emplazamiento idóneo para que sus obras puedan ser observadas.

L'ambiente creato in questo spazio consente l'esposizione di opere grandi e piccole di pittori e artisti, i quali ritengono che questo sia il posto adatto per esporre le loro creazioni.

Thèatron Restaurant
Restaurante Thèatron / Ristorante Thèatron

Philippe Starck

Beyond its immediate functions, the Thèatron restaurant, located in the National Auditorium, is theatrical. Clients come not only to have dinner, a drink and spend the evening, but they also come in search of a maximally theatrical evening. The clients star in their own plays. The Thèatron is an idea generated by Philippe Starck, who has worked along with the head of construction of the Mexican architect, Baltasar Vez.

The spaces boast humor; the sceneries are humorous and inoffensive. Complicity with the spectator is sought. One room is lit by a nineteenth century chandelier, the next by a bulb hanging from the ceiling by a thread. One goes up a disproportionate, monumental stairway and then goes through a dark, narrow hallway. The restaurant is immersed in an amusing atmosphere. Filmy white curtains cover the spaces in serpentine forms from the ceiling to chair level, partially dividing the space.

Despite its more than 300 m², the vestibule has only three decorative elements: a large Richad Avedon photograph approximately 10 meters high by 6 meters wide, a large stairway, and a gray velvet theater curtain with a scarlet lining, which is more than 12 meters high by 16 meters wide.

El restaurante Thèatron, situado en el Auditorio Nacional, tiene, más allá de su función inmediata, un carácter escenográfico. Los clientes no acuden únicamente para cenar, tomar una copa y pasar la velada, sino para que la noche alcance su máxima teatralidad. Los clientes se convierten en protagonistas de sus propios actos. El Thèatron es una idea nacida del propio Philippe Stark, quien ha trabajado junto a la dirección de obra del arquitecto mexicano Baltasar Vez.

Los espacios rebosan humor, las escenografías tienen un carácter lúdico, son inofensivas. Se busca la complicidad del espectador. Una sala se encuentra iluminada por una lámpara de araña decimonónica, la siguiente por una bombilla colgada del techo por un hilo. Se sube por una escalera desproporcionada, monumental, y después se pasa por un corredor oscuro y estrecho. La sala del restaurante está sumergida en una atmósfera brumosa: unas cortinas blancas y vaporosas corren los espacios con formas serpenteantes, desde el techo hasta la altura de las sillas, de modo que dividen el espacio tan sólo a medias.

A pesar de tener más de 300 m² de superficie, el vestíbulo se organiza únicamente con tres elementos decorativos: un gran marco de aproximadamente 10 metros de altura por 6 metros de ancho, con una fotografía de Richard Avedon, una gran escalera y un telón de terciopelo gris con el reverso de seda escarlata, de más de 12 metros de altura por 16 metros de ancho.

Il ristorante Thèatron, situato nell'Auditorio Nacional, oltre alla sua funzione più immediata possiede un carattere scenografico. I clienti non vi si recano solo per cenare, bere qualcosa o trascorrere la serata, ma anche perché la notte acquisti la massima teatralità. I clienti diventano i protagonisti dei propri atti. Il Thèatron è un'idea concepita dallo stesso Philippe Starck, che ha collaborato alla direzione dei lavori dell'architetto messicano Baldasar Vez.

Gli spazi traboccano di umorismo, le scenografie hanno un carattere ludico, sono inoffensive. Si cerca la complicità dello spettatore. Una sala è illuminata da un lampadario a gocce di cristallo ottocentesco, la seguente da una lampadina appesa al soffitto con un filo. Si sale per una scalinata sproporzionata, monumentale e poi si passa a un corridoio stretto e scuro. La sala del ristorante è sommersa in un'atmosfera brumosa: tende bianche e vaporose percorrono lo spazio con forme serpeggianti, dal soffitto fino all'altezza delle sedie, quindi dividono lo spazio solo a metà.

Sebbene occupi una superficie di oltre 300 m², l'atrio possiede solamente tre elementi decorativi: un'enorme cornice, alta 10 metri e larga 6, con una fotografia di Richard Avedon, una grande scalinata e un telone di velluto grigio con il rovescio di seta scarlatta, di oltre 12 metri di altezza e 16 di larghezza.

Architect: Philippe Starck

Location: Mexico DF, Mexico

Photographs: Alfredo Jacob Vilalta

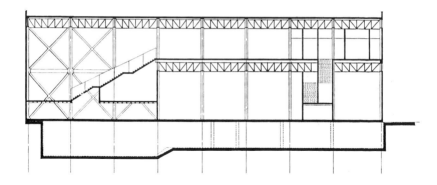

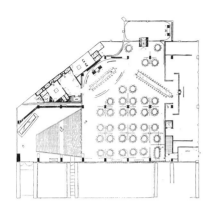

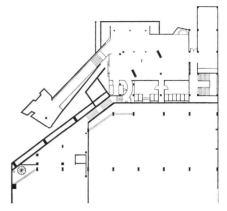

Restaurant floor plan
Planta del restaurante
Pianta del ristorante

Basement
Planta sótano
Pianta del sotterraneo

Thèatron is essentially divided into three spaces: the vestibule, the restaurant, and the bar. The restaurant can accommodate up to 280 diners, while 250 fit into the bar. The furniture is mainly designed by Starck, although it is combined with period pieces and chandeliers that are more than 2.5 meters high.

El Thèatron se divide esencialmente en tres espacios: el vestíbulo, el restaurante y el bar. El restaurante tiene una capacidad de 280 comensales, mientras que en el bar caben 250 personas. El mobiliario en su mayoría está diseñado por Starck, aunque combinado con muebles de época y lámparas de araña de más de 2,5 metros de altura.

Il Thèatron si divide essenzialmente in tre spazi: l'atrio d'entrata, il ristorante e il bar. Il ristorante ha una capienza di 280 persone, mentre il bar ne può ospitare 250. La maggior parte dell'arredamento è stato disegnato da Starck ed è stato combinato con mobili d'epoca e lampadari con gocce di cristallo di oltre 2,5 metri di altezza.

Belgo Centraal

Ron Arad,
Alison Brooks

Arad always demonstrates his constant search for beauty in his immediate surroundings—aesthetic dignity for daily life.

The concept of the Belgian restaurant that he tested in Chalk FarmBelgo Noord is transferred here to an old wine cellar on London's West End, this time with a triple function: a sidewalk café, a beer shop, and offices.

The experience begins outside the restaurant: the kitchen, which operates exclusively using steam, is a public space visible from the façades of the six-meter high glassed-in entrance. The two entrances to the restaurant and the bridge connecting them create a pedestrian trench between the two bustling streets in Covent Garden.

The solution adopted in the restaurant's roof deserves special attention; its structural concept consists of a tilted glass plane, shown in a piecemeal fashion via a series of molded boards, with a distance of depth in a 4 to 1 proportion. The exterior walls, painted in a vivid red as far up as the entrance, also stand out. The original design of chairs and tables, the repeated touches of steel that appear throughout the space, and the decorative elements placed in attention-getting shapes are yet more inherent elements from Ron Arad's rebellious and aggressive signature style.

Arad muestra siempre una constante búsqueda de la belleza en el entorno inmediato, una dignidad estética para la realidad cotidiana.

El concepto de restaurante belga que ensayó en Chalk FarmBelgo Noord se traslada ahora a una antigua bodega del West End londinense, esta vez con una triple función: un café en la acera, una tienda de cervezas y oficinas.

La experiencia empieza fuera del restaurante; la cocina, que opera totalmente con vapor, es una obra pública visible desde las fachadas de la entrada acristalada, de seis metros de alto. Las dos entradas del restaurante y el puente que las conectan crean una trinchera pedestre entre dos bulliciosas calles del Covent Garden.

Merece una especial atención la solución adoptada en la cubierta del restaurante, cuyo concepto estructural consiste en un plano inclinado de cristal, mostrado a cortes a través de series de tablas moldeadas, con una distancia de profundidad en proporción 4 a 1. También destacan las paredes exteriores, pintadas con un vivo rojo a la altura de la entrada. El original diseño de sillas y mesas, los reiterados complementos de acero que recorren toda la estancia, los elementos decorativos, dispuestos en llamativas formas son otros tantos elementos inherentes a la firma rebelde y agresiva de Ron Arad.

Arad è sempre alla ricerca della bellezza nell'ambiente più prossimo, di una dignità estetica per la realtà quotidiana.

Il concetto di ristorante belga che sperimentò in Chalk FarmBelgo Noord viene adesso trasferito in un antico magazzino del West End londinese, questa volta con una tripla funzione: un caffè all'aperto, una birreria e uffici.

L'esperienza comincia fuori dal ristorante; la cucina che funziona solamente con vapore, è un'opera pubblica visibile dalle facciate dell'entrata di vetro, alta sei metri. Le due entrate del ristorante e il ponte che le collega creano una trincea pedonale tra due strade rumorose di Covent Garden.

Merita una menzione speciale la soluzione adottata per il tetto del ristorante, il cui concetto strutturale consiste di un piano inclinato di vetro, visibile a tratti attraverso tavole modellate, con una distanza di profondità in una proporzione di 4 a 1. All'altezza dell'entrata, spiccano le pareti esterni dipinte con un rosso vivo. L'originale design delle sedie e dei tavoli, i reiterati accessori di acciaio sparsi per tutta la sala, gli elementi decorativi, disposti in forme suggestive sono altrettanti elementi che distinguono la firma ribelle e aggressiva di Ron Arad.

Architects: Ron Arad, Alison Brooks
Location: London, United Kingdom
Photographs: F. Busam/Architekturphoto

It was decided that daylight should enter through the roof and that the new roof would have to drain over the already existing curved roof.

Se decidió que la luz de día debería introducirse a través del techo y que la nueva cubierta debería drenar sobre el curvado techo existente.

Secondo il progetto, la luce doveva passare attraverso il soffitto e che la nuova copertura doveva far filtrare la luce sopra il tetto curvo esistente.

Belgo Restaurant
Belgo Restaurant / Ristorante Belgo

FOA. Foreign
Office Architects

Belgo Zuid is located in small old dance theater in London's Notting Hill Gate. The project's intervention strategy consisted of playing with all the elements that the clients who frequent the restaurant use, in an attempt to exploit their formal, structural and organizing qualities, beyond their intentional kitsch origins.

Given the unstable condition in which the building was found, the majority of it had to be demolished in order to adapt it to the requirements of its new use. Both the walls and the roof of the main dining space were reconstructed, as well as a new supporting structure and walls. Covered on the outside by stainless steel, the inside of the walls and roof are lined with oak boards that characterize the main dining room.

Belgo Zuid está situado en un antiguo y pequeño teatro de danza en el Notting Hill Gate de Londres. La estrategia de intervención del proyecto consistió en jugar con todos los elementos que manejan los clientes que frecuentan el restaurante, intentando explotar sus cualidades formales, estructurales y organizadoras, más allá de sus intencionados orígenes *kitsch*.

Dadas las precarias condiciones en que se encontraba el edificio, la mayor parte tuvo que ser demolida para adaptarse a las exigencias del nuevo uso. Tanto las paredes como la cubierta del espacio principal del comedor fueron reconstruidas, así como una nueva estructura de soporte y cerramientos. Revestidos exteriormente con chapa de acero inoxidable, el interior de los muros y la cubierta están forrados con tablas de madera de roble que caracterizan el comedor principal.

Belgo Zuid si trova in un vecchio e piccolo teatro di danza di Notting Hill Gate a Londra. La strategia del progetto è stata quella di giocare con tutti gli elementi che hanno a che fare con i clienti che frequentano il ristorante, tentando di sfruttare le loro qualità formali, strutturali e organizzative, oltre alle sue origini kitsch.

Date le precarie condizioni dell'edificio, la maggior parte di esso è stata demolita per soddisfare le nuove esigenze. Sia le pareti che il tetto dello spazio principale dell'area ristorante sono stati ricostruiti, così come la nuova struttura di supporto e i tramezzi. Rivestiti esteriormente con una lamiera di acciaio inossidabile, l'interno dei muri e il tetto sono ricoperti con listelli di legno di rovere che caratterizzano la sala principale del ristorante.

Architects: FOA. Foreign Office Architects

Location: Notthing Hill Gate, London, United Kingdom

Photographs: Valerie Bennett